# Roman Laughter

# Roman Laughter

## THE COMEDY OF PLAUTUS

*Second Edition*

Erich Segal

New York Oxford
OXFORD UNIVERSITY PRESS
1987

Oxford University Press

Oxford   New York   Toronto
Delhi   Bombay   Calcutta   Madras   Karachi
Petaling Jaya   Singapore   Hong Kong   Tokyo
Nairobi   Dar es Salaam   Cape Town
Melbourne   Auckland

and associated companies in
Beirut   Berlin   Ibadan   Nicosia

Preface to the Second Edition and Appendix © 1987 by Oxford University Press, Inc.

First edition published in 1968 by Harvard University Press.

First issued in paperback in 1971 by Harper Torchbooks, Harper & Row, Publishers.

Second edition first published in paperback in 1987 by Oxford University Press, Inc., 200 Madison Avenue, New York, New York 10016

Oxford is a registered trademark of Oxford University Press

Library of Congress Cataloging-in-Publication Data
Segal, Erich, 1937–
Roman laughter.
Bibliography: p.
Includes indexes.
1. Plautus, Titus Maccius—Criticism and interpretation.   I. Title.
PA6585.S4   1987      872'.01      86-23682
ISBN 0-19-504166-6

Printing (last digit): 9 8 7 6 5 4 3 2 1

Printed in the United States of America

*To My Mother
and to the Memory
of My Father*

# Preface to the Second Edition

In the years since this book first appeared, over a thousand articles and reviews have been written about Plautus.[1] They were mainly the result of the "Menandrian explosion," the sudden discovery and publication of substantial portions of the Greek New Comedy master who was the model for so many Roman playwrights, not merely Plautus and Terence. What was once a collection merely of aphorisms and a few long fragments is now a full-fledged Oxford Text.[2] Perhaps the most important single piece of scholarship was E. W. Handley's *Menander and Plautus: A Study in Comparison.* Among other things, it invalidates my claim (p. 7) that there is no extant Greek model to which a Plautine play — or even scene — might be directly compared in order to see precisely what Plautus did in his process of adaptation (or, as he calls it, *vortere.*)

Handley published forty-four lines of Menander's *Dis Exapaton* ("The Double Deceiver") and set them beside the Plautine scene they inspired, *Bacchides* lines 494–562. Even from such a relatively small sampling, Handley was able to demonstrate a great deal of Plautine technique. We see, for example, that the Latin playwright changes some of the names of bland stereotypical characters, endowing them with new, colorful ones.[3] Plautus excises a scene — for the sake of speed, perhaps — and places jocular quips in the mouth of the youth at a point where Menander had him speak pensively. As Handley concludes, "We have seen, on a small scale but by direct observation, how Plautus likes his colors stronger, his staging more obvious, his comedy more comic" (p. 18).

Handley's stylistic observations confirmed some of the intuitive conjectures on Plautine expansion and elaboration made by Eduard Fraenkel nearly half a century earlier.[4]

The new corpus of Menandrian drama also reinforced another of Fraenkel's theories, namely, that Plautus "invented" —
or at least greatly amplified — the role of the clever slave.
There have been scholarly attempts to find *servi callidi* hidden in the lines of Menander, but to no avail.[5] As a recent
study concluded, "there is no comparable emphasis in ancient
Greek comedy." [6]

As a consequence, the essential thesis of this book — that
Plautus presents a "saturnalian" reversal of Roman values to
evoke Roman laughter — has found tangible support.[7] Still, a
valid criticism of this book when it first appeared was that it
tended to be overschematic.[8] While allowing that I may have
been too dogmatic at times, I have nonetheless tried to re-
spond to this opinion head-on by appending three essays on
Plautine "problem plays," that is, those apparently least likely
to fit the scheme set out in the book itself. (Economic realities
made extensive internal revisions of the book unfeasible.)

I would like to thank W. G. Arnott, Eric Handley, Mal-
colm Willcock, Gordon Williams, and John Wright, who
were kind enough to go over the new material and offer helpful comments. I am also grateful to Professor G. P. Goold, my
chairman at Yale, and to its former president, A. B. Giamatti
for their friendship and generous support, which allowed me
the time to complete this work.

Finally, an expression of heartfelt appreciation to William
Sisler and Robin Denniston of Oxford University Press, who
allowed this book to be born again.

*Wolfson College, Oxford*                                    E.S.
*January 1987*

# Preface

Laughter is an affirmation of shared values. It is, as Bergson constantly reminds us in his essay, a social gesture. Comedy always needs a context, a community, or at least a communal spirit. Moreover, the fact that ancient comedy was presented to an audience which constituted an entire citizenry suggests that laughter might at times even be a national gesture. Certainly this notion is implicit in the time-honored view of Aristophanes as "soul of an age." How to know Athenian democracy? Plato suggested a reading of Aristophanes. No one has ever suggested anything of the sort for Plautus. In fact, few people suggest reading Plautus at all.

A study of Rome's most popular playwright has certain occupational hazards, for he seems to contradict the convenient stereotype of what Romans and their literature ought to be. Hence Ennius is hailed as the "father of Latin literature," although Plautus was writing before Ennius could read. It is undeniable that without Plautus the history of Latin literature is ever so much neater. But Plautus is not isolated merely because he wrote for the stage. "Neat Terence" (as Ben Jonson praised him) has never been out of favor — except during his lifetime. But Terence was *puri sermonis amator*; he wrote good, decorous Latin. Fastidious Horace, who could barely brook the vulgarisms of Catullus and refused to admit him into the ranks of Latin lyric poets, vehemently argued (*Ars Poetica* 270ff) that both Plautus' wit and metrical skill were vastly overrated. Doubtless the Dean of Roman Critics was also outraged by Plautus' playful pleonasms, his wanton waste of words, complex comic *coronae* woven out of inexcusable verbal extravagance; *Persicos odi, puer, apparatus*. Worst of all, Plautus is conspicuously lacking in "high seriousness." *Dulce*, perhaps (*in loco*, that is), but

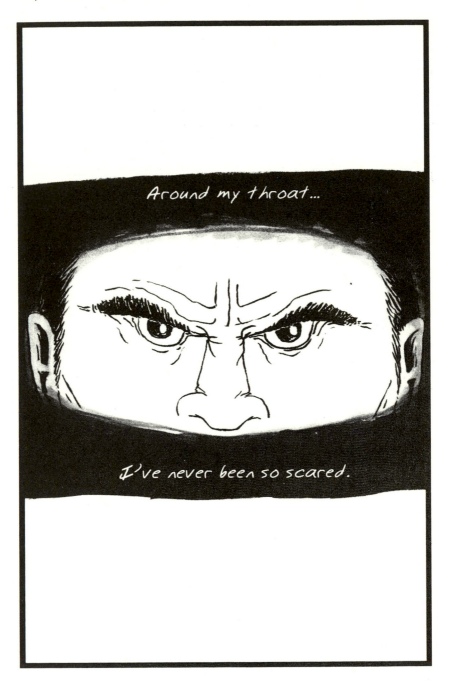

*utile?* And of course *levitas* could not be a shared value of a people renowned for *gravitas*. But then why did they love Plautus so?

Although no book in English has been devoted solely to the comedy of Plautus, several great continental scholars have dealt with aspects of his art, particularly in relation to Greek New Comedy. Still, no one has studied Plautus in relation to contemporary Roman culture or to the comic tradition. Is it merely chance, as some critics would have it, that so much of Plautus is extant and so much of Ennius lost? Is the immense "influence" of Plautus attributable merely to the fact that he happened to be part of the curriculum in Stratford England and at the Collège de Clermont? Is there any inherent value to Plautus *ipsissimus?* Obviously, my own answer to this last question is affirmative, or else this would not be a preface to a book, but an apology for not writing one.

A word about the translations, which, except for instances duly signaled, were prepared by the author for this volume. In a study of the comic significance of Plautus, it seemed to me inappropriate to follow the standard scholarly practice of rendering quotations into literal prose. His happy repartee deserves live dialogue, and his musical moments should be translated into song. Following the principles I set out for my translation of *The Braggart Soldier* (Samuel French 1963), I have tried to approximate the length and rhythm of the Latin verse, adding rhyme where the analogous situation on the English stage would call for it. I have taken no liberties with the Latin, except to omit a conjunction or expletive now and then. Very rarely a metaphor was altered, in the hopes of better conveying Plautus' comic intent. I hope no anachronisms have intruded. My argument is, of course, based on the Latin text, but I confess that my translations were, to some extent, based on my argument.

## PREFACE

If I have contributed anything toward an understanding of Roman comedy, Romans, or comedy, it is due in large measure to guidance and insights received from Harry Levin and Mason Hammond, both of whom read many versions of this book, each time offering valuable advice, new ideas, and welcome stylistic corrections. My colleague A. Thomas Cole also pored over these pages more than once, leading me on many occasions from the path of error to areas of fruitful inquiry. Some of his memos have become paragraphs, others footnotes; all were helpful. Needless to say, the errors that remain are my own.

I am also grateful to Cedric Whitman, who read an early draft, and to Craig LaDrière, who read a later one, for their comments and their constructive criticism. My good friends Frederick H. Gardner and Julius Novick cast sharp eyes on my prose and did much to improve it. C. L. Barber has not read my book, but anyone familiar with the brilliant *Shakespeare's Festive Comedy* will see that I have read *his* and found much inspiration. This volume was patiently and perceptively edited by Anne Miller Whitman of the Harvard Press, to whom I will be ever grateful for giving my manuscript so much of her *t. l. c.* (*tempus, labor, cura*).

Finally, may I thank Eric Havelock, Chairman of the Yale Classics Department, for arranging a leave in the fall of 1965, which enabled me to put much of this book in order. During this time, my research was "subsidized" by various theatrical assignments, for which I am indebted to Mrs. Sylvia Herscher and the William Morris Agency. Very special thanks go to Mrs. Lillian Christmas, who with unflagging good cheer typed draft after draft, and to the friends who encouraged me along the way.

E. S.

Ezra Stiles College
Yale University
January 1968

# Contents

# Roman Laughter

# Introduction

Of all the Greek and Roman playwrights, Titus Maccius Plautus is the least admired and the most imitated. "Serious" scholars find him insignificant, while serious writers find him indispensable. He deserves our careful attention, not merely because his twenty complete comedies constitute the largest extant corpus of classical dramatic literature (more plays than Euripides, nearly twice as many comedies as Aristophanes, more than three times as many as Terence), but because, without any doubt, Plautus was the most *successful* comic poet in the ancient world. We know of no setback in his artistic career comparable to Aristophanes' frustrations with the *Clouds*, or to Terence's inability to hold his audiences in the face of competition from gross athletic shows. What is more, Plautus is the first known professional playwright. Like Shakespeare and Molière (to name two who found him indispensable), Plautus depended upon the theater for his livelihood. Terence could afford to have the *Hecyra* fail twice. Subsidized by the aristocrats of the so-called Scipionic circle, he had merely to satisfy his patrons. Plautus the professional had to satisfy his public.

It was primarily his economic motives which put Plautus into disrepute with the "classicists." Horace threw one of the first stones when he taxed the Roman comedian for seeking only to make money, and therefore ignoring all the rules for proper dramatic construction.[1] But it was easy for Horace to criticize, doubtless in the comfort of the Sabine farm given him by the eponymous Maecenas, far away from the *profanum vulgus* to whom Plautus had to cater — in order to eat. For, if such an attitude be a fault, Plautus must share Boileau's objection to Molière, that of being "trop ami du peuple." Terence could afford to call the Roman audience *populus stupidus* (*Hecyra* 4), but Plautus knew only too well that those "who live to please must please to live." Even the characters within his plays keep an eye on the mood of the spectators. "Be brief," says one of them as the plot nears its conclusion, "the theatergoers are thirsty." [2]

One of the few indisputable statements which can be made about Plautus the man is that he enjoyed great popular success. The ancient biography states that he twice amassed a fortune in the theater. Having lost his first profits in a disastrous shipping venture, he bailed himself out of a Roman version of debtors' prison by writing once more for the comic stage.[3] Thereafter, he entertained no further business schemes; he merely entertained the Romans.

Plautus' popularity reached such phenomenal proportions that his very name acquired a magic aura. It seems that the mere words "I bring you Plautus" were enough to captivate a huge, unruly — and probably drunken — crowd.[4] In contrast, the prologues of Terence, which work feverishly for the spectators' attention, never once mention their author's name, although they refer to *Plautus* three times. And it is well known that unscrupulous producers would put Plautus' name on plays by others to enhance their market value. A century after the playwright's death, there were in circulation over 130 comedies of allegedly Plautine authorship. It had long since become a scholarly enterprise to determine the authenticity of these plays.[5] And Varro's diligent triple cataloguing of definitely-, probably-, and probably-not-Plautus was by no means the final word. Several centuries thereafter, Aulus Gellius is found passing judgments on Plautinity, as is Macrobius still later, on the threshold of the Dark Ages.

The tribute of such prolific plagiarism and forgery is unique in the annals of literature. One never hears of any Aristophanic apocrypha, of pseudo-Menander or pseudo-Terence. The only valid analogy would seem to be with the Spanish Golden Age, when Lope de Vega's name was forged on dramatic manuscripts to increase their commercial value. Even the Shakespearean apocrypha cannot be considered in this regard, since the counterfeits were never so numerous, nor did they entice vast audiences into the theater, as the names of Plautus and Lope obviously did.

No less amazing than the strength of Plautus' name is the durability of his comedy. This phenomenon of vitality is evident not only on the pages of works like Karl von Reinhardtstoettner's exhaustive chronicle of *Spätere Bearbeitungen*,[6] but on the stages wherever comedy has flourished. The Roman playwright is still very much alive in our own day. As recently as 1962, an unabashed *contaminatio* of the *Pseudolus*, *Casina*, and *Mostellaria* entitled *A Funny Thing Happened on the Way to the Forum* delighted Broadway audiences for almost a thousand performances, repeated its triumph throughout the world, and was transformed into a motion picture. Horace might boast that he created a *monumentum aere perennius*, but Plautus created a perennial gold mine.

And yet few scholars of the last century have been willing to examine Plautus for what he undeniably was — a theatrical phenomenon. While the ancient professors like Varro (*diligentissimus*, as Cicero praised him for his research methods) concerned themselves with giving Plautus his due credit by rescuing his name from inferior Latin comedies, the modern approach has shifted from integrity to disintegration. Plautine comedy has become the child in the Judgment of Solomon. From Friedrich Ritschl in the mid-nineteenth century to T. B. L. Webster in the mid-twentieth, a possessive family of scholars have stressed the Roman playwright's "echt-attisches"

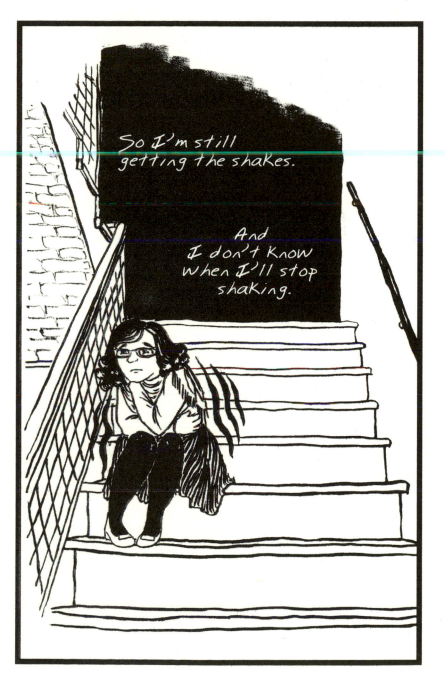

parentage, considering the value of Plautus to consist solely in what may be discerned of his Greek models which lie beneath an exterior defaced by jokes, puns, songs, and anachronisms.[7] Webster states his views in temperate terms, and a few sentences from his *Studies in Later Greek Comedy* may serve to epitomize the attitude of the Hellenists toward Roman comedy in general. He begins by stating that "the Roman copyists . . . are known quantities," and continues:

> Plautus may elaborate the particular scene to the detriment of the play as a whole; he remodels his text to produce song and dance where there was plain dialogue before; he substitutes elaborate metaphor and mythological allusion for the plain and "ethical" language of the original. But this colouring and distortion is a recognizable quality for which allowances can be made.[8]

And Webster is far more objective than was Gilbert Norwood, who argued:

> When the plays are strongly suffused by Plautus' own personality and interests, they are mostly deplorable . . . The result is that we find only one rational principle for discussing his work. The genuinely Greek passages should be distinguished from the far larger bulk where the original has been smothered by barbarous clownery, intolerable verbosity, and an almost complete indifference to dramatic structure.[9]

Norwood's views have not gone out of fashion. And, although recent discoveries of Menander have done little to strengthen the myth of "the perfection of New Comedy," many scholars still attribute everything that sparkles in Plautus to his models, and everything that falters to his fault.[10]

But the case for Roman artistry has not lacked partisans. Eduard Fraenkel's monumental *Plautinisches im Plautus* demonstrated, even to the satisfaction of the Hellenists, that certain turns of phrase, rhetoric, and imagery are uniquely Plautine — and praiseworthy.[11] Indeed, Webster himself acknowledges a debt to Fraenkel's perceptive work.[12] Moreover, in recent years, sound and persuasive studies, particularly by D. C. Earl, Gordon Williams, and John Arthur Hanson, have pointed out the dramatic purpose of many seemingly random Roman references in the comedies, thereby directing Plautine studies into the area which the present writer considers the most vital: the playwright's relation to his public.[13] And yet the Greco-Roman tug of war still occasions extreme arguments on both sides. Thus, in passionate defense of his countryman's art, Raffaele Perna can loose Plautus entirely from his Greek moorings and eulogize "l'originalità di Plauto." [14]

But what exactly is the "originality" being debated? The "fresh new jokes" which Aristophanes keeps boasting of? That "novel something" which Boccaccio presents in each of his hundred tales? If innovation alone were a standard of excellence, King Ubu would take the palm from King Lear. Clearly this is a notion both unclassical and unsound. Ancient theories of art were based on mimesis within traditional genres: an imitation of life. To this Platonic-Aristotelian concept, Roman aesthetics added a second mimetic principle: imitation of the Greeks. Horace in the *Ars Poetica* states it as the first rule of artistic composition. But this had been Roman practice long before it became Horatian precept. One thinks of Catullus and Sappho, or (more to Horace's liking) Virgil and Homer or, for that matter, the odes of Horace himself. Conscious emulation of Greek models was the tradition in Rome from the very beginning.

And for us Plautus *is* the beginning, the very earliest surviving Latin author. After all, Livius Andronicus is some lines and a legend; Plautus is a literature. There is nothing which distinguishes his treatment of Greek models from that of later

Roman artists. The *Ars Poetica* enjoins the poet: *exemplaria Graeca . . . versate manu* (lines 268–269). Plautus frequently describes his technique of composition in a similar manner, e.g. (*Trinummus* 19):

> Philemo scripsit: Plautus vortit barbare.

> Philemon wrote it: Plautus made the "barbarian" version.

What a paradox that Horatian *versare* is a praiseworthy practice and Plautine *vortere* (the same root, after all) is looked upon as a reverse alchemy which transmutes the gold of Athens into Roman dross.[15] The problem is not eliminated even when a scholar of Fraenkel's stature sets out to redeem the Plautine *vortere*,[16] for this merely aggravates the general tendency to anatomize the playwright, to separate "Plautinisches" and "Attisches." But the real Plautus only exists as the sum of his parts — whatever these parts be: *invenies etiam disiecti membra poetae.*

We cannot deny the value of studying a playwright's sources. It is interesting, for example, to know that Shakespeare took Enobarbus' colorful description of Cleopatra on the barge directly from North's Plutarch. The bard copied it almost word for word, altering it chiefly to turn (*vortere?*) prose into pentameter.[17] But are these lines, once in the play, any less Shakespearean? Did it matter to the groundlings who wrote them first? Surely the Roman audience did not care whether what they heard was copied or concocted, as long as it made them laugh. Like Shakespeare and Molière, Plautus begs, borrows, and steals from every conceivable source — including himself.[18] But we must acknowledge that once the play begins, everything becomes "Plautus" just as Plutarch becomes "Shakespeare."

Another circumstance cannot be left unnoticed: Shakespeare's sources fill several well-edited volumes, but there is

not a single Greek original to which a Plautine version may
be directly compared. There is not even a scene or a speech *
that we might contrast with its Latin counterpart in the way
Gellius is able to compare Menander and Caecilius.[19] But we
do have twenty-one thousand lines of Plautus, twenty Latin
plays which share many common elements, regardless of
origin. Of course our view of Roman popular comedy, like
that of Old Attic comedy, is somewhat distorted, since the
work of only one of its many authors is extant. What will be
said of Plautus in the succeeding pages may well have been
true of the comedy of Naevius and Caecilius.[20] Terence, of
course, represents an entirely different tradition: drama for
an aristocratic coterie.[21] The Elizabethans who paid their
penny at the Globe would not have stood for the theatricals
composed in the polite circle of the Countess of Pembroke
any more than the Roman groundlings put up with the
*fabulae statariae* of Terence.

Even if he disagrees with some of the conclusions put forth
on the pages that follow, the reader should not view this study
as yet another round in the *agon* between "Plautinisches" and
"Attisches." For whether we insist upon calling Plautus'
comedy Greek, or dissect it so minutely that we can term it
"Greco-osco-etrusco-latin," [22] there is one undeniable fact to
be faced: Plautus made them laugh. And the laughter was
Roman.

It is impossible to understand Plautine comedy without
appreciating the context in which it was presented; for Roman drama from the earliest times is inextricably connected
with Roman holidays. Livy (7.2) associates the beginning of
theatrical activity with the *ludi Romani* in 364 B.C., when
Etruscan *ludiones* were imported to perform for the populace.
At this same September holiday in 240 B.C., Livius Andronicus

* See now E. W. Handley, "Menander and Plautus: A Study in Comparison" (London 1968).

introduced the first (Greek-into-Latin) "play with a plot." But there is evidence that some kind of performance took place at this harvest festival long before Livy's traditional dates, in the *lusus iuvenum*, which Varro regarded as the true ancestor of Roman dramatic art.[23] Horace describes the "rustic banter" that delighted the farmers during September holidays of a bygone age (*Epist.* 2.1.145–148):

> Fescennina per hunc inventa licentia morem
> versibus alternis opprobria rustica fudit,
> libertasque recurrentis accepta per annos
> lusit amabiliter . . .[24]

From this tradition [of primitive holidays] the Fescennine verses developed, and rustic abuse poured forth in dialogue-verse. This freedom, playing happily along, was welcomed year after year . . .

What characterized these festive occasions (and we need not discuss the precise nature of the "entertainment") was *licentia* (line 145) and *libertas* (line 147), attitudes which also describe the *ludi* in the poet's own day (*Ars Poetica* 211ff), as well as the "libertà e licensiozità carnevalesca" of later Italian festivals.[25] Sir James Frazer found this phenomenon in various cultures throughout the world:

> Many people observe an annual period of license — when the customary restraints of law and morality are thrown aside [for] extravagant mirth and jollity. Though these festivals commonly occur at the end of the year, they are frequently associated with one or another of the agricultural seasons, especially the time of sowing and harvest.[26]

The best known of such festivals is, of course, the Roman Saturnalia held in December.[27] There is a strong possibility that this holiday may have originally taken place in September, that is, at the time of the *ludi Romani*. Many scholars even see in the name Saturnus the suggestion of an agricultural deity.²⁸ Fowler cites the frequent incorporation of winter "saturnalian" customs into harvest holidays — like the *ludi Romani*.²⁹

But I am not arguing for the direct influence of specific holiday customs on Roman comedy. The important connection is the fact that "the holiday occasion and the comedy are parallel manifestations of the same pattern of culture."³⁰ With this principle as his point of departure, C. L. Barber has provided brilliant new insights into Shakespearean comedy. But if Barber's premise is at all valid for Elizabethan drama (which was basically a year-round activity), how much more so would it be for ancient Rome, when the holiday occasion and the comedy are not merely "parallel manifestations" but simultaneous occurrences. All Plautus is literally "festive comedy," since the various *ludi* were the only occasions for dramatic presentations, a condition which prevailed even as late as Juvenal's day.³¹

The festive feeling, as Freud described it, is "the liberty to do what as a rule is prohibited,"³² a temporary excess which implies everyday restraint. Comedy, likewise, involves a limited license, a momentary breaking of society's rules. Man's inner urge to "misbehave," the psychological tension between restraint and release, is not a concept new with Freud. Plato long ago recognized this unconscious desire as one of the prime appeals of comedy.³³ Moreover, if there is truth in Max Beerbohm's statement that "laughter rejoices in bonds,"³⁴ that the joy of the release is in direct proportion to the severity of the restraint, then Roman comedy must have given rise to a laughter of liberation which even the art of Aristophanes (albeit *fecundissimae libertatis*, according to Quintilian)³⁵ could not equal.

For the "bonds" in Plautus' day were literary as well as social. Greek Old Comedy was distinguished for its παρρησία, that celebrated freedom of speech which licensed even the most brutal personal attacks on individuals of high rank. But the Roman Twelve Tables (those antique *tabulae vetantes*, as Horace calls them) [36] forbade the merest mention of an individual by name — even to praise him. Cicero mentions this in the *De Republica* (4.10): *veteribus displicuisse Romanis vel laudari quemquam in scaena virum, vel vituperari,* "the ancient Romans looked askance if a particular person was either praised or criticized on the stage." [37] "Censorship" is, after all, a Roman invention and originally involved much more than jurisdiction over words. The Roman censor was essentially a guardian of behavior.

We must constantly bear in mind that the age of Plautus was also the age of Cato the Elder. In fact, when he wishes to describe the historical period of the late third century B.C., Aulus Gellius links the names of comic author and authoritarian censor in what at first glance seems a most curious tandem (*N.A.* 17.21.46):

> Ac deinde annis fere post quindecim bellum adversum Poenos sumptum est . . . M. Cato orator in civitate, et Plautus poeta in scaena floruerunt.

> And then, almost fifteen years after the beginning of the Punic War, the men of prominence were Marcus Cato the orator in the state, and Plautus the poet on the stage.

The atmosphere in Rome of this era is constantly described by scholars as "spartan" or "puritanical," and it was, without question, conservative in the extreme. Early Roman society was distinguished for its "thou shalt not" attitude which was embodied in a unique series of restrictive, moralistic ordinances, about which Crane Brinton comments in *A History of Western Morals*:

We here encounter clearly for the first time another persistent theme in the moral history of the West, and one that
confronts the sociological historian with some difficult
problems: sumptuary, prohibitory, "blue law" legislation
accompanied by official or semi-official educational propaganda toward a return to "primitive" virtues.[38]

Plautus was just beginning his theatrical career when the first
of these laws, the *Lex Oppia*, was enacted in 2 1 5 B.C. And the
date traditionally given for Plautus' death — 1 8 4 B.C. — was
the famous year in which Cato and Valerius Flaccus assumed
the censorship, to wield their power with a reactionary rigor
that became a legend. Plutarch reports that they expelled one
man from the senate for kissing his wife in public.[39] What
actual effect these "blue laws" had on the Romans does not
bear upon our arguments.[40] Whether or not they were strictly
adhered to is less important than the fact that the rules were
promulgated; they were there. And to appreciate what Plautus' characters are doing, we must be aware of what his contemporary Romans were not supposed to do.

Of course conservatism by definition yearns for the good
old days, and Byron's wry observation is quite true: "all days
when old, are good." Yet in Rome the conservative conscience
was very special. For the Romans had created an impossible
ideal and transferred it to the past, making myths out of the
men who were their forefathers. The Roman obsession with
the greatness of their ancestors is epitomized in Cicero's well-
known apostrophe (*Tusc. Disp.* 1.1):

Quae enim tanta gravitas, quae tanta constantia, magnitudo
animi, probitas, fides, quae tam excellens in omni genere
virtus in ullis fuit ut sit cum maioribus nostris comparanda?

What people ever had such dignity, such stoutheartedness,
greatness of spirit, uprightness, loyalty, such shining qual-

ities of every kind that they could possibly compare with
our ancestors?

The guiding principle for behavior was *mos maiorum*, our
forefathers' precedent. But which forefathers? Cicero lavished
praise on Cato's day, and Cato himself evokes the precedent
of still earlier *maiores nostri*.[41] No Roman of any age could
fulfill the dictates of *mos maiorum* any more than Sisyphus
could push his rock to the summit. Roman *gravitas* (at least
as it is celebrated in literature), was more than seriousness and
avoidance of frivolity. It was a pervasive melancholy nurtured
by a vague sense of guilt and personal unworthiness. The final
lines of Horace's Roman Odes express this (*Carm.* 3.6.46–49):

> Damnosa quid non imminuit dies?
> aetas parentum, peior avis, tulit
>     nos nequiores, mox daturos
>         progeniem vitiosiorem.


> What has ruinous Time not tainted?
> Our parents' age, worse than their ancestors',
>     Bore us, less worthy, soon to bear
>         Children still unworthier.[42]

We find this sentiment everywhere. Cicero begins Book
Five of *De Republica* with the same thoughts. The Roman
mentality was suffused with guilt feelings analogous to Chris-
tian original sin. In the ode quoted above we hear of *delicta
nondum expiata*.[43] In Virgil's *Aeneid* it is voiced even more
strongly; the sins being purged in Elysium are described as
*vetera mala, scelus infectum, concreta labes* (6.735–746).[44]
The fact that these are poetic references to the recent civil
wars, as well as to the mythical sin of Romulus, does not ad-
equately explain the omnipresence of this motif. It was more
than Adam's transgression which caused the medieval loathing

for the flesh. In both societies, the guilt is even more psychological than historical. *Gravitas* may describe a paragon of behavior, but it may also reveal a pathology.

A Freudian psychologist would describe the early Romans as a people with an overdeveloped superego. The superego, as A. A. Brill defined it, is

> a precipitate of all the prohibitions and inhibitions, all the rules which are impressed upon the child by his parents and parental substitutes. The feeling of *conscience* depends altogether on the superego.[45]

These very same words serve as a precise definition of *mos maiorum*, the rules imposed upon the Romans by various parental figures, not the least of whom was *pater* Aeneas! Every Roman institution was a sacred patriarchy, every family the state in miniature. But Aeneas was a myth, and the ideal he embodied an impossibility. It is small wonder that *mos maiorum* is linked with *gravitas*.[46] The superego is the father of melancholy.

But comedy has been described by the psychiatrist Ernst Kris as a "holiday for the superego," [47] and Plautus, reflecting as he does the festive spirit, banishes Roman melancholy, turning everyday attitudes and everyday values completely upside down. To a society with a fantastic compulsion for hierarchies, order, and obedience, he presents a saturnalian chaos.[48] To a people who regarded a parent's authority with religious awe and could punish any infringement with death, Plautus presents an audacious irreverence for all elders. The atmosphere of his comedy is like that of the medieval Feast of Fools (product of another highly restrictive society), which some see as "providing a safety valve for repressed sentiments which otherwise might have broken their bonds more violently." [49] But we need not stress the cathartic value of Plautine comedy; we need only appreciate the fascination

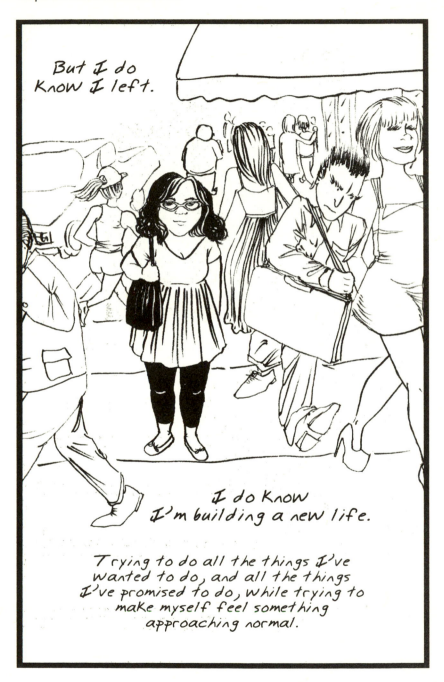

which a flouting of the rules would have had for people so bound by them in everyday life. This very appeal to what Shakespeare called "holiday humor" accounts in large measure for the unequaled success of Plautus.

If we are to understand the whole tradition of popular comedy, we must see Plautus in the proper perspective, and acknowledge that his work is a significant milestone.[50] If it seem bold to compare him with Aristophanes, let us not forget that Cicero did so.[51] Nor should we hesitate to compare to Molière a writer who had also mastered "le grand art de plaire." The most passionate partisan would never place Plautus' achievement on a par with Shakespeare's, but no reasonable man should deny that Plautus was like Noah: great in his age. His art does not give rise to "thoughtful laughter," but Meredith may not be correct in seeing this as the aim of True Comedy. For True Comedy should banish *all* thought — of mortality and morality. It should evoke a laughter which temporarily lifts from us the weight of the world, whether we call it "das Unbehagen," loathèd melancholy, or *gravitas*.

Plautus is our only example of popular Roman entertainment, comedy "as they liked it." His twenty plays show us what delighted a nation on the verge of world domination, in the only age when its theater lived and flourished. Rome went on to build much that remains vital and viable in our own day. The most obvious monuments to her craftsmanship are the aqueducts which still carry water, the bridges and highways which can still be traveled. But when Zero Mostel as Pseudolus trod nightly on his way to the Broadway forum, he was walking another Roman road of astounding durability.

# CHAPTER I

# "O Tempora, O Mos Maiorum!"

The most common dilemma presented in Plautine comedy is that of a young man *amans et egens*, "in love and insolvent," turning to his clever slave for salvation. The desperate youth is usually assured of deliverance, especially if his bondsman happens to be the wily Pseudolus (lines 117–120):

CALIDORUS:  Dabisne argenti mi hodie viginti minas?
PSEUDOLUS:  Dabo. molestus nunciam ne sis mihi.
atque hoc, ne dictum tibi neges, dico prius:
si neminem alium potero, tuom tangam patrem.


CALIDORUS:  Will you get me twenty *minae* — cash —
today?
PSEUDOLUS:  Of course. Now don't annoy me any more.
But so you won't deny I said it, let me say:
If I can't swindle someone else — I'll fleece your father.

The young man's reaction to Pseudolus' plan is vehement indeed (line 122):

Pietatis causa — vel etiam matrem quoque!

Remember love and loyalty — fleece mother too!

This particular comic twist has more significance than the

usual Plautine παρὰ προσδοκίαν, for Calidorus' words have a special Roman moral connotation.[1] The expression *pietatis causa* appears on monuments that Roman sons raised to their fathers out of genuine devotion (in contrast to *ex testamento*, which meant that the father's will had ordered it). Plautus has invoked a pious formula only to reverse it: swindle mother as well as father.[2]

This irreverent outburst typifies the attitude of Plautine sons toward their parents. We find another ready example in the *Bacchides*, where young Mnesilochus vows to revenge himself on the mistress he believes has been unfaithful to him. But since he still loves her, this will be a very special retaliation (lines 505–508):

Ego faxo hau dicet nactam quem derideat.
nam iam domum ibo atque — aliquid surrupiam patri.
id isti dabo. ego istanc multis ulciscar modis.
adeo ego illam cogam usque ut mendicet — meus pater.


She'll never say she played me for an utter fool.
I'll go right home and then — I'll steal something from
                                      father
To give to her. I'll punish her in countless ways.
I'll drive her to the point of poverty — for father.[3]

There is surely no need to emphasize that the young man's plan involves a breach of *pietas*, the very cornerstone of Roman morality. This quality alone led Aeneas (*insignis pietate*) to the founding of Rome. The entire *Aeneid* is in fact epitomized by the exclamation of the patriarch Anchises when he greets his son in the Elysian Fields (6.687–688):

Venisti tandem, tuaque expectata parenti
vicit iter durum pietas.

You've come at last. The *pietas* your father hoped for
Conquered every hardship on your way.

But, whereas love and loyalty inspire Virgil's hero to brave
the dangers of an underworld journey merely to talk to his
father, the sons in Plautus have quite different aspirations. Far
from desiring parental communion, they would prefer their
sires to embark for Elysium as soon as possible, that is, to drop
dead. Philolaches in the *Mostellaria*, for example, sees his
mistress and cries out (lines 233–234):

> Utinam nunc meus emortuos pater ad me nuntietur,
> ut ego exheredem meis bonis me faciam atque haec
> sit heres.

> I wish someone would bring me news right now that
> father's dead
> So I could disinherit myself and give her all my
> goods!

In addition to longing for his father's swift demise, he is eager
to act the prodigal, to give away all his property, an action
which would have been almost as shocking to the Roman
audience. Nor is Philolaches alone among Plautine *adulescentes* in dreaming of parricide and bankruptcy. In fact young
Strabax in the *Truculentus*, like Calidorus, the *pietatis causa*
fellow in the *Pseudolus*, is careful to include his mother as
well in his aggressive agenda (lines 660–662):

> Eradicarest certum cumprimis patrem
> post id locorum matrem. nunc hoc deferam
> argentum ad hanc, quam mage amo quam matrem
> meam.

> My plan is this: I'll first completely wipe out father.
> And then I'll wipe out mother. Now I'll take this cash
> And bring it to the girl I love much more than mother.

Freud considered the hostile impulse against the father to be the very origin of all totemism and taboo.[4] Since the breaking of restrictions is at the heart of all comedy, it is not surprising that this primal taboo should be assaulted here. But the frequent parricidal utterances in Plautus gain special significance when we recall that Roman fathers had absolute power over their children and could have *them* killed if they deemed fit.[5] Typically Roman is the story of Manlius Torquatus, who in 340 B.C. during the Great Latin War had his son executed for disobeying orders, even though the son's courageous but unauthorized attack resulted in a great military victory.[6] The history of Rome is replete with examples of fathers killing disobedient sons. Lucius Junius Brutus, founder of the Roman republic, had his rebellious sons put to death in the year of his consulship.[7] Whether the latter story be fact or legend,[8] its very existence testifies to the Roman preoccupation with filial deference. Of course father-son conflict is a universal psychological configuration, Freud's Oedipus complex being its most famous formulation. But it is of significance that in the Roman version, unlike such legends as the sons of Noah and the son of Kronos (not to mention the son of Laius), it is the father who prevails.[9]

Fears of parricide typify what certain anthropologists call a "patrist" society (as opposed to a "matrist" one, in which the fear of incest dominates).[10] In Rome, where the patriarchal organization maintained its pristine vigor far longer than elsewhere in Europe, veneration for old age was no less intense than at Sparta. Moreover, patriarch and patriotism were associated in the most literal sense. Take, for example, the speech which Livy places in the mouth of Scipio Africanus, a man renowned for his filial devotion.[11] Scipio cites the actions of Coriolanus, another (potential) Roman parricide. Coriolanus, he says, was driven by injustices to assault his fatherland (*ad oppugnandam patriam*) but his Roman loyalty prevailed (Livy 28.29.1):

Revocavit tamen a publico parricidio privata pietas.

Nevertheless, personal *pietas* prevented him from public
parricide.

Rome is truly the fatherland. When Cicero brands a man a
traitor, he calls him *parricida*. And of course in daily life *pietas*
would prevent a Roman from wishing his father dead, just as
it prevented Coriolanus from acting out the parricidal urge.

There is a reason why Plautine characters so often mock
Rome's most solemn and fearful institution. As Dr. Grotjahn
writes, "Jokes grow best on the fresh graves of old anxi-
eties." [12] Freud himself observed that wit attacks those institutions or religious precepts which are so respected that they
can be opposed in no other way.[13] It is worth noting that
there are no outrages to *pietas* in Terence.[14] One may compare
the Plautine "drop dead" scenes we have discussed with a
similar one in the *Adelphoe*, when the young man is informed
of his father's inopportune arrival in town (lines 519–520):

Quod cum salute eius fiat, ita se defetigarit velim
ut triduo hoc perpetuo prorsum e lecto nequeat surgere.

I wish — as long as he stayed healthy — he would tire out
And lie in bed for three whole days, unable to get up.

It sounds very much like a parody of Plautus. It may in fact
be a reaction to the general irreverence which characterized
all Roman popular comedy. When Donatus comments on this
Terentian "anti-father" passage, he contrasts to its mild sentiments the harsh ("Plautine") outburst of a young man from
a play by Naevius: *deos quaeso ut adimant et patrem et matrem meos*, "I pray the gods to snatch away my father and
my mother." [15] Clearly, such an assault on parental *pietas* had
a special appeal for the Roman audience.

Teachers, in Quintilian's words, are "parents of the mind,"

and since Plautus' characters openly flout the Roman dictates
of respect for elders, it is not surprising that Lydus, the tutor
in the *Bacchides*, does not command the traditional veneration
(lines 447–448):

> . . . hocine hic pacto potest
> inhibere imperium magister, si ipsus primus vapulet?

> Just how can a teacher
> Show authority — if he himself's the first one to be
> punched?

Where we should expect deference, we find defiance. In a
comic reversal, the teacher feels the hickory stick. Homer
shows how even Achilles at the height of his wrath was
courteous to his tutor Phoenix, but in Plautus the dignity of
pedagogue as well as parent is ignored or, as in the case of
Lydus, literally assaulted.

We have already seen that many Plautine sons wish their
absent fathers dead. But here in the *Bacchides* young Pistoclerus threatens to kill his tutor face to face (lines 154–155):

LYDUS:    Magistron quemquam discipulum minitarier?
PISTOCLERUS:    Fiam, ut ego opinor, Hercules, tu autem
Linus.

LYDUS:    Does a pupil dare to menace his own teacher?
PISTOCLERUS:    I think I'll act like Hercules. You'll be my
Linus.

As educator, Lydus might take some ironic consolation in the
fact that the murderous threat is couched in a clever mythological reference to Hercules brutally murdering his own
tutor,[16] but this hardly mitigates the shocking breach of
*pietas*. Real-life Rome would not countenance such disregard
for an elder's authority, not the people who spoke admiringly

of the *Manliana imperia*, in praise of the general who put his respectful, loving, victorious, yet "nobly" disobedient son to death.[17]

But *pietas* signifies more than merely respect for one's elders; it is an all-inclusive moral term.[18] In addition to respect for parental authority, it also describes the loyalty of wife to husband, as well as devotion to the gods. The scene in Roman literature that conveys most vividly the totality of what this term connotes is the end of *Aeneid* 2, the exodus from the flaming city of Troy. *Pius* Aeneas (only later to become *pater* Aeneas) leads with his right hand his son Ascanius, in whom the future of Rome resides, and at the same time carries his father on his back. He is, in the most literal sense, shouldering the burden of *mos maiorum*; for his father, in turn, is holding an armful of sacred objects as well as their ancestral gods, *sacra . . . patriosque penatis* (line 717). Aeneas was truly weighed down with *gravitas*; who else but a hero could carry it all? To be a complete Roman was a heavy task indeed.

Following several paces behind Aeneas (and knowing her place) is Creusa, his wife. In a way, she is the archetypal Roman matron, especially when she appears to Aeneas in a vision and bids her *dulcis coniunx* accept their parting in submission to the will of the gods, saying, "Let the love for our son be the bond that joins us."[19] Her tender words are very similar to those which Propertius places in the mouth of Cornelia, paragon of Roman wives, as she addresses her grieving husband from beyond the grave.[20] This too is *pietas*. What is more, the position of the ideal Roman wife was conceived of as Creusa-like — following dutifully several steps behind. Her husband was supreme head of the household and when they were married she came to him *in loco filiae*. In the "good old days," Roman women were never legally independent; they were subject either to a father's *potestas* or to a husband's *manus* ("custody").[21] Andromache's farewell

to Hector, in which she calls him parents and brother as well
as husband, epitomizes what the Romans would later regard as
the ideal wifely attitude.[22]

Plautine comedy (and New Comedy in general) deals
primarily with family life: *res privata*, as Gilbert Murray
described its matter, to distinguish it from the *res sacra* of
Greek tragedy and the *res publica* of Old Comedy.[23] But how
vastly Plautus' families (especially the wives!) differ from the
ideals of the Catonic period. With minor exceptions, Plautine
*matronae* are the antitheses of Creusa and Cornelia. The wives
who appear briefly in the *Stichus* are among the minority who
do believe in conjugal loyalty (lines 7–8a):

> Nostrum officium
> nos facere aequomst
> neque id magis facimus
> quam nos monet pietas.

> It's only our duty
> That we remain true
> What *pietas* bids us
> Is all that we do.

Alcumena in the *Amphitruo* is likewise concerned with
what is *meum officium facere* (line 675). But she is a very
special case, embodying everything the Romans admired in a
wife, especially the virtue of *obsequentia*, loving submission,
a quality celebrated on many epitaphs and one of the three
marital ideals which Gordon Williams describes as "Roman
and in no way Greek."[24] Alcumena sings a song in praise of
her husband's (Roman) *virtus* (lines 642ff), a theme not
elsewhere heard on the lips of a Plautine *matrona*. Amphitryon's wife is loving and *morigera* (dutiful), as she herself argues in the eloquent speech describing her "dowry of
honor" (lines 839–842).

But the typical Plautine matron is *irata*, not *morigera*. She is quite unlike the sympathetic ladies depicted by Terence, Sostrata in the *Hecyra*, for instance. Even Nausistrata in the *Phormio* displays remarkable good nature when confronted with evidence of her husband's bigamy. But in Plautus, the henpecking wife and cringing husband are commonplace. Menaechmus, for example, is hardly blessed with a *dulcis coniunx*. His spouse is a constant source of irritation, as he complains to her: *me retines, revocas, rogitas* (line 114), "You detain me, delay me, demand every detail." When his wife later asks the parasite how to behave toward Menaechmus, he tells her *idem quod semper, male habeas* (line 569), "the same as always, make him suffer." In similar fashion Cleostrata, the wife in the *Casina*, prepares to meet her husband *maledictis, malefactis* (line 152), in short (line 153):

Ego pol illum probe incommodis dictis angam.

I'll torture him with words that cause him great distress.

No wonder a wife is so often likened to a barking dog. It is enough to keep old Periplectomenus in the *Miles* a celibate (lines 680–681):

Licuit uxorem dotatam genere summo ducere
sed nolo mi oblatratricem in aedis intro mittere.


Could've led a wealthy wife of high position to the altar,
But I wouldn't want to lead a yapping dog into my house.

The bitchy wife is hardly a Plautine invention. She is, in fact, the basis of the most ancient "joke" on record, reputedly spoken by Susarion, the legendary inventor of comedy.[25] But she seems to have been an especially popular figure in Roman comedy. We know that Caecilius in adapting Menander's *Plokion* to Roman tastes emphasized and augmented the "anti-

wife" elements in the Greek.[26] He presents a bothersome woman much like those of Plautus:

> Ita plorando, orando, instando, atque obiurgando me optudit.

> My wife bombarded me with crying, sighing, prying, and vilifying.

When Harry Levin called the marriage of Menaechmus "a Punch and Judy relationship," he could have been describing every Plautine household.[27] No blows are literally exchanged on stage, but the militant air is rarely absent. Menaechmus boasts in soldierly fashion, *uxorem abegi ab ianua* (line 127) and *pugnavi fortiter* (line 129).[28] The *Casina* presents a situation closest to an actual husband-wife fistfight, when old Lysidamus urges his slave to strike his wife's servant, while he stands toe-to-toe with Cleostrata, arguing violently (lines 404–407):

LYSIDAMUS: Percide os tu illi odio. Age — ecquid fit?
CLEOSTRATA: Cave obiexis manum.
OLYMPIO: Compressan palma an porrecta ferio?
LYSIDAMUS: Age ut vis.
OLYMPIO: Em tibi!
CLEOSTRATA: Quid tibi istunc tactio est?
OLYMPIO: Quia Iuppiter iussit meus.
CLEOSTRATA: Feri malam, ut ille, rursum.
OLYMPIO: Perii, pugnis caedor, Iuppiter! [29]


LYSIDAMUS (*to Olympio, his slave*): Break that awful fellow's face. Go on — what's wrong?
CLEOSTRATA (*to Olympio*): Don't raise your hand.
OLYMPIO: Shall I use my fist or shall I slap him?

LYSIDAMUS:  As you wish.
OLYMPIO (*hitting the wife's slave*):  Take that!
CLEOSTRATA:  How could you dare touch that man?
OLYMPIO (*pointing to his master*): An order from my Jupiter.
CLEOSTRATA (*to her own slave*): Smash his face right back.
OLYMPIO (*getting beaten*): I'm being punched to death. (*to his master*) Help, Jupiter!

Husband and wife pummel each other by proxy, and it is well worth noting whose slave gets the worst of it; Juno beats Jupiter. This bellicose behavior is completely at odds with the ideal of *obsequentia*, these barking dogs so unlike the celebrated "silent women of Rome." [80] Plautine wives are nothing but a parade of untamed shrews. It is small wonder that a son can turn to his father during a party and ask (*Asinaria* 900–901):

ARGYRIPPUS:  Ecquid matrem amas?
DEMAENETUS:  Egone illam? Nunc amo, quia non adest.
ARGYRIPPUS:  Quid cum adest?
DEMAENETUS:  Periisse cupio.


ARGYRIPPUS:  Don't you love my mother?
DEMAENETUS:  Yes, I love the fact she *isn't* here!

ARGYRIPPUS:  What if she were?
DEMAENETUS:  I'd wish her dead!

Lysidamus in the *Casina* echoes this same sentiment when he remarks, "my wife is torturing me — by staying alive" (line 227). Plautus also deals ironically with the acknowledged wifely virtue of obedience (*Cistellaria* 175):

Ea diem suom obiit, facta *morigera* est viro.

She died — and finally behaved to please her husband.[31]

Clearly the Romans loved this sort of joke, for Caecilius, in the passage quoted on p. 24, presents the very same pleasantry with a few words changed:

> Placere occepit graviter, postquam emortuast.

> She really pleased me as a wife — after she died.

The wish-she-were-dead joke provides the premise for an entire scene in the *Trinummus*, involving a breach of religious as well as family *pietas*. As he leaves home, Callicles, an upstanding *paterfamilias*, instructs his wife in the worship of their Household God with what at first seems like genuine devotion (lines 39–42):

> Larem corona nostrum decorari volo
> uxor, venerare ut nobis haec habitatio
> bona, fausta felix fortunataque evenat —
> teque ut quam primum possim videam emortuam.


> Be sure a wreath adorns our Household God, dear wife.
> And pray, beseech him reverently to bless this house.
> May it be filled with fortune, faith, felicity —
> (*aside*) And may I see you dead as soon as possible.

The twist in line 42 is similar to the sacrilegious outburst of young Calidorus quoted at the beginning of this chapter. The comic principle is the same; this prayer to the *Lar Familiaris* is merely a variation of the *pietatis causa* theme. Another religious formula is invoked only to be overturned. The adjectives employed in line 41 all suggest holiness and fertility, but the comic husband's conception of a blessed house involves a deceased wife.

Of course a noble Roman needs a living wife. Both Creusa and Cornelia urge their husbands to remarry. When Creusa appears to Aeneas in a vision and he rushes to embrace her, Virgil describes the action with the same three lines he employs to depict Aeneas embracing his father.[32] But on the Plautine stage, the attitude of sons to fathers as well as husbands to their wives, is the exact opposite of the exemplary behavior of *pius* Aeneas. There are several parallels to be observed in these comic rebellions against everyday virtue.

To begin with, sons are always overjoyed when their fathers are away. The *Mostellaria* is the classic example, where the patriarch's absence affords the chance for limitless revels. Similarly, husbands are never happier than when their wives are not present. Among innumerable such instances are old Demaenetus' good humor *quia non adest* (*Asinaria* 900, quoted above), and the jubilation in the *Mercator, quia uxor rurist* (line 543). Or as Menaechmus puts it, *clam uxoremst ubi pulchre habeamus atque hunc comburamus diem* (line 152),[33] "hidden from my wife we'll live it up, and burn this day to ashes." And Cylindrus the cook testifies to Menaechmus' change of humor when he is "free" (line 318):

Quam vis ridiculus est, ubi uxor non adest.

How merry he can be — that's if his wife is gone.

The departure of father or wife is always the occasion for a Plautine party.

Secondly, while the sons have no compunction whatsoever about robbing and/or ruining their sires (cf. young Mnesilochus in the *Bacchides*, quoted above on p. 16), husbands never hesitate to steal from their own wives. Menaechmus is one such culprit, although he realizes that he is bankrupting himself in the long run (line 133), and Demaenetus has been plundering his wife Artemona for years, and the woman never even suspected (*Asinaria* 888–889):

Ille ecastor suppilabat me, quod ancillas meas
suspicabar . . .

Oh by Castor, *he's* the one who's pilfered my belongings
and I
Thought it was the maids . . .

In fact the entire plot of the *Asinaria* centers about the
old man's latest attempt at intramarital thievery: *iussit . . .
nos uxorem suam defraudare* (lines 365–366).

Thirdly, there is always antagonism, direct or indirect,
between father and son and between husband and wife. The
first may be a mere battle of wits (with the clever slave acting
as the youth's champion), as in the *Pseudolus* or *Mostellaria*,
or a battle of wills, as in the *Cistellaria*, where the young man
objects to the wife his father has chosen for him. The con-
tention between father and son is more direct in the *Mercator*,
since both are fighting for the same girl, Pasicompsa. In the
delightful "bargaining scene," each pretends to be buying the
lass on behalf of a friend (lines 425–427):

DEMIPHO:  Tace modo, *senex est quidam* qui illam mandavit
mihi
ut emerem aut ad istanc faciem.
CHARINUS:  At mihi *quidam adulescens*, pater,
mandavit ad illam faciem, ita ut illaec est emerem sibi.


DEMIPHO:  Wait — *a certain older man's* commissioned me
to buy the girl
Or a girl of just her type.
CHARINUS:  But sir — *a certain younger man*
Has commissioned me to buy this very type of girl for
him.

It is a marvelously ironic *agon* between the generations, with
neither father nor son aware of who his adversary is.[34] The

*Casina* not only presents the husband-wife pugilistics mentioned earlier but also has an implicit father-son contest.[35] ·The object of the youth (who never appears), as well as his sire, is "droit du seigneur" with lovely Casina (who also does not appear). Here the wife is battling as her son's champion, but Plautus' *matronae* usually need no specific call to war. Their every breath is an ill wind on the sea of matrimony.[36]

Finally, in most irreverent fashion, often adding religious blasphemy to filial or conjugal impiety, sons wish their parents dead, husbands pray that their wives will die quickly. Such mockery of religious practice impugns still another important aspect of *pietas*, devotion to the gods.[37] The harsh attitude toward parents is shocking enough, for as Menander says, "To curse one's parents is to blaspheme the gods." [38] But Plautine characters do not stop at indirect heresy; they blaspheme the gods themselves. The plays contain a great many religious allusions and innumerable references to various deities. This practice contrasts sharply with the style of Terence, who rarely even mentions a god by name.[39] As John Hanson remarks, "Plautus impresses the student of Roman religion with the sheer quantity of material which he presents. No other Latin author, with the possible exception of St. Augustine, can match him in this respect." [40]

Hanson has studied Plautus' abundant use of religious language, not merely in expletives like *edepol*, *hercule*, or *luppiter*, which are as neutral as "for heaven's sake," but phrases like *ita di me ament*, which appears frequently in the dialogue.[41] While this too may have been a cliché to the Roman spectator, he still would have noticed the formula *abused*, as in the *Poenulus*, where young Agorastocles exclaims (line 289):

Ita di me ament — ut *illa* me amet malim quam di!

May the gods love me — oh no! May *she* love me
                                        and not the gods!

Later in the play, old Hanno, a character who strikingly resembles Naevius' description of the patriarch Anchises, *senex fretus pietatei*,[42] calls reverently to Jupiter to show him a "reward for his *pietas*" (line 1190). This same brash youth mocks the old gentleman's appeal, boasting (lines 1191–1192):

> Omnia faciet Iuppiter faxo
> nam mi est obnoxius et me
> metuit . . .

> Jupiter will do whatever I say
> He's in my control, he's under my sway
> And he fears me . . .

Roman religion was notoriously strict: "taboos inherited from the stone age were observed with outer scrupulousness which bordered on absurdity."[43] Long after faith disappeared, *fear* remained. When Plautus was in mid-career, his countrymen were still performing human sacrifice right in Rome.[44] Polybius says that the Roman terror of the gods was a kind of superstitious panic, or δεισιδαιμονία (6.56.7). In light of this, what would the reaction of Plautus' audience be to the remarks of the brash youth who claims that Jupiter fears *him*? One of Agorastocles' subsequent outbursts is still more outrageous (lines 1219–1220):

> . . . ita me di amabunt, ut ego, si sim Iuppiter
> iam hercle ego illam uxorem ducam et Iunonem
>                          extrudam foras!

> May the gods love me, if I were Jupiter himself
> I would marry that girl and kick Juno right
>                          straight out!

We imagine, with horror, Punch and Judy on Olympus.[45] The mother of the gods will be driven from her home by force.[46] Once again in Plautus we find a bellicose relationship between man and wife, here further tainted with blasphemy. And it is worth recalling that even at his most irreverent moments, Aristophanes never abuses Hera.[47]

In sum, the very foundation of Roman morality is attacked in word and deed on the Plautine stage. What is more, in subverting filial devotion, marital concord, and respect for the gods, Plautus' characters express their awareness of the outrages they are perpetrating. The *pietatis causa* joke invokes the very standard it assaults. Sacred practices are parodied with devilish accuracy calculated to remind the audience that ritual is being deliberately stood on its head.[48] When parricide is mentioned in the *Epidicus*, the clever slave not only jokes with the word itself but with a cadenza of puns mocks the brutal Roman punishment for this crime of crimes.[49] Nothing is sacred in the world of Plautus; irreverence is endemic.[50] Scholars have suggested that the impiety of Plautus' characters is the Latin poet's own invention, nowhere to be found in his Greek models, and certainly not drawn from contemporary Roman life.[51] This is very likely. But to denounce Plautus as an artist because, to quote Gilbert Norwood, "his whole morality is utterly un-Roman"[52] is to miss the basic principle of his comedy.

Plautus himself is the first to remark that his own characters are not behaving in the good Roman manner. He often reminds us that his plays are *palliatae*, that is, Greek stories in Greek dress, bearing no relation whatever to Roman practice. Hence those who believe that the purpose of drama (especially comedy) is "to hold the mirror up to nature" (a misguided notion whether argued by Cicero, Quintilian, or Hamlet)[53] therefore consider Plautus to be reflecting the nature of Hellenistic Greece.[54] The Plautine world cannot be Rome, since this was the city which Ennius praised in his famous verse as standing staunchly on its time-honored

morality: *moribus antiquis res stat Romana virisque.*[55] Quite
the contrary, the scene on stage is Athens, described by one
Plautine character as a city *ubi mores deteriores increbrescunt
in dies* (*Mercator* 838), "where every day morality gets worse
and worse." [56] Lines frequently cited to support this view are
those spoken by the slave Stichus, who, after arranging a
dinner party, breaks the dramatic illusion and apologizes to
the audience (*Stichus* 446–448):

> Atque id ne vos miremini, hominis servolos
> potare, amare atque ad cenam condicere.
> licet haec Athenis nobis.


> Don't be surprised that lowly little slaves like us
> Can drink, make love, and ask our friends to supper.
> At Athens we're allowed to do this sort of thing.

This is not the only such passage in the comedies.[57] Moreover,
many critics believe that Plautus feels bound to add an edi-
torial reminder that the dramatic locale is Athens, lest the
spectators be shocked by the antics of slaves like Stichus: "to
make such a sight tolerable, Plautus declares that such things
did happen at Attica." [58]

But there is nothing about Stichus' party which would
offend Roman sensibilities, especially if it is compared to the
practices of the Roman Saturnalia. Our oldest extant description of this festival comes from the playwright Accius, who
was born in the decade after Plautus died. In his day, the
mid-second century, it was a far more sedate holiday than it
became in later ages when, as Seneca saw it, the entire city
went insane (*Epistle* 18). At first the Saturnalia was merely
an occasion when masters waited on their servants, and *cum
dominis famuli epulantur ibidem.*[59] Accius speaks of banquets,
*epulae*, suggesting a more lavish meal than Stichus' *cena*,
which merely means "supper." Moreover, the Roman slaves

dined at the same table as their masters, a thought far from
Stichus' mind. In fact the play specifically states that the
masters are feasting in another house (*Stichus* 662–665). Most
important of all, the masters in Accius' account serve their
own servants in true "saturnalian" fashion, certainly a more
unusual phenomenon than a bondsman drinking with his
fellow slaves, behavior for which Stichus must "apologize,"
assuring the audience that it takes place in distant, dissolute
Athens. Indeed, Stichus doth protest too much.

As further proof that Plautus is not presenting Roman practices, critics note that to describe revels and loose living the
playwright has coined the verbs *pergraecari* and *congraecare*.
As, for example, in the *Mostellaria* (lines 22–24) when the
puritanical Grumio accuses Tranio, his fellow slave, of leading
their young master down the primrose path:

> Dies noctesque bibite, pergraecamini,
> amicas emite liberate, pascite
> parasitos, obsonate pollucibiliter.

> Keep drinking day and night, and Greek-it-up like mad,
> Buy mistresses and free 'em, feed your flatterers,
> Buy groceries as if you were a caterer! [60]

Needless to say, Terence never uses these verbs. *Convivarier*
can describe the same high living without any nasty racial
slurs.[61]

Plautus, of course, is deliberately excusing himself for
comic effect. Stichus' remarks and the playwright's ironic
use of *pergraecari* reflect a technique similar to that of Beaumarchais, who protests that the setting of his *Barber of Seville*
is truly Spain. In Act II, scene xv, for example, Bartholo
remonstrates Rosine, "nous ne sommes pas ici en France, où
l'on donne toujours raison aux femmes." I know of no critic
who has missed Beaumarchais's irony, but there are many who

# AFTERMATH
## EXPLORATIONS OF
## LOSS & GRIEF
Edited by Radix Media

PRINTING & PUBLISHING

NEW YORK

Stacya Silverman's Father

take Stichus' apology at face value. In fact Stichus describes
his behavior even more specifically than *pergraecari*. At the
start of the festivities he cries (line 670), *Athenas nunc
colamus!* Obviously, to "Greek-it-up" to the fullest, one must
go to the capital.

But if the Roman audience really saw this comic world as
Greece, there would be no need to invoke "Athenian license."
What is more, in Athens there is nothing unusual about acting
"in the good old Athenian way," certainly nothing which
would characterize the holiday of which Stichus has been
dreaming. For this day, he says, will be his *eleutheria*, his
festival of freedom. He will be at liberty to celebrate it in any
way he wishes (lines 421–422):

> Nunc hunc diem unum ex illis multis miseriis
> volo me eleutheria capere advenientem domum.

> This "now," this single day, after so many cares,
> Will be my Freedom Day because I made it home.

His holiday will involve not merely the espousal of Athenian
ways but the explicit rejection of all "foreign" elements (lines
669–670):

> Volo eluamus hodie, peregrina omnia
> relinque, Athenas nunc colamus!

> Let's cleanse ourselves today, forget all foreign cares.
> Let's cultivate the great Athenian way!

To be free from care is here equated with being Athenian — at
least for twenty-four hours, *hunc diem unum.*

Stichus' speech may have been in the Menandrian original
on which Plautus based part of his comedy.[62] Praise of Athens

was, after all, common in Greek drama at least as early as the days of Aeschylus. But the passages we are discussing are much disputed; many scholars consider the whole slave party, and especially the lines we have quoted, to be Plautine inventions.[63] Still, whatever their source, these words would have a special connotation for the Roman audience. Plautus frequently gibes at his countrymen in pseudo-Greek manner, calling them "foreigners," *barbari*. (Cato, unlike Plautus, was not amused that those corrupt Grecians would thus refer to noble Romans.) [64] Italian towns are alluded to as *barbaricae urbes* (*Captivi* 884), Italy itself is *barbaria* (*Poenulus* 598), and of course Plautus calls his own plays "barbarian versions" (*Trinummus* 19, quoted earlier).

In light of Plautus' "barbarian irony," I do not think it extravagant to claim that Stichus' Greek-it-up statements would be construed by his audience as an abjuration of things Roman, *peregrina omnia*, as the overture to *pergraecari*. In much the same way, Milton banishes loathèd Melancholy before invoking Mirth, Laughter, and Sport. To Stichus' mind, "all things foreign" represent the cares and woes of duty, which he hopes to forget during this day of merriment. Surely if there is such a strict limitation of being Athenian, it must be because the other days of the year are "Roman."

Another example may help to support this interpretation. In the *Casina*, the slave Olympio is also planning a wild, sensual revel. Whereas Stichus' holiday meant merely a vacation from slavery, Olympio is also celebrating his wedding (and the fact that his master has claimed *ius primae noctis* does not alter his enthusiasm). He wants a luxurious feast, as he shouts to the cooks (lines 744–746):

> Propere cito intro ite et cito deproperate.
> ego iam intus ero. facite cenam mihi ut ebria sit
> sed lepide nitideque volo.
> nil moror barbarico bliteo.

> Hurry quickly go inside and quickly hurry up.
> I'll be right in. Prepare a drunken dinner for me.
> Something fine and fancy.
>                        Keep your bland barbarian stuff!

For this special party, Olympio will have no "flat Roman fare" (as Nixon renders the line). [65] Plautus elsewhere jokes about the colorless Roman diet, as in *Mostellaria* 828, where a Roman carpenter is called *pultiphagus opifex . . . barbarus*, "porridge-eating barbarian workman." In fact, on another occasion the playwright uses similar language to describe himself.[66] Here in the *Casina*, the slave's request for a *cena ebria* is a veritable invitation to vertigo. Contrasted to his intoxicating bill of fare is the Roman meal he so vehemently rejects and, along with it, Roman sobriety. In a Plautine context, the adjective *barbarus* means not only "Roman," but "unfestive" as well.[67] The words of Olympio suggest that *Romanitas* and *festivitas* are incompatible. Paradoxical as it may sound, Greece must be the scene of a Roman holiday.

While Olympio is explicit in his renunciation of things Roman, the constant subversion of *pietas* in Plautine comedy reflects a similar attitude. In their festive mood, Plautus' characters reject everyday morals no less than everyday menus. The constant protestation that the plays are "Athenian" is less a geographical than a psychological phenomenon. Calling a character Greek is merely a convenient way of licensing behavior that is un-Roman. That this was typical of the *palliata* convention may be seen from Plautus' ironic statements in the *Menaechmi* prologue (lines 7–9):

> Atque hoc poetae faciunt in comoediis:
> omnis res gestas esse Athenis autumant
> quo illud vobis graecum videatur magis.

> Now here's what authors do in every comic play:

"It all takes place in Athens, folks," is what they say.
So this way everything will seem *more Greek* to you.

The poet's own scruples inspire him to carry this practice to
absurdity, to tell his audience the complete and accurate
"truth" (lines 10–12):

Ego nusquam dicam nisi ubi factum dicitur.
atque adeo hoc argumentum graecissat, tamen
non atticissat, verum sicilicissitat.


But I reveal the real locations when I speak to you.
This story is quite Greekish, but to be exact,
It's not Athenish, it's Sicily-ish, in fact.

In sporting with a convention, the playwright affirms that it
is only convention. By placing the action in a precise area of
the Hellenistic world, Plautus is really not worried about his
spectators' Roman sensibilities, *ne id vos miremini*, as it were.
For despite this meticulous geographical pinpointing, he never
adds any distinguishable ethnic touches to his Greeks. The
Menaechmus brothers are originally boys from Syracuse, but
the scene of the play is not "Sicily-ish" at all. Epidamnus is
the modern Durazzo in Albania.

But Plautus had no need of characterization or caricature.
His audience knew perfectly well what a Greek was like: he
was their exact opposite. While the Romans were god-fearing
and renowned for keeping their word,[68] to the Greeks *iusiur-
andum iocus est, testimonium ludus* (Cicero *Flacc.* 9.12), "an
oath is a joke, the truth a plaything." This moral antithesis was
already a cliché in Plautus' time.[69] All Greeks were descendants of Sinon, the arch liar who deceived the people of
Aeneas. Virgil is anything but gentle in his treatment of this
incident. He insists on the baseness and guile of all Greeks; to
know one is to know all. They are the embodiments of anti-

*pietas.*[70] The Romans labeled all vice as Greek in much the same way that the English called "French leave" what was known across the channel as "sortie anglaise," and Shakespeare's Englishmen would refer to venereal disease as "the malady of France."

Polybius in 6.56 disguises this prejudice as history; you can always trust a Roman, you can never trust a Greek. In Plautus there are more than seventy-five different expressions to denote Greek perfidy.[71] Perhaps the most famous example is *Graeca fides* (*Asinaria* 199), an instance where a single adjective can transform the Latin word for honesty, devotion, and faithfulness [72] to its polar opposite. The Roman stereotype of the lascivious Hellene even influenced Elizabethan comedy; as early as Udall's *Ralph Roister Doister* (c. 1550) there is a character named Matthew Merrygreek. And Ben Jonson is merely translating *pergraecari* when he has Mosca say to Volpone, "let's die like Romans / Since we have *lived like Graecians*." [73]

Plautus' suspicion of aliens extends to other nationalities. Witness his description of Hanno, the Carthaginian (*Poenulus* 112–113):

> Et is omnis linguas scit, sed dissimulat sciens
> se scire. Poenus plane est. quid verbis opust?

> And he knows every language. Yet he knowingly
> Pretends he doesn't know. It's clear — he's one of *them*.

Beware of non-Romans, they are all "Greeks," ethnic differences notwithstanding.[74] Very little distinguished what Plautus calls *Graeca fides* from what Polybius labels Φοινικικὸν στρατήγημα, "Punic scheming" (3.78.1), in referring to the many disguises of Hannibal. Cicero's view of *Poeni foedifragi*, "faith-breaking Phoenicians," is the same as his attitude toward the Greeks.[75] Both descriptions anticipate that of the most famous dissimulator, Juvenal's *Graeculus* who, like Plautus' *Poenulus*, "knows every science." [76] Since all foreigners (especially rivals) are viewed with suspicion, Juvenal's Greekling can become Dr. Johnson's "starving monsieur," with hardly a change of adjective (*London* 111–112):

> Obsequious, artful, voluble and gay
> On Britain's fond credulity they play.

True to the pattern, the Englishman, to whom duplicity is so alien, falls easy prey to the foreigners because of his noble, trusting nature.

The Roman was god-fearing, faithful, and forthright, a plain dealer. His conversation followed the famous Catonic formula, *rem tene verba sequuntur*, "Stick to the subject, the words follow." At the other end of the scale, rhetorical no less than moral, stood the Greek, "artful, voluble and gay." Similarly, far from being Catonic and laconic, Plautine people are prodigal with words. As Duckworth remarks, "Plautus never uses one phrase if three or six will be more effective." [77] His language is a luxurious feast of words in contrast to the "bland barbarian stuff," the spare Roman style advocated by Cato.[78] This verbal excess — and excess is a primary characteristic of festivity [79] — complements the overindulgent behavior on stage. Both attitudes are excused by invoking "Athenian license," the temporary permission to be un-Roman.

In the world of Plautus, Cato's dictates are always rejected. Here *verba non sequuntur*, but rather, *verba dantur*, that is, the life-style is not simplicity, but duplicity. Both volubility and dissimulation are vices characteristically Greek, so much so that Juvenal regarded these people in totality, as a *natio comoeda*, a race of playactors.[80] And the people of Plautus are a race of players, *acting Greek*. This principle gives Plautus the freedom to mock all that is Roman. Scholars like Leo fail to appreciate these advantages in the *palliata* convention when they lament that Plautus might have become a great Roman writer, that is, of *togatae*, but "did not follow the voice which wished to make him a true poet, and remained a translator, to the grave loss of Roman literature." [81] But perhaps one of the reasons why drama in Roman dress never won real favor at Rome was precisely because its toga-wearing characters were too Roman. Donatus observes that in a *fabula togata* a slave could never act smarter than his master.[82] Is it any wonder that Plautus avoided a tradition which would banish his most vivid creation from the stage?

And yet the *palliata* was Roman comedy. Its basic premise, "it all takes place in Athens, folks," licensed behavior that was ordinarily forbidden. The censorship of Cato might prevail in every corner of the city of Rome, but it could not restrict the revels on the comic stage. Plautus therefore delivers to his spectator a taste of that *other* city, condemned by Cato as a place "filled with every sort of illicit enticement." [83] Witness the prologue to the *Truculentus* (lines 1–3):

> Perparvam partem postulat Plautus loci
> de vestris magnis atque amoenis moenibus
> Athenas quo — sine architectis — conferat.

> Plautus petitions a paltry and paddling portion of space
> Within your great and pretty city walls. A space
> Where he'll deliver Athens — without using big machines.

Now, in his holiday state of mind, the Roman spectator can exchange his toga for the pallium, because this Greek "disguise" permits him to revel with impunity. Freud and countless other psychologists describe comedy as "a disguise to evade censorship." [84] As Dr. Ernst Kris explains it:

If the comic process is to succeed, we may conceive of

this as dependent on two factors. The claims of the instinctual life are satisfied by its content, the objections of the superego by the manner of its disguise.[85]

Is this not precisely what occurs in a Plautine *fabula palliata*? The Roman superego is satisfied by the Greek masquerade, and the audience enjoys an inward revel. For a few hours, the people Virgil eulogized as *Romanos rerum dominos, gentemque togatam*, the lords of the earth, the toga-ed people, doff their noble destiny and don the pallium to act like "good old Athenians." What is a real Roman holiday, after all? In Juvenal's metaphor it is *togam effugere*,[86] "to escape the toga." And so the Roman flees from restraint to release, from censorship to sensuality, from Rome to Athens.

# CHAPTER II

# From Forum
# to Festival

The primary characteristic of "holiday" is its distinct separation from "every day." Ordinary activities cease, the agenda completely changes. In a mood of sincere admiration (not, as so often, sarcastically) Horace praises the ideal "Roman day" (*Epist.* 2.1.103–107):

> Romae dulce diu fuit et sollemne reclusa
> mane domo vigilare, clienti promere iura
> cautos nominibus rectis expendere nummos,
> maiores audire, minori dicere per quae
> crescere res posset, minui damnosa libido.

At Rome it was a pleasure and a practice of long standing to be up and about in the early morning, with the house doors open, giving legal aid to clients, carefully investing money with good-risk creditors, heeding one's elders and teaching the younger generation how to increase their wealth and decrease the ruinous urge to be profligate.

In light of the preceding chapter, it is interesting to note that Horace is here comparing the responsible Romans with the fun-loving Greeks (whom he has just described in lines 93–102). The latter, he intimates, are a "holiday race," whose everyday activities are play, not work. Such noble practices as *clienti promere iura* are contrasted to a Greek agenda filled with games and levity. Horace describes Greek behavior as *nugari* (line 93) and *ludere* (line 99), words which always had pejorative connotations to the Roman.[1]

Horace's "Roman day" also stands in direct opposition to the activities of a "Plautine day." As the previous chapter demonstrated, the people of Plautus do the precise opposite of "heeding one's elders." Such an attitude was a prime characteristic of *pietas*, and this virtue is turned topsy-turvy by the comic playwright. Unlike the economical, obedient sons whom Horace eulogizes, the younger generation in Plautus is always in passionate pursuit of *damnosa libido*. And if Horace epitomizes as *ludere* all activities that contrast with the duties of a "Roman day," it is understandable that the Roman festivals were all called *ludi*.[2]

The *Menaechmi* illustrates in dramatic terms the longing of an ordinary citizen for temporary escape from his everyday agenda. The two houses on stage represent the conflicting forces in the comedy. They are not unlike the statues of Artemis and Aphrodite which frame the setting of Euripides' *Hippolytus*. In both plays, the action takes place in a magnetic field between personifications of restraint and release. It is no mere coincidence that the house of Menaechmus I stands at the exit nearer the forum. The Epidamnian twin is bound by innumerable ties, legal, financial, and social obligations, not to mention his marital bond to a shrewish wife who is constantly "on the job." Menaechmus describes his wife's behavior as excessive *industria* (line 123), a term which almost gives allegorical overtones to the action of the comedy.

Across the stage, and nearer the harbor whence visitors come, dwells a lady of pleasure aptly named Erotium. (Menaechmus' spouse has no name at all, she is merely called *matrona*. Shakespeare reverses this situation in the *Comedy of Errors*, creating a nameless "courtesan.") Menaechmus always seems to have *le mot juste*, for he refers to his mistress as

# THE MARK

Stacya Shepard Silverman

MY FATHER WAS A CON MAN.

When I was twelve, the phone rang one day, and a man asked for my father. When I said he wasn't home, the man said, "Sure he's not."

"But he's not," I said.

"Your father's a crook, did you know that?" His voice was shaking but full of intensity. "He ripped off my entire life savings."

The caller repeated the word *crook* several times before hanging up. I stayed on the phone, the dial tone drilling into my ear. Were we in trouble? My heart pounded and I started to panic; part of me knew that the man wasn't lying. Lately, my dad kept blaming the post office for his lost rent checks, and we'd made a frenzied move from one house to another. I left the phone off the hook, afraid the man might call back.

I looked for my mother, and found her pulling weeds in the back yard. She always treated me like an adult, and was ruthlessly *voluptas*, which is not only an endearment, but the most appropriate description of the atmosphere at Erotium's house, one which contrasts diametrically with the *industria* across the stage. In going from one side to the other, Menaechmus is "acting out" the inner direction of the comic spirit. The comedy itself presents the conflict of *industria* and *voluptas*, holiday versus everyday, or, as Freud would describe it, the reality principle versus the pleasure principle.

As the parasite Peniculus remarks, today's celebration is much overdue, there has been a long "intermission" (*intervallum iam hos dies multos fuit*, line 104). But when Menaechmus gives a party it is almost a national holiday. His parasite, who must be regarded an expert in these matters, says as much (lines 100–101):

> Ita est adulescens: ipsus escae maxumae
> Cerialis cenas dat . . .

> That young chap is like this: the greatest of all eaters,
> The feasts he gives are festivals of Ceres . . .

To Peniculus, his patron's entertainments are like those gala Roman occasions when banquets were served in the Circus; this will be quite a day indeed.

We first meet Menaechmus battling soldier-like against domestic oppression.[3] To him, the precondition for holiday is the absence of his wife (line 152):

> Clam uxoremst ubi pulchre habeamus atque hunc
> comburamus diem.

> Hidden from my wife, we'll live it up and burn this
> day to ashes.[4]

He describes her restrictive behavior in no uncertain terms (lines 114–118):

Nam quotiens foras ire volo,
                me retines, revocas, rogitas,
quo ego eam, quam rem agam, quid negoti geram,
quid petam, quid feram, quid foris egerim.
portitorem domum duxi, ita omnem mihi
rem necesse eloqui est, quidquid egi atque ago.


However often I try to go out, you detain me, delay me,
        demand such details as:
Where I'm going, what I'm doing, what's my business
                                all about,
Deals I'm making, undertaking, what I did when I
                                was out.
I don't have a wife — I've wed a customs office
                        bureaucrat,
For I must declare the things I've done, I'm doing, and
                                all that!

His wife is the antithesis of the holiday spirit; she is both rule
book and conscience, always questioning his behavior. Her
*industria* has driven Menaechmus to seek festive release, as he
himself tells her (lines 122–124):

Malo cavebis si sapis,
virum observare desines.
atque adeo, ne me nequiquam serves, *ob eam*
                                *industriam*
hodie ducam scortum ad cenam atque aliquo
                        condicam foras.


Watch out for trouble, if you're wise,
A husband hates a wife who spies.
But so you won't have watched in vain, for all your
                        diligence and care,
Today I've asked a wench to dinner, and we're eating
                        out somewhere.

The playwright himself understood the psychological motivations for his hero's behavior, as indicated by the remarks of Menaechmus' father-in-law later in the play. When his wife sends for him to complain about her husband's antics, the *senex* blames her, not Menaechmus (lines 788–791):

SENEX: . . . Quotiens monstravi tibi viro ut morem geras,
    quid ille faciat, ne id observes, quo eat, quid rerum gerat.
MATRONA: At enim ille hinc amat meretricem ex proxumo.
SENEX:                                 Sane sapit,
    atque *ob istanc industriam* etiam faxo amabit amplius.


OLD MAN: . . . How often have I warned you to behave
                                        yourself with him.
    Don't watch where he's going, what he's doing, what his
                                           business is.
WIFE: But he loves a fancy woman next door.
OLD MAN:                                He's very wise!
    And I tell you thanks to all your diligence, he'll love her
                                           more!

The old man echoes Menaechmus' opening tirade almost verbatim (especially lines 115 and 122). He excuses the husband's desire to revel, seeing it as the natural result of the wife's excessive vigilance: *ob eam industriam* (Menaechmus, line 123), *ob istanc industriam* (Old Man, line 791).[5]

In contrast to the wife's *industria*, the mistress represents its polar opposite, pleasure personified. When he first spies her, his explanation emphasizes this antithesis, counterpoising as it does *uxor* and *voluptas*, withholding the verb, and hence the entire meaning of the outcry until the last possible moment (line 189):

Ut ego uxorem, mea voluptas, ubi te aspicio, odi male!

Oh my wife, my joy, when I look at *you*, how I hate *her*!

Wife and mistress dwell at the antipodes of human experience;
Plautus states this in no uncertain terms. To visit Erotium is
*pulchre habere* (line 152), whereas life with his wife is a
perpetual atmosphere of *male habere* (line 569). This contrast
— the essential conflict of the *Menaechmi* — goes even further. Just as Erotium is nothing at all like Menaechmus' wife,
so too the day which will be devoted to her will differ totally
from an ordinary day. Even the banquet which the wayward
husband orders would underscore for the Roman audience in
a very specific way that the usual rules would be set aside
(lines 208–213, 215):

Iube igitur tribus nobis apud te prandium accurarier,
atque aliquid scitamentorum de foro opsonarier,
glandionidam suillam, laridum pernonidam,
aut sincipitamenta porcina aut aliquid ad eum modum,
madida quae mi adposita in mensa miluinam suggerant;
atque actutum . . . propera modo.


Please arrange a feast at your house, have it cooked for
three of us.
Also have some very special party foods bought in
the forum.
Glandiose, whole-hog, and a descendant of the lardly ham.
Or perhaps some pork chopettes, or anything along
these lines.
Let whatever's served be "stewed," to make me hungry
as a hawk.
Quickly too . . . and hurry up.

In many ways Menaechmus' menu resembles the slave's request for festive food in the *Casina* (see p. 35). His desire for
something "stewed" echoes Olympio's call for a "drunken
dinner," and in both instances there is an emphasis on "holiday

haste." [6] Most important, each celebrant rejects ordinary
Roman fare. For Olympio, this merely meant "something fine
and fancy" as opposed to "bland barbarian beans." But the
delicacies which Menaechmus orders and all food "along
those lines" were specifically forbidden to Romans by the
current sumptuary laws. These, according to Pliny, forbade
the eating of *abdomina, glandia, testiculi, vulvae, sincipita
verrina.*[7] Not only do these outlawed items figure prominently
on Menaechmus' bill of fare, but Plautus plays with them
verbally, concocting dishes like *sincipitamenta*, and the comic
patronymics *glandionida* and *pernonida*. Apparently Menaechmus is savoring his words in anticipation of the breaking-
of-the-rules banquet.

According to Pliny, Cato's orations constantly inveighed
against gastronomic luxury, especially eating certain cuts of
pork.[8] In spite of this (perhaps because of this), Plautine
gourmets went whole hog, and so, it appears, did the characters of Naevius. Just as the fragments of Plautus' comic
predecessor reveal traces of *pietas* abused, so too they mention
some of the unlawful delicacies.[9] Once again we discover a
Plautine characteristic which may well have been common to
the general *palliata* tradition: a holiday from the rules (here
dietary), further emphasized when the playwright calls attention to the very prohibition being violated.[10]

After ordering his un-Roman banquet, Menaechmus leaves
for the forum. A split second later, his long-lost twin enters
from the harbor. And by artful coincidence, the visiting
brother's very first word upon arrival in Epidamnus is
*voluptas* (line 226). He is little aware of the reverberations
that word will have for him and how apt a description it is
for the whole way of life in this place. For with the exception
of his twin brother's house, this is the ultimate in "party
towns." When the slave Messenio describes it to his master,
he uses only superlatives (lines 258–264):

Nam ita est haec hominum natio: in Epidamnieis
voluptarii atque potatores maxumi;
tum sycophantae et palpatores plurumi
in urbe hac habitant; tum meretrices mulieres
nusquam perhibentur blandiores gentium.
propterea huic urbi nomen Epidamno inditumst,
quia nemo ferme huc sine damno devortitur.


Now here's the race of men you'll find in Epidamnus:
The greatest libertines, the greatest drinkers too,
The most bamboozlers and charming flatterers
Live in this city. And as for wanton women, well —
Nowhere in the world, I'm told, are they more dazzling.
Because of this, they call the city Epidamnus,
For no one leaves unscathed, "undamaged," as it were.

The visiting twin does indeed encounter "voluptuaries,"
especially the dazzling Erotium, but unlike an ordinary tourist
on an ordinary day he will suffer no damage (*dammum* literally
means financial ruin). This boy from Syracuse belongs to a
great comic tradition: a lowly stranger who arrives in town,
is mistaken for someone of greater importance, and fulfills the
comic dream: everything for nothing, or more specifically,
food, sex, and money. Xanthias in the *Frogs* is the first of
such types in surviving ancient comedy, and true to this
tradition is Khlestakov, Gogol's humble government clerk who
is mistaken for the Inspector General and treated accordingly.
Like Gogol's hero, the traveling Menaechmus has come to
town virtually penniless. What ensues seems too good to be
true. A lovely courtesan calls him by name and invites him
to a lavish feast of all the senses . . . at no cost. What
Menaechmus II receives is the precise opposite of *damnum*.
In fact he profits in every imaginable way. Having reveled to
the fullest and been given an expensive dress (supposedly to

be taken to the embroiderer for improvements), he emerges from Erotium's house drunk, garlanded and euphoric; no man, he says, has ever received more favors in just a single day (lines 473–477).

But someone has to pay the bill. And here the local twin suffers a double *damnum*, physical as well as fiscal, for the significant reason that he has gone to work on a holiday. Acting "the good Roman," Menaechmus I has gone to the forum and ended up defending a client in court. According to Horace, *clienti promere iura* was one of the primary duties of the ideal Roman day (see above, p. 42). The fate of Menaechmus I emphatically demonstrates how inimical this activity is to the festive agenda. He finally reenters with a barrage-in-song against the patronage system (lines 571ff).[11] It is a bothersome thing to have clients (lines 588–589):

> Sicut me hodie nimis sollicitum cliens quidam habuit,
> neque quod volui
> agere aut quicum licitumst, ita med attinuit, ita detinuit.

> I was just now delayed, forced to give legal aid,
> no evading this client of mine who had found me.
> Though I wanted to do you know what — and with who —
> he just bound me and tied ropes around me.

Fulfilling one's civic obligations is a form of restraint, it "tied up" Menaechmus (*ita med attinuit, ita detinuit*) and prevented him from following his instinct (*quod volui agere*).[12] In the famous *canticum* which follows, the twin of Epidamnus realizes that his great error was even thinking of business on a holiday. It is as much his fault as his client's (lines 596–599):

> Di illum omnes perdant, ita mihi
> hunc hodie corrupit diem,
> meque adeo, qui hodie forum

umquam oculis inspexi meis.
diem corrupi optimum.
iussi adparari prandium,
amica exspectat me, scio.
ubi primum est licitum, ilico
properavi abire de foro.


By all the heavens, cursed be he
Who just destroyed this day for me.
And curse me too, a fool today,
For ever heading forum's way.
The greatest day of all destroyed,
The feast prepared, but not enjoyed.
My love awaits, I know. Indeed,
The very moment I was freed
I left the forum with great speed.

Plautus stresses the haste with which Menaechmus rushes away from the commercial center (*ubi primum . . . ilico / properavi*). From business in the forum, he dashes to pleasure at its polar opposite: across the stage, at the house of Erotium. The antipodes of the Plautine world are *industria* and *voluptas*, forum and festivity. At Rome, the first step in a holiday direction was always (as quickly as possible) *abire de foro*.

Forum and festivity are also specifically counterpoised in the *Casina*. Like young Menaechmus, old Lysidamus has set this day aside for merrymaking (*ego cum Casina faciam nuptias!* line 486), and has ordered a luxurious banquet. But again like Menaechmus, Lysidamus has been detained by a lawsuit in the forum. He finally reenters, having learned his lesson (lines 563–568):

Stultitia magna est, mea quidem sententia,
hominem amatorem ullum ad forum procedere,

in eum diem quoi quod amet in mundo siet;
sicut ego feci stultus. contrivi diem,
dum asto advocatus cuidam cognato meo;
quem hercle ego litem adeo perdidisse gaudeo.

It's folly, that's what I would call it, total folly,
For any man in love just to approach the forum,
The very day his love awaits, all fancied up.
That's what I've done, fool that I am. I've ruined the day,
While acting as attorney for a relative.
By Hercules, I'm overjoyed we lost the case!

*Ad forum procedere* has destroyed Lysidamus' festive plans
(*contrivi diem*) just as a similar journey had spoiled Menaechmus' day (*diem corrupi optimum, Menaechmi* 598a). Again,
like the twin of Epidamnus, Lysidamus has been defeated in
court.[13] Totally devoid of professional pride, Lysidamus is
happy to have failed. These lawyers' laments prove con-
clusively that funny things happen only on the way *from* the
forum.[14]

The prologue to the *Casina* affirms this interpretation of the
festive rule.[15] It demonstrates that the lesson which Menaechmus and Lysidamus learn the hard way is actually the first
principle of Roman holiday. The prologue's appeal to the
public is very specific (lines 23–26):

Eicite ex animo curam atque alienum aes,
ne quis formidet flagitatorem suom.
ludi sunt, ludus datus est argentariis;
tranquillum est, Alcedonia sunt circum forum.

Just kick out all your cares, and as for debts, ignore 'em.
Let no one fear fierce creditors will sue.
It's holiday for everyone — for bankers too.[16]
All's calm, a halcyon quiet floats around the forum.

The prologue speaks not merely of the play, but of the day as well. The *ludi* are on, here in Rome, and there is an unusual silence even in the very center of business. So unequivocal is this statement that all commerce has ceased that each of the lines quoted contains a financial or business reference: to debts, creditors, bankers, and the banking district. During the *ludi* all ordinary activity came to an absolute standstill, a practice which Cicero, in the heat of prosecuting Verres, vehemently objects to, but could do nothing to change.[17] On a Roman holiday there was simply no business — but show business. The forum was empty because the theater was packed. The sons of Aeneas, longing like Menaechmus to loose their everyday ties, to travel from the regions of *industria* to the realm of *voluptas*, had all beaten a path to that festive place which may best be described as being as far as possible from the forum.

The Roman may have flatteringly pictured himself as a paragon of *pietas*, but an objective view sees him as more pragmatic than pious. His materialistic attitude is evident even in Horace's idealized "Roman day," where the poet lauds the noble practice of heeding one's elders. The parents he pictures are not imparting to their children *mos maiorum* in the spiritual sense but are rather lecturing them on sound investment policy: *per quae / crescere res posset* (*Epist.* 2.1.106–107). And *this* was in fact considered a Roman virtue. In the oft-quoted eulogy by Quintus Metellus at his father's funeral (221 B.C.), the son claims that his father achieved the ten greatest things (*decem maximas res optimasque*) which wise men strive for, and these include not only being first in war and first in peace, but being first in finance as well: *pecuniam magnam bono modo invenire*.[18] It is well attested that the Romans were extremely fond of money and would pass up no opportunity for financial gain.[19] Horace's picture of the straightforward with me. I told her about the man and the accusations he'd made. A small part of me wanted her to say that it wasn't true.

"Your father did rip off that old man," she said. She didn't soften the blow.

When my father came home, I was in a rage. I felt humiliated and ashamed, as if the whole world knew, and I hated him for it. I confronted Dad, calling him what the man said he was—a crook.

Dad looked at me, and his face went slack. He opened his mouth as if to say something and his arms fell limp to his side, the ashes from the cigar in his hand dropping to the floor. I expected him to either defend himself, or tell me that I was in trouble for yelling at him. Instead, a look of fear spread across his face, as if *he* were the child in trouble. He stood frozen like this for a while, smoke swirling around him, eyes wide, and he didn't or maybe couldn't speak. He turned around and left, slamming the front door behind him. I felt powerful. My anger had spooked my father out of the house. I was proud of myself for telling him off, and, for a while anyway, glad that I had made him slink away.

My father was charming and folksy. He used his North Carolina drawl, cowboy hat, and early success in the music business (he told people he wrote "Blue Christmas") to make others feel instantly comfortable and impressed with him. He often bragged that he could have started his own religion, though he was hostile towards believers privately. If I could journey back in time, I'd tell everyone I'd ever met not to give my dad any money. Even my mother tried to warn the people whom dad singled out as easy marks, but she eventually decided that if they didn't want to listen to her, then it was their problem. If I had told people the truth, they wouldn't have taken my skinny, buck-toothed, little-girl word over his smooth talk, anyway. Even I didn't know the extent of my dad's scams until the day the man called.

When I was a teenager and got my first paying job, Mom told me to hide my money, and I did, usually in the pages of a book in my room or in a shoe box under my twin bed. Mom said that if Dad knew I had any cash, he'd borrow it and never pay me back, that I should lie to him and say I spent it. She complained about him endlessly and I began to tune her out; I eventually stopped listening to her at all.

Roman father teaching his son to enlarge his patrimony serves
well to describe Cato the Elder, who, according to Plutarch,
considered a man who increased the capital he inherited to
be "marvelous and godlike," θαυμαστὸς καὶ θεῖος.[20]

Polybius, like Terence, was a protégé of Scipio Aemilianus
and could hardly be praised for writing *sine ira et studio*; yet
in his Universal History he punctuates what is essentially a
panegyric celebrating the superiority of Roman qualities to
Greek with the candid observation that the Roman was
extremely difficult, in fact a stickler when it came to financial
matters. As Polybius sees it, this quality is not unpraise-
worthy; it suggests that the Romans were hyperefficient and
kept a good house. He states in no uncertain terms that at
Rome you get nothing for nothing (31.26.9):

ἁπλῶς γὰρ οὐδεὶς οὐδενὶ δίδωσι τῶν ἰδίων ὑπαρχόντων
ἑκὼν οὐδέν.

Absolutely no one gives anyone *anything* he possesses of his
own free will.

Polybius' emphatic language demonstrates how antithetical
the typical Roman outlook was to the comic spirit. Max
Eastman observes that in comedy it is "the *too* much —
always and absolutely — not the *much* that is funny." [21] But
according to Polybius "too much" is a completely un-Roman
concept. In the pragmatic "nothing-for-nothing" atmosphere
of workaday Rome, there could be none of the laughter
which Freud saw as inspired by the aspect of "an excessive
expenditure of energy." [22] The Romans had a violent aversion
to spending anything, as Polybius notes further: "their punctiliousness about expenditures is as intense as their compulsion
to turn every second of time into profit" (31.27.11). One of
Plautus' most brilliant characters, Euclio the miser, reflects
this trait, caricatured to absurdity. He would not only refuse

to expend the energy for laughter, but he is parsimonious even with his ordinary breath (*Aulularia* 302–303):

PYTHODICUS:  Quin cum it dormitum, follem obstringit ob
gulam.

ANTHRAX:  Cur?

PYTHODICUS:  Ne quid animae forte amittat dormiens.

PYTHODICUS:  Why when he sleeps he strings a bag around
his gullet.

ANTHRAX:  What for?

PYTHODICUS:  So he won't lose a bit of breath while
sleeping.

Euclio is also madly possessive about his bath water (line 308), his hunger (line 311), and his fingernails (lines 312–313). When he is viewed with Polybius' description in mind, Euclio seems very much a "Roman parody." In the next chapter we will discuss other Plautine characters who are comically compulsive about time and money — if not the air they breathe.[23] The Romans were notoriously stingy (we need not paint the lily by calling them "economical"). Plautus even mocks their well-known miserliness in one of his prologues. As mentioned in the previous chapter,[24] the *Truculentus* opens with an invitation to the audience to make room in their imaginations so that Plautus can deliver Athens to Rome (lines 1–3). The prologue then muses light-heartedly about what would happen if Plautus would ask the spectators to *pay* for this delivery. He quickly concludes that Romans would refuse to hand over any cash whatever, noting further that the spectators would be following in the footsteps of their forefathers (line 7):

Eu hercle in vobis resident mores pristini!

By Hercules, the great traditions live in you! [25]

Although in the "Roman day" which we have been discussing he lauds the pursuit of wealth, Horace the moralist more often deplores the Roman predilection for material gain at the expense of spiritual enrichment.[26] But whether we believe the poet when he is admiring or critical, we are none the less presented with a Roman society imbued with the doctrine of acquisition. And "doctrine" it was. This attitude seems to have been characteristic of the Romans from the earliest times, and at least one scholar sees it as an implicit aspect of *mos maiorum*.[27]

Moreover, while the Roman praised profit-making by noble means, as in the elder Metellus' accumulation of wealth *bono modo* (see above), in point of fact he gathered his lucre *quocumque modo*, by means fair or foul. Witness Horace's deprecation of a current maxim (*Epist.* 1.1.65–66):

> . . . rem facias rem
> si possis, recte, si non quocumque modo, rem.

These are the very lines that Ben Jonson renders in describing the materialistic atmosphere of his contemporary London (*Every Man in His Humour* II v 49–51):

> The rule, "get money"; still, "get money, boy,
> No matter by what means; money will do
> More, boy, than my lord's letter."

Thus while the Romans may have extolled *virtus* in word, in deed they placed money before morality, *virtus post nummos*. Horace imagines this as a phrase which echoes and reechoes from one end of the forum to the other.[28] Even Cato, for all his celebrated asceticism, chased huge profits in the most disreputable manner.[29] Ironically, Livy praises him as a *contemptor . . . divitiarum* (39.40.11), an ambiguous compliment, suggesting that he had no regard whatever for wealth, in the very manner Virgil described his ideal hero Aeneas, who responded nobly to King Evander's request, *aude, hospes, contemnere opes*.[30] But Livy surely means that Cato was unawed by the riches of others, probably because he had gathered so much for himself, and *quocumque modo*, at that.

In direct contrast to Horace's picture of the forum resounding noisily with shouts of *quaerenda pecunia*, we may have the situation described by the *Casina* prologue, *tranquillum est, Alcedonia sunt circum forum* (line 26). This atypical calm, this empty business district, characterizes a Roman holiday, the only occasion on which the city did not echo with the cry, "get money."

The characters of Plautus display an attitude diametrically opposed to the markedly Roman regard for profit. His comedies almost always involve money matters, but never the pursuit of wealth for its own sake. The typical Plautine youth may be *amans et egens*, but he only seeks money enough to win his beloved. Quite unlike Balzac in his *Comédie Humaine*, Plautus never presents a scheming protagonist in search of "une femme et une fortune." His young men are lunatic-lovers who scorn material things. Phaedromus in the *Curculio* (*verum totum insanum amare*, line 177) provides a ready example: *sibi sua habeant regna reges, sibi divitias divites* (line 178), "let kings have kingdoms, rich men have their riches." This is, of course, a cliché, a romantic outburst that in most contexts would be taken with a grain of salt (although it specifically reminds the student of Latin poetry of that unRoman poet Tibullus).[31] But these Plautine lovers live up to their word; they want the girl, not the gold.

Nowhere in Plautus do we find an ambitious young man like Balzac's Eugène de Rastignac. Though there are several marriages in the plays, the affluence of the girl's family is never a motivating factor.[32] Yet this affects even Shakespeare's suitors from time to time, as, for example, Fenton in *The Merry Wives of Windsor* (III iv 13–16):

> Albeit I will confess thy father's wealth
> Was the first motive that I wooed thee, Anne,
> Yet wooing thee, I found thee of more value
> Than stamps of gold, or sums in sealèd bags.[33]

The attitude of Plautus' lovers toward dowries stands in sharp distinction to what actually went on in Roman society at the time, where the size of the bridal portion greatly influenced most marriages. Polybius makes this point, describing very complicated dowry arrangements, the payments to be made in three precise installments, and so forth.[34] Not only does the behavior of the Plautine hero differ from the practices of the audience, but it contrasts with the outlook of almost all comic heroes, perhaps typified by Beaumarchais's scheming barber, of whom the countess remarks, "Figaro n'est pas homme à laisser échapper une dot." In fact Figaro is after *two* dowries and ends up with *three*, a triumph celebrated in the final song,

> Triple dot, femme superbe
> Que de biens pour un époux! [35]

Even if a dowry is mentioned in Plautus (which is seldom), it is dismissed with a shrug or rejected without regret. Thus Megadorus in the *Aulularia* is not only willing, but anxious, to take Euclio's daughter *sans dot*, a condition which became a famous *mot de caractère* in Molière's adaptation.[36] The plot of the *Trinummus* involves arranging a dowry for a young man who wants none at all. Lysiteles tells his father that he would marry into his best friend's family (lines 374–375, 378):

LYSITELES:  Soror illi est adulta virgo grandis: eam cupio,
pater,

ducere uxorem sine dote.

PHILTO: Sine dote uxorem?

LYSITELES: Ita.

. . . . . . . . . . . . .

PHILTO: Egone indotatam te uxorem ut patiar?

LYSITELES: Sir, his sister is a grown-up girl, and she's the
one I'd like to

Take to wife without a dowry.

PHILTO (*choking*): Without a dowry? Wife?

LYSITELES: That's right.

. . . . . . . . . . . . .

PHILTO: Can I really bear to let you wed a wife without
a dowry? [37]

The sire is far from pleased, but the son convinces him.[38] Even
when the girl's father arrives unexpectedly from abroad and
offers a marriage portion, Lysiteles insists, *dotem nil moror*
(line 1158). He finally relents, but the subject is dismissed
forever three lines later. In the *Cistellaria*, young Alcesimarchus rejects great riches and a huge dowry for his true love
Silenium. His father is distraught and beseeches his son to
abandon a sweetheart who "keeps you from great wealth, a
dowry both fat and plentiful," *prohibet divitiis maximis, dote
altili atque opima* (line 305), but not even the most passionate
pleas can impress upon the Plautine lover the (everyday)
value of money.[39]

If a dowry is suddenly reduced, as in the *Truculentus*,
because the young man has been too forward with his fiancée,
the youth cares little (lines 844–846):

CALLICLES: . . . verum hoc ego te multabo bolo:
sex talenta magna dotis demam pro ista inscitia.

DINIARCHUS: Bene agis mecum.

CALLICLES:　. . . you'll be fined a pile for this:
　Six whole talents from her dowry for your little
　　　　　　　　　　　　　　　　indiscretion.
DINIARCHUS:　Oh, you're very kind to me.

And the situation in this play differs vastly from that of the *Cistellaria*. Here young Diniarchus is not a rhapsodic Romeo willing to give all for love and the world well lost. When the above-quoted conversation takes place, he has already ravished Callicles' daughter, given her a child, and then broken the engagement. From a pragmatic point of view, he has a very strong bargaining point, since the old man is anxious to give his grandchild legitimacy. Yet here again, and this time without strong motivation, a Plautine lover pays no attention to the practical matters that concerned his audience almost to the point of obsession.

Scholars have called attention to the multitude of commercial references in Plautus, to the countless mentions of contracts, debts, lawsuits, business trips, and so forth. But few have noted that this is rarely "business as usual." The only meaningful transactions are those which bring the youth the girl he longs for. In almost every instance, the sum of money for which the clever slave is scheming turns out to be just enough to buy his master's sweetheart and nothing more. Profit for its own sake is never a factor; gold is merely the means to an end. Here again Plautine and Balzacian worlds stand in direct contrast. At the end of *Eugénie Grandet*, for example, Judge de Bonfons marries the heroine for her fortune, but agrees to forgo all conjugal rights. In Plautus the situation is just the reverse: *connubium* always takes precedence over *commercium*.[40] As one of his typical *adulescentes* expresses it (*Poenulus* 328):

Namque edepol lucrum amare nullum amatorem addecet.

A lover should love love, by Pollux, not love lucre.

Plautus presents a world where *ludi sunt argentariis*, whereas in Balzac, as old Grandet tells his daughter, "la vie est une affaire."

In Plautus, money is meaningless, coins are merely tokens to be redeemed for pleasure. It is more than coincidence that in the *Asinaria* the amount needed to purchase the girl Philaenium is precisely the sum being delivered as payment for the asses: twenty *minae*. This price is mentioned no less than eighteen times during the play, but its "value" lies only in what it represents, a yearlong holiday with a beautiful courtesan (*Asinaria* 636–637):

> ARGYRIPPUS: Videtin viginti minae quid pollent quidve possunt?
> ille qui illas perdit salvos est, ego qui non perdo, pereo.

> ARGYRIPPUS: You see what power and potential twenty *minae* have?
> To spend them is to save myself; with none to spend, I'm spent! [41]

The aim is to gain the money with a view toward "losing it" again. The sum they are after is just enough; but to the Plautine lover, "just enough" is *satis superque*.

An even stranger phenomenon is that the prime mover in the plots, the clever slave, is never after profit for himself.[42] This is especially odd considering that slaves in Plautus' day were not only permitted, but encouraged, to amass their own *peculium* (personal savings). Bondsmen who did not try to save toward their ultimate freedom were looked upon with disdain and suspicion.[43] Yet Plautine slaves do not care for cash. Epidicus executes his particular scheme so well that he obtains more money than his master needs. Triumphantly, he hands the sack of gold over to his young *patronus*, asking for no financial reward (*Epidicus* 345–347):

EPIDICUS:  . . . accipe hoc sis.
STRATIPPOCLES:  Quantum hic inest?
EPIDICUS:                Quantum sat est, et plus satis:
                                  superfit.
decem minis plus attuli quam tu danistae debes.


EPIDICUS:  . . . now take this please.
STRATIPPOCLES:  How much is here?
EPIDICUS:            Enough and more — an extra overflow.
I've even brought you ten more *minae* than you owe the
                                  broker.

How would the Roman audience react to this? Polybius
claimed that absolutely no one in Rome would refuse any
opportunity for any sort of profit, yet here a slave rejects an
ideal occasion to add to his *peculium*. For Plautine slaves,
however, the playing's the thing. Toxilus in the *Persa* best
expresses this attitude when he shouts, *iam nolo argentum!*
(line 127).[44] Like Epidicus and other slaves with like esprit,
the only profit he seeks is nonmaterial.

The *Poenulus* presents an interesting variation on this
theme. Here the young lover is not *egens*, but *affluens*. His
riches could easily buy the lovely Adelphasium from the
pimp. But his clever slave Milphio would never permit such
an ordinary procedure (lines 163–169):

MILPHIO:  . . . Vin tu illam hodie sine dispendio
tuo tuam libertam facere?
AGORASTOCLES:               Cupio, Milphio.
MILPHIO:  Ego faciam ut facias. sunt tibi intus aurei
trecenti nummi Philippi?
AGORASTOCLES:             Sescenti quoque.
MILPHIO:  Satis sunt trecenti.
AGORASTOCLES:        Quid iis facturu's?

MILPHIO: Tace.
totum lenonem tibi cum tota familia
dabo hodie dono.

MILPHIO: . . . How would you like, today,
To free her at no cost to you?
AGORASTOCLES: I'd really love to.
MILPHIO: I'll see to it you will. Do you have gold inside —
Three hundred *nummi*?
AGORASTOCLES: I could give you *double* that.
MILPHIO: Three hundred is enough.
AGORASTOCLES: What will you do?
MILPHIO: Just wait.
Today I'll take that pimp with his entire household
And give him to you as a gift.

From a practical point of view, all the trickery in the *Poenulus* is absolutely superfluous. Agorastocles can afford to purchase whatever he desires. But one of the prime characteristics of "holiday" is its sharp distinction from the ordinary. Thus Milphio, who insists upon extraordinary, *un*businesslike methods, will have his way. Like Epidicus, Milphio uses cash merely as a stage prop in his merry masquerade. In fact, later in the *Poenulus*, Plautus has one of the lawyers whom Milphio has hired for his trickery step forward and break the dramatic illusion to emphasize, paradoxically, that "it is all illusion" (lines 597–599):

Aurum est profecto hoc, spectatores, comicum
macerato hoc pingues fiunt auro in barbaria boves;
verum ad hanc rem agundam Philippum est: ita nos
adsimulabimus.

Folks, this money here is strictly "player's gold."
When the stuff's dissolved, it's used by foreigners to
fatten bulls.

When Dad came around asking for cigar money, I always handed over what I had, exposing my carefully thought out hiding place and he'd always say the same thing: "Pay you back with interest, kid." He valued my loyalty, and I felt that our emotional connection meant more than his dishonesty, unpaid loans, and broken promises. I told myself that I understood him better than anyone else.

I was proud to be the one my father chose. I know that he'd had several children with different women before I was born, children that he did not keep in contact with. He had been married four times before meeting my mother in the 1960s, and I was the only child he raised. He abandoned the others either before they were born, or by age three or four. Dad told me I couldn't meet my brothers and sisters because the mothers didn't want him around anymore. It made me feel sad for him, but I also wondered if he might some day vanish from my life, never to be seen again.

Even if his other kids had tried to contact him, our constantly changing addresses made him difficult to find. He used eighteen different names over his lifetime, and had several Social Security cards. During their first nine years together, he'd made my mother promise not to contact anyone she'd ever known, not even family. We never seemed to have money, and we were often evicted.

Right after Dad stormed out of the house on the day I called him a crook, he sat in his beat-up Oldsmobile smoking his cigar. He stayed out there for a long time, even through dinner. When he came back inside, he said, "My own daughter thinks I'm a crook? Who keeps food in this house? Who pays the rent? Where do you suppose you're gonna live?" He didn't speak to me for the rest of the night. I went to bed more anxious than angry.

For breakfast the next morning, he made me buttermilk pancakes with homemade syrup. Dad was no longer pouting, he was chatty and engaging. He told me that I reminded him of his grandmother, Martha Amelia Merritt Tindal, and went on to say what a strong woman she was and how much he admired her. It was a stark contrast to the previous night.

"You're gonna be rich—I'm leaving all my royalties to you, kid," He told me. He said that his projects would pay off the investors with

But, to act this whole thing out, we'll just pretend
                King Philip coined it.[45]

This is quite in the spirit of the prologue to the *Casina*, which
reminded the audience that all businesses were closed, while
at the same time referring to many commercial activities.
Here too, at the very moment the actor is assuring the
audience that all is "play," he also alludes to Roman ("barbarian") husbandry, noting that the lupine seeds being used
on stage as money were ordinarily soaked and fed to fatten
oxen. Today is a holiday for *farmers* too.

But we still have not explained why Milphio has cooked up
this theatrical scheme, this game with *aurum comicum*, when
his young master Agorastocles could have solved all problems
— that is, purchased the lovely Adelphasium — in a normal
businesslike manner. Indeed, there has been much critical discussion on this matter. Why does the playwright present such
"psychological improbabilities"? This is a question posed by
Legrand, who then adds: "Occasionally the devices and tricks
by the actors have no *raison d'être*, or else there is no possibility for their resulting in any good." [46] What Legrand here
objects to is precisely what Johann Huizinga in *Homo Ludens*
defines as "play," an activity with no *raison d'être*, "and no
profit can be gained by it." [47] We are near the very fountain-
head of comedy, which developed, as Freud saw it, from
"play." [48] The profitless trickery which Plautus presents reflects a levity quite the opposite of *gravitas*: the spirit of
holiday, and especially that of the Roman *ludi*.

Plautus' heroes go even further than ignoring monetary
gain. They rush with holiday haste toward financial disaster.
Prodigality replaces pragmatism as the order of the day. As
mentioned earlier, good business sense was an implicit aspect
of *mos maiorum*. A fine Roman son will increase his patrimony, *bono modo* if he is a noble Metellus being praised
posthumously, but *quocumque modo* if he is anything but

dead. In the *Mostellaria*, Plautus uses the verb *patrissare* to suggest this "business tradition." When old Theopropides returns from abroad, he is told that his son has purchased a house. Overjoyed at the youth's sound judgment, he exclaims (line 639):

Patrissat! iam homo in mercatura vortitur.

Taking after father! Now the boy's become a businessman.

The truth, of course, is that his son has turned in precisely the opposite direction. The verb which best describes young Philolaches' behavior is not *patrissare*, but *pergraecari* (line 960), as well as *potare* (lines 946 and 964) and *perpotare* (line 977). In a phrase, instead of taking after father, he is taking *from* him: *suom patrem . . . perdidit* (line 979), a contrast which Plautus drives home with abundant alliteration.[49]

In reality, *mos maiorum* was more mercantile than moral. Young Charinus in the *Mercator* acknowledges as much. His father had set a shining precedent, investing his own patrimony in *mercatura* and acquiring prodigious wealth (lines 73–78). Charinus realizes that his sire expects him to turn to commerce as well: *me idem decere, si ut deceret me forem* (line 79). And much to his parent's delight, the boy embarks on a commercial voyage. At first he seems his father's son (lines 93–97):

Rhodum venimus ubi quas merces vexeram
omnis ut volui vendidi ex sententia.
lucrum ingens facio praeterquam mihi meus pater
dedit aestimatas merces: ita peculium
conficio grande.


We came to Rhodes, where all the goods I brought along
I sold — and just the way I wanted to. I made
A great enormous profit, far above the price

That father specified. So for myself I gained
A lot of extra money.

The youth's spectacular success has realized a double reward, *lucrum ingens* for his father, and *peculium grande* for him. But the subsequent fate of this money exemplifies what happens to all income in Plautus (lines 98–99):

Hospes me quidam adgnovit, ad cenam vocat.
venio, decumbo acceptus hilare atque ampliter.


An old friend spied me and invited me to dinner.
I came, relaxed, received a lush and lovely welcome.

The initial intent to *patrissare* is overcome by the irresistible urge to *pergraecari*.[50] The youth succumbs to the holiday spirit *hilare atque ampliter*, and by the morning, *lucrum* has been sped to its polar opposite, *damnum*. The Mercator's son has surrendered to the same *damnosa libido* against which the elders in Horace's "Roman day" have preached. He has squandered all his earnings on a girl whose very name, Pasi-compsa ("Omni-pleasant"), suggests that she is pleasure personified. Since it is not unlikely that Plautus invented her name,[51] the metamorphosis of *peculium* into *pasicompsa* would then be a conscious echo of the *industria* to *voluptas* theme in the *Menaechmi*, another victory of the pleasure principle over the reality principle.

The voyage of Charinus, the Mercator's son, typifies the behavior of innumerable other Plautine characters toward matters pecuniary. Moreover, they are reckless with *pecunia* in its most literal sense: *pecus*, farm animals.[52] Very often in Plautus we find the un-Roman tendency to forsake livestock in pursuit of liveliness. One thinks of three ready examples which would have made the author of *De Agri Cultura* shudder, if he couldn't laugh. Asses in the *Asinaria*, oxen in the *Persa*, and sheep in the *Truculentus* all become debit items to pay for pleasure.[53] In the first play, as mentioned earlier, the asses have been sold for the magic sum of twenty *minae*. This payment is en route to Demaenetus' wife and the plot revolves around a masquerade to have the right price fall into the wrong hands. In the *Persa*, the slave Sagaristio has been given money by his master to purchase *domitos boves* (line 259), but these funds will serve bachelorhood, not husbandry (lines 262–264):

SAGARISTIO: nam hoc argentum alibi abutar: boves quos
emerem, non erant;
nunc et amico prosperabo et genio meo multa bona
faciam,
diu quo bene erit, die uno absolvam . . .


SAGARISTIO: Yes, I'll waste this money somewhere else. The
oxen won't exist.
Now I'll help a friend and do myself a few good turns.
We'll *live*!
In a single day we'll burn it all . . .

Sagaristio fully realizes he is putting good money to bad uses, *argentum abutar*, but proper business procedure will be ignored for one splendid day of pleasure.[54]

In the *Truculentus*, the sheep represent earnings from a deal which Strabax' farmer-father has negotiated. But here again, profit is quickly reversed to loss. Forgetting the frugal ways his parent has taught him, Strabax hastens from country simplicity to city luxury, in passionate pursuit of "joy" (he states his desire to *gaudere* three times in lines 922–924). His own account bears quoting in full, since he displays many of the (disgraceful) characteristics we have previously noted in Plautus' young men (lines 645–657, 660–661):

Rus mane dudum hinc ire me iussit *pater*,
ut bubus glandem prandio depromerem.
post illoc quam veni, advenit, si dis placet,
ad villam argentum meo qui debebat *patri*,
qui ovis Tarentinas erat mercatus de *patre*.
quaerit *patrem*. dico esse in urbe. interrogo
quid eum velit.
homo cruminam sibi de collo detrahit,
minas viginti mihi dat. accipio libens,
condo in cruminam. ille abit. ego propere minas
ovis in crumina hac in urbem detuli.
fuit edepol Mars meo periratus *patri*,
nam oves illius hau longe absunt a lupis.

.   .   .   .   .   .   .   .   .

eradicarest certum cumprimis *patrem*,
post id locorum matrem . . .


This morning early father sent me to the country,
He ordered me to give the cows some nuts for breakfast.
But when I reached the farm, a man came — praise the gods!
A man who owed a sum of money to my father,
Because he'd bought some sheep a while ago from father.
He asks where father is. I say he's in the city.
I ask him what he wants.
He takes a leather wallet from around his neck,
He gives me twenty *minae*. I accept. Why not?
I put them in my wallet. Then he goes. I rush.
I bring the wallet with the sheep-cash to the city.
By Pollux, Mars was surely angry with my father,
These sheep of his are not far from "the house of wolves."

.   .   .   .   .   .   .   .   .   .

My plan is this: I'll first completely wipe out father
And then I'll wipe out mother . . .

No son could be more aware of his filial obligations. Strabax mentions his father four times in the first six lines. Like young Charinus in the *Mercator* (line 79), he fully realizes that he should be taking after father, not taking from him. But he suddenly receives the magic sum of twenty *minae*, which is precisely the cost of the girl (and the asses) in the *Asinaria* and the same amount which Pseudolus must swindle to win his master's sweetheart. And in young Strabax we note once again the holiday haste (line 654) toward merriment reminiscent of Menaechmus, Olympio, and so many others. In but a few seconds, pragmatic provincial becomes prodigal parricide,[55] as Strabax throws his father's sheep-money "to the wolves."

To state the comic paradox succinctly: pound-foolishness in Plautus is as common as penny-pinching was in the Rome of his day. And the Latin poet is not merely presenting an extravagant revel, for this is at the heart of every comedy. Yet Aristophanes can present a *komos* without mentioning who is paying the bill. In Plautus, however, part of the pleasure seems to be that *someone else's money is being wasted*. To explain why this appealed to his audience we may invoke Freud or *Schadenfreude*: the stingy Roman enjoys a vicarious prodigality similar to the secret pleasure he derived from seeing *pietas* abused. For the parsimonious, *industria*-bound spectator, Plautus provides an imaginary excursion to a land of *voluptarii maxumi* much like the place where Menaechmus lives, there to succumb to what might be termed *Epidamnosa libido*. But prodigality of the imagination involves no real loss; on holidays, joy comes *sine damno*. In fact, since these revels are paid for in *aurum comicum*, they bring dividends of laughter.

# CHAPTER III

# Puritans, Principles, and Pleasures

We have thus far seen that Plautine comedy reflects the kind of holiday attitude described by the prologue to the *Casina*. The rules are put aside, reality rejected, and pleasure pursued. But at any festival there is always a minority so strongly attached to the business of everyday life that it cannot join the merrymaking. This group of "spoilsports," incapable of play, constitute the antagonists to the comic spirit. In one way or another, but usually in a literal sense, they remain "on the job." But, as Bergson observed, the precondition for comedy is quite the reverse: it is an atmosphere in which one's thoughts are "absent . . . away from his work." [1] These non-players are also non-laughers, and in the discussion to follow they will be referred to as "agelasts," [2] following Meredith's definition:

> We have in this world men whom Rabelais would call "agelasts," that is to say, non-laughers, men who are in that respect as dead bodies, which, if you prick them, do not bleed . . . In relation to the stage, they have taken in our land the form and title of Puritan. [3]

The most famous "Puritan" on the English stage, the agelast par excellence, is Shakespeare's Malvolio. In *Twelfth Night* his prime antagonist, Sir Toby Belch, is a passionate defender of cakes and ale, the embodiment of holiday. In fact, the conflict between Malvolio and Toby is not unlike that in the *Menaechmi* between *industria* and *voluptas*, and the implicit theme of all Plautine comedy, Roman austerity versus *pergraecari*. A further coincidence is the fact that "Puritanical" has always been a convenient adjective for describing Roman social attitudes of Plautus' day.[4] Shakespeare's picture of Malvolio (III iv 4), as "sad and civil," that is, serious and sedate, is also an epitome of the *gravitas* in which the Romans prided themselves. But on the comic stage, whether Plautine or Shakespearean, such a character is bound to be unpopular; since a *komos* involves universal levity, all gravity must be put to flight.

In Plautus the agelast is sometimes an enemy to festivity because he is a Catonic Puritan carrying his *gravitas* to absurdity, but more often because he embodies the typical Roman attitude toward money, since, as we have seen, the Romans paid lip service to *pietas* but real service to "payment." In a word, the Plautine spoilsport is a caricature of actual Roman attitudes who stands in violent contrast to the atypical "Greek" holiday atmosphere passionately celebrated on stage.

One character who closely resembles Malvolio is Lydus, the straitlaced tutor in the *Bacchides*. This "comic Cato" is a humorless, inflexible defender of the old *disciplina* (lines 135, 421), a man so obsessed with the ancestral, ascetic way of life that he completely forgets the golden mean; his concern with past virtue precludes all present laughter. Like Malvolio, Lydus equates all celebration with damnation. When he accompanies his young pupil Pistoclerus to the home of the courtesan Bacchis, the tutor inquires who lives behind these doors. The youth's reply suggests that the building is a shrine where dwell (*Bacchides* 115–116):

Amor, Voluptas, Venus, Venustas, Gaudium,
Iocus, Ludus, Sermo, Suavisaviatio.

Affection, Luxury, Love, Loveliness, Joy,
Fun, Games, Conversation, and Kissy-kissy-kissy.

In deifying these abstractions, young Pistoclerus is mocking a common Roman religious practice; we are reminded once again of the *pietatis causa* jokes discussed in Chapter I.[5] And this youth is a devoted acolyte who considers any attitude which disparages the sanctity of his shrine to be blasphemy (lines 118–119). His pantheon of pleasures includes many of the festive joys which attract Plautus' protagonists, including Menaechmus' *Voluptas*, the *Gaudium* which appeals to young Strabax in the *Truculentus*, as well as the *Sermo* and *Venustas* which figure among the divine pleasures at Pseudolus' revel.[6] It follows that a Puritan like Lydus the tutor does not believe in this kind of indulgent "religion" and can only preach incessantly the abstemious cloistered virtue of *mos maiorum*. But a party is no place for pious admonitions.[7] In *Twelfth Night* the revelers begin the fun by banishing all thoughts of virtue, even in song. When Feste is first asked to sing, he inquires what subject matter would please his audience most (II iii 32–35):

FESTE:  Would you have a love song, or a song of good
life?

TOBY:  A love song, a love song.

ANDREW:  Ay, ay, I care not for good life.

Thoughts of the good (that is, moral) life, *disciplina*, if you will, do not fit the festive mood. Sir Toby and company prefer Pistoclerus' pantheon: *Amor, Gaudium, Iocus, et al.* And like Lydus in the *Bacchides*, "virtuous" Malvolio denies the existence of these divinities of joy. In his view, Toby's party has desecrated the somber atmosphere of mourning that prevails in Olivia's home (II iii 80–85):

My masters, are you mad? Or what are you? Have you

no wit, manners, nor honesty, but to gabble like tinkers at this time of night? *Do you make an alehouse out of my lady's house*, that ye squeak out your coziers' catches without any mitigation or remorse of voice? Is there no respect of place, persons, nor time in you?

Lydus has an attitude which is strikingly similar. He sees Bacchis' abode as anything but celestial. In fact, after a brief look inside, as he furiously rushes from the courtesan's house, the tutor literally makes a hell of his pupil's heaven (lines 368, 373–374):

Pandite atque aperite propere ianuam hanc *Orci*, obsecro.
. . . . . . . . . . .
omnis ad perniciem instructa domus opime atque opipare,
quae ut aspexi, me continuo contuli protinam in pedes.


Hurry quickly, open wide, unbar these awful gates of Hell!
. . . . . . . . . . .
That whole house was built for ruin — sumptuous and
                                                    scrumptuous.
And the second I beheld it, speedily, I speeded out!

Like Malvolio, Lydus sees the "holiday house" as an inferno to escape as quickly as possible. Moreover, the speed with which he *rejects* these joys contrasts to the "holiday haste" of the typical Plautine merrymakers. His frantic dash *from* pleasure, *propere . . . continuo . . . protinam*, reminds us (in reverse) of Olympio in the *Casina* (*propere cito intro ite et cito deproperate*, line 744) and, of course, Menaechmus' anxiety to flee the forum.[8] Agelast and reveler react with similar urgency but rush in opposite directions. While the reveler seeks release, the spoilsport cries for restraint. In fact, "restraint" is the watchword of the agelast, as may be observed in the words of Lydus as he complains of Pistoclerus' a lot left over, and not to worry. I was still confused, but I started to feel bad about yelling at my dad. Besides, he was right—I had nowhere else to live. This dark and complicated experience had to be packed up and put away, a memory to recall when I had the luxury to do so.

Dad ended up leaving my mother after twenty-three years. He told her he was taking a short trip to Los Angeles, but he never returned. I'm the one who tracked him down over a year later, in an effort to keep our dysfunctional relationship afloat. Had I not done that, I don't know if he would have ever contacted me.

When my father died in 2009, I impulsively dashed out an obituary and included many of the other names he used, his many marriages and other children. Sending the obituary to the small town newspaper felt like a betrayal. It took me a long time to see the impact of being raised by him. It is still deeply confusing to me, even as a full-grown woman, to understand why I tolerated his behavior, or why anyone else would.

My last visit with him was in the nursing home where he spent his final years, in a small town in California. The former mayor of the town was there, too. He was one of the few friends my father still had. We chatted for a while about my dad's health before he said, "Your father ripped off everyone I ever introduced him to." I wondered why the hell he kept introducing him to people, but said nothing. I didn't know what to say. I couldn't explain his continued faith in my dad's bullshit anymore than I could explain mine.

Later, my mother told me other things about my dad's past, like that he had been caught stealing from his family's grocery store in Wilmington, North Carolina when he was maybe ten or eleven years old. His grandmother—the one he claimed I take after—sent him off to a boy's home in a nearby town called Rocky Mount as punishment. The home was later known as "The Fountain School," which makes it sound nicer than the cruel place it was in the late 1920s. I'm not sure how long he had been there—it may have been months, maybe a year. Even a week in that place would have been a severe punishment for a child. Dad had confided in my mother that it was a horrible place, and that he had been beaten and raped by the older boys. The experience, rather than reforming my father's penchant for stealing, made him a roistering to the young man's father: *non sino, neque equidem . . . sinam,* "I won't allow it, no indeed, I won't allow it" (line 419). But Pistoclerus' father defends pleasure in moderation (lines 416–418):

Paulisper, Lyde, est libido homini suo animo obsequi

.   .   .   .   .   .   .   .   .   .   .

dum caveatur, praeter aequom ne quid delinquat, *sine.*


Lydus, for a little while, why can't a man indulge himself?

.   .   .   .   .   .   .   .   .   .   .

If he's careful and he doesn't go too far — allow the spree.

This advocacy of limited license acknowledges holiday as a natural human need. But the agelast is totally unnatural; he cannot comprehend or accept the briefest lapse into pleasure, since he himself is incapable of relaxing his own iron grip on pragmatic realities, and let go even *paulisper.*

In his perceptive essay, Northrop Frye describes "the argument of comedy" as essentially the reintegration of society, the movement toward a harmonious dance in which everyone joins hands.[9] What we have here labeled the agelast, Frye calls the "blocking character," because this dour person impedes the comic hero's progress and delays the universal celebration. As Frye sees it, this anti-comic character may be dealt with in one of two ways: he may either be purged of his "ruling passion" (what Ben Jonson would call a "humor" and modern psychologists a "compulsion") and be included in festive society, or else, if he is too rigid to be converted, he must be expelled.[10] In the latter instance, the obstructing antagonist resembles the scapegoat in the primitive rituals which F. M. Cornford compared to Attic comedy.[11] This is, in fact, a configuration discernible in all comedy and has a parallel in the plays we are discussing.

The Plautine plot very frequently involves the banishment of a blocking character. In fact the playwright seems to be translating the festive exhortation of the *Casina* prologue [12] into dramatic terms (line 23):

Eicite ex animo curam atque alienum aes.

Kick out all your cares, and as for debts, ignore 'em.

The verb *eicere* suggests vigorous physical action [13] and gives this phrase greater force than a similar invocation to revelry by Martial, where the poet merely asks his pale cares to "go away": *pallentes procul hinc abite curae* (11.6.6.). In Plautus, the agelasts personify the *curae* which the holidaymaker should expel from his mind. Moreover, the association of *cura* and *alienum aes* in the *Casina* prologue is not a casual one. As we have already demonstrated, the average Roman was preoccupied with financial matters, and to enjoy himself he would have had to banish from his mind not some vague "loathèd Melancholy" but a very specific concern about money. This fact explains why the Plautine agelast is almost always connected with *alienum aes*, a bill to be paid.

Next to the clever slave, the spoilsport is Plautus' favorite figure.[14] A. McN. G. Little has noted the playwright's predilection for characters who can easily be turned into butts. This, says Little, conforms to the entire tradition of popular comedy, and the nature of the comic victim has varied little through the centuries.[15] Nor has the treatment given the agelast type differed from age to age, as may be seen from the following verses, which began an "Asses' holiday" in thirteenth-century France:

Lux hodie, lux laetitiae, me iudice tristis
quisquis erit, removendus erit solemnibus istis,
sint hodie procul invidiae, procul omnia maesta,
laeta volunt, quicunque colunt asinaria festa.[16]

Let there be joy today, nothing but joy today.
    Anyone serious
Should be removed from these services, I judge him
    quite deleterious.
Far away be all our troubles, everything sad far away.
Everywhere joy, not a thing to annoy those who
    worship the Asses today.

Here the spoilsport will be ejected for being *tristis*, "sad and civil" like Malvolio. On the Plautine stage, we have seen such a figure in Lydus the tutor, shouting for gravity. But the most common trait of the Plautine agelast is greed, an obsession with *lucrum*, making him a caricature of the typical materialistic Roman. Euclio, the miser in the *Aulularia*, is perhaps the most famous example. His compulsive avarice prevents him from letting go, either with his purse or his person. Even though he makes an effort, he cannot even provide a wedding party for his daughter. When he returns from "shopping," he protests to the audience that he had really tried to make this a special day. In fact, Euclio's use of *bene habere* reminds us of Menaechmus' festive plans to *pulchre habere* [17] (*Aulularia* 371–372):

Volui animum tandem confirmare hodie meum
ut bene me haberem filiai nuptiis.


I really wanted to convince myself today
To let myself be merry for my daughter's wedding.

Though he intended to buy all sorts of lovely delicacies, he found everything to be "too expensive"; it was impossible to make a single purchase (line 377). Quite the opposite of a man on holiday, Euclio simply cannot take his mind off tomorrow, especially tomorrow's bills. He rationalizes his abnormal behavior with the maxim (lines 380–381):

Festo die si quid prodegeris
profesto egere liceat.


On holiday the cash that flows
Is cash a man tomorrow owes.

But the very act of rationalizing is itself, according to Dr. Sandor Ferenczi's analysis, a kind of mental miserliness, "a means of preventing a squandering through action." [18] This observation would certainly be supported by the behavior of Euclio, who embodies the ἀκρίβεια ("punctiliousness") which Polybius saw as so typically Roman.[19]

Plautus' miser displays the whole gamut of anti-holiday attitudes. His personality quirks even hinder the "caterers" he has hired to prepare the meager fare which will serve as a nuptial "feast." Euclio's concern with finances makes him harass and admonish the cooks, until one of them asks with exasperation whether in fact the old man is trying to *restrain* them (line 431):

Volo scire *sinas* an non *sinas* nos coquere hic cenam?

Will you allow or not allow us to cook dinner?

A second chef wonders (line 435) just what it is that makes Euclio "prohibit" them from preparing the party. They do not realize that he is struggling vainly with himself to "let go."

Euclio's money-mania prevents him from any sort of enjoyment, try as he may (lines 371–372), for when it comes to *bene habere*, the cry of the agelast is not *volo*, but *nolo*. Even when there is no longer a question of his paying the bill, when it is merely a case of having fun at someone else's expense, Euclio is incapable of giving in; he must remain "on the job." Thus, when the would-be bridegroom Megadorus offers him some splendid wine, Euclio will not savor it, even though it is free. Fearing that his precious pot of gold will be stolen unless

he remains vigilant and in control of his senses, the miser
refuses to join the party (lines 569–572):

MEGADORUS:   Potare ego hodie, Euclio, tecum *volo*.
EUCLIO:   Non potem ego quidem hercle.
MEGADORUS:                                At ego iussero
   cadum unum vini veteris a me adferrier.
EUCLIO:   *Nolo* hercle, nam mihi bibere decretum est aquam.


MEGADORUS:   Euclio, I want to drink with you today.
EUCLIO:   No, I won't drink, by Hercules.
MEGADORUS:                                But I insist!
   I'll have some vintage wine brought over from my house.
EUCLIO:   I won't, by Hercules. I'll stick to drinking water.

For this stingy agelast, the ensuing banquet will be the exact
opposite of the *cena ebria* which the slave Olympio orders for
his own nuptial feast (*Casina* 746, quoted earlier). Because of
his obsession, Euclio's bill of fare would emphatically exclude
the "stewed" items that Menaechmus longs for.[20] His avarice
denies him any relaxation whatever; he is tied to business, to
the obligation of being "on guard." As he himself describes
his behavior in watching his treasure (frag. 4):

   Nec noctu nec diu
   quietus umquam servabam eam [aulam] . . .


   Not night or day
   I never had a moment's peace while guarding it.

The miser's ceaseless vigilance (*servabam*) is not unlike the
attitude of Menaechmus' "industrious" wife, whose own
energies are totally absorbed in *servare* and *observare*.[21] Such
characters are slaves to the reality principle, and are usually
unaware of what natural pleasure they are missing. Euclio is

different in this regard, in that he ultimately realizes what his obsession has deprived him of. He confesses as much when his pot of gold is stolen (lines 724–726):

> Perdidi quod concustodivi
> sedulo. egomet me *defraudavi*
> *animumque meum geniumque meum.*
> nunc eo alii laetificantur
>     meo malo et damno.

> It's lost, though I guarded hard night and day for it
> Cheating my soul and my self as a whole.
> Now others are hearty, they're having a party
> And using my losses to pay for it.

There is a faint echo of Menaechmus I's complaint, when the unlucky twin discovers he has paid for a revel which another has enjoyed.[22] And true to the "festive rule," the man who thinks of business loses pleasure as a result. Euclio, however, seems to end up happier than most Plautine agelasts, who are usually punished and excluded from the final party. From what we can deduce of the lost finale to the *Aulularia*, he is one of those rare blocking characters in Plautine comedy who are converted and, in Frye's terminology, "integrated into society."[23]

The most common agelast figure in Plautus is the pimp, a character who displays the worst anti-comedy attitudes, namely ill humor and greed. Of all the people in the happy-go-lucky Plautine world, only the *leno* arouses the playwright's genuine indignation; Plautus hates this kind of spoilsport. Even in the *Rudens*, a play of generally serene emotions, when the slave Trachalio is asked for a *brief* description of Labrax the pimp (line 650), he makes the following vitriolic reply (lines 651–653):

Fraudis sceleris parricidi periuri plenissimus
legirupa impudens impurus inverecundissimus
uno verbo absolvam, lenost: quid illum porro praedicem?

Foully full of fraud and falsehood, parricide and perjury
Unbelievably untruthful, unrestrained, unlawful too.
In a single word: the man's a pimp. What need to tell
you more?

This *animus* is universal in Plautus.[24] Witness the diatribe
he places in the mouth of Curculio, a tricky parasite who
happens to be dealing with the kindest, most humane procurer
in all Roman comedy. The following is merely a part [25] of his
attack (*Curculio* 499–502):

Item genus est lenonium inter homines meo quidem animo
ut muscae, culices, cimices pedesque pulicesque:
odio et malo et molestiae, bono usui estis nulli,
nec vobiscum quisquam in foro frugi consistere audet.

Here's what I think the pimpish breed is in the world
of men:
Just like mosquitoes, gnats and bugs, like lice and flies
and fleas.
You're hateful, damned and damaging, no good to anyone
at all.
No decent man could stand to stand up with you in
the forum!

The pimp arouses this kind of wrathful bitterness because he
makes a business of pleasure. What is play to others is work
to him. While Plautus' young men blithely empty their
coffers to fill their couches, the churlish pimps remain in
earnest pursuit of profit.[26]

Nothing deters a Plautine *leno* from seeking gain. His

watchword is truly *quaerenda pecunia primum est*. Ballio in
the *Pseudolus*, for example, a character so infamous that his
name was to become a generic term,[27] says that even if he
were sacrificing in the temple, he would drop everything
should a chance for profit come along, for money-making is
— *pietas* (lines 267–268). Ballio and his colleagues of the
pimpish breed provide Plautus' prime targets for attacking
anti-holiday sentiment. Because they reflect the workaday
Roman attitude toward *lucrum*, the pimps suffer physically
and financially and are finally expelled from the festivities.
In brief appearances (their very brevity a significant contrast
to Plautus) Terence's two *lenones*, Dorio in the *Phormio*
and Sannio in the *Adelphoe*, are paid in full. The Plautine
pimp is *always* punished. True enough, Labrax in the
*Rudens* does get invited to the final banquet, but not
before he suffers a great monetary loss as well as a harsh
roughing up by the burly slaves of the man who ultimately
becomes his host.[28] Labrax' case is a unique exception, and the
tone of the *Rudens*, like that of Shakespeare's *Tempest* (to
which it is often compared), is one of universal forgiveness
and reintegration.

A closer look at but one of Plautus' agelastic pimps will
give an accurate impression of the entire *genus lenonium* in
his comedies. Dordalus in the *Persa* is a dour procurer par
excellence, a man so obsessed with profit that he simply
cannot enjoy himself, and his watchword, like that of Euclio
the miser, is *nolo*. The plot of the *Persa* is a very simple one:
the slave Toxilus wishes to free his sweetheart and hold an
unrestrained revel. The tone of the play is established by the
opening repartee in which Toxilus invites his fellow slave
Sagaristio to come join his party (lines 30–31):

> Si tu tibi bene esse
> pote pati, veni: vives mecum
> basilico accipiere victu.

> If you can endure to
> Live it up, come on! You'll live with me, as
> Stylish as a king of kings!

Toxilus' playful remark, "if you can *endure* enjoyment" has ironic reverberations when we consider the pimp's behavior in the final scene. For, despite the fact that a universal *komos* is planned, Dordalus, like every agelast, is unable to *bene esse*. Menander's Knemon was terribly chagrined at having to "endure" (ὑπομένειν) merrymaking at the end of the *Dyskolos* (lines 957–958), but Plautus' *leno* cannot be forced to join the revels at all.

This pimp is a blocking character for innumerable reasons, not the least of which is that he owns the girl whom Toxilus wants to liberate. Moreover, Dordalus pays attention only to fees, not pleas. He wants the six hundred *nummi* owed him, and words mean nothing. His pragmatic philosophy is like that of Ballio in the *Pseudolus* (line 308): *dicta non sonant*. The playwright emphasizes how much Dordalus' materialistic attitude is at odds with the holiday spirit, by calling attention to the fact that the *leno* is literally a foreigner, that is, not an Athenian: "Six months ago, that pimp came over from Megara / To set himself up here . . ." (*Persa* 137–138). Significantly, Plautus almost always makes his unpleasant characters *aliens* to the locale of the play. As we suggested in Chapter I, his audience would construe the elements which Plautus labels as "foreign" to be everyday Roman things and "Athenian matters" to be un-Roman holiday humor. The manner in which he presents his greedy agelasts adds further support to this interpretation. Not one of these spoilsports "belongs"; they are all strangers.[29] This is because normal Roman attitudes are alien to the festive atmosphere. Therefore a character like Dordalus, who embodies these attitudes, begins as an outsider and ends as an outcast.[30]

At his initial entrance, the pimp's ruling passion is presented in no uncertain terms. Dordalus is a true ancestor of the great Molièresque monomaniacs. The moment he spies Toxilus, he spares no words. Nothing for nothing at Rome, said Polybius, and waste of anything was a Roman sin.

DORDALUS: Cedo sis mi *argentum*, da mihi *argentum*, impudens,
possum a te exigere *argentum*? *argentum*, inquam, cedo,
quin tu mi *argentum* reddis? nilne te pudet?
leno te *argentum* poscit . . .

(lines 422–425)

DORDALUS: My money please, give me my money, nasty
man.
I must demand my money from you. Money please.
Will you deliver money, please? Oh shame on you!
The pimp demands his money.

This compulsive money-mania is by no means unique in the gallery of Plautine agelasts. In fact, Dordalus' dunning demand is very like that of Misargyrides, the banker who appears in the *Mostellaria*. The behavior of this latter agelast merits a brief examination. Misargyrides' name itself is a capsule characterization,[31] perhaps to be construed ironically as *contemptor divitiarum*, Livy's ambiguous description of the Elder Cato. Of course this banker does anything but spurn wealth. In fact, like Dordalus the pimp, he dispenses even with superfluous talk (lines 568–569):

TRANIO: Salvere iubeo te, Misargyrides, bene.
MISARGYRIDES: Salve et tu. *quid de argentost?*

TRANIO (*cheerily*): Hello, Misargyrides, hope you're
feeling well.

more careful criminal. "I learned not to get caught. Never again," he said. Mom knew to pack up whenever Dad said it was time to go.

A few years ago, a widow contacted me, hoping to recover the investments that she and her husband had made in Dad's *Encyclopedia of Folk Music*. She wondered if it could still be published. It was a project that he had worked on throughout my childhood, and I didn't know just how many "investors" he had. My mother said he was inspired to sell shares in the *Encyclopedia* after seeing the movie *The Producers* in 1967. The plot of the movie is that two Broadway producers bilk several investors by creating a show that will bomb so badly, it will close the same night it opens.

It's hard to admit that you were wrong to trust a person, to look back and realize you were taken for a ride—especially if you were strung along for an extended period of time. Many remain silent when this happens to them, unlike the man who called our house all those years ago. How long did my father work on that man, earning his trust? Most people would never admit to being scammed, and people like my dad count on that. It takes a lot more effort to convince someone they've been fooled than it does to fool them.

The look of fear on my father's face when I called him a crook forty years ago wasn't because he was afraid of me. In that moment, I reminded him of the terrible consequences that he could face. Not long after the man called our house, we packed up and moved, perching in a small town where no one knew us. Until the next call came.

MISARGYRIDES:   Hello to you. *Now what about my money?*

Never mind the salutations, this agelast cares about one thing only: *quin mihi faenus redditur?* (line 575), "when do I get my interest back?" The banker mentions the payment of interest in the first line of his entrance speech, and he repeats the word *faenus* over and over until it culminates in a comic cadenza very similar to the *argentum* speech of Dordalus quoted above. In fact, Misargyrides' pursuit of money is even more impassioned (lines 603–606):

MISARGYRIDES:   Cedo *faenus*, redde *faenus*, *faenus* reddite.
daturin estis *faenus* actutum mihi?
datur *faenus* mihi?
TRANIO:          *Faenus* illic *faenus* hic.
nescit quidem nisi *faenus* fabularier.


MISARGYRIDES:   My interest please, give me my interest,
                                        interest please.
Now will you give my interest to me right away?
Give me my interest.
TRANIO:          "Interest" here and "interest" there.
The only interest this man has in life is "interest."

Like the pragmatic Romans described by Polybius, this banker avoids excessive expenditure of time and energy as well as money. When he is told to return at noon for his *faenus*, he decides to wait on the scene, so as not to waste any effort (lines 581–582). (Of course he is not quite as compulsive as the miser Euclio, who was afraid to waste his breath while sleeping.) [32] Here in the *Mostellaria*, Misargyrides the banker inspires the same sort of abuse that Plautus elsewhere heaps upon agelast-pimps (lines 657–658):

TRANIO: Nullum edepol hodie genus est hominum taetrius
nec minus bono cum iure, quam danisticum.

TRANIO:  By Pollux, you won't find a fouler class of men
Or men less lawful than the moneylending breed.

Tranio's attack on the *genus danisticum* is very similar to Curculio's verbal barrage against the *genus lenonium*.[33] In Plautine comedy, any character connected with financial matters is regarded as the most despicable individual in the world.

To return to the *Persa*. Dordalus' *mot de caractère* is *lucrum*, and the multitudinous repetitions of this word constitute what is perhaps Plautus' best use of this particular comic device. Paraphrasing what Tranio said of the banker in the *Mostellaria*, we may well describe Dordalus as a man "whose only interest in this life is . . . profit." To this pimp, *lucrum* is a thing divine, an outlook which contrasts with that of the Plautine youths who worship the pantheon of pleasure and have no concern for everyday Roman divinities.[34] As Dordalus expresses it, *quoi homini di propitii sunt, aliquid obiciunt lucri* (line 470), "When the gods show favor to a man, they show the man a profit." This echoes Ballio's assertion that he would drop everything, even a temple sacrifice, if a lucrative enterprise came his way (*Pseudolus* 267, cited above). Here in the *Persa*, Toxilus cleverly exploits the pimp's obsession, luring him into a trap with the promise of great gains (lines 493–495):

TOXILUS:  Nam est res quaedam, quam occultabam tibi
dicere: nunc eam narrabo,
unde tu *pergrande lucrum* facias: faciam, ut mei memi-
neris, dum vitam
vivas.
DORDALUS:  Bene dictis tuis bene facta aures meae auxilium exposcunt.

TOXILUS:  Listen, let me advise a brand new enterprise.
I've not mentioned it to you before,
having hid it.

> If my counsel you take, what a profit you'll make,
>    and you'll always remember
>       the fellow who did it.
> DORDALUS:  Good words. Both my ears would obey them,
>    so pay them with facts.

The slave continues to emphasize the fortune forthcoming, repeating *lucrum* with ever increasing irony. He even invents a most appropriate deity (lines 514–516):

> TOXILUS:  . . . nescis quid te instet boni
>    neque quam tibi *Fortuna* faculam *lucrifera* ad*luc*ere volt.
> DORDALUS:  Quae istaec lucrifera est Fortuna?

> TOXILUS:  . . . you don't know what goods await you
>    Now that Fortune's Shining Prophet is incoming just for
>                                                        you.
> DORDALUS:  What? A fortune? Shining profit? Income?

What is supposedly about to brighten Dordalus' life (and Plautus cleverly reinforces the promise of *lucrum* with the verb *adlucere*) is a beautiful "Persian" lass whom the pimp will be able to sell at a tremendous markup. This lovely creature's name just happens to be *Lucris* ("Profitta," line 624), an appellation coined by the clever Toxilus. The effect on Dordalus is precisely as planned, as the pimp punningly remarks while admiring the girl (lines 626–627):

> Si te emam,
>    mihi quoque "Lucridem" confido fore te.

> If I buy you,
> I'm quite sure you'll "Profitta" me a lot.

After the pimp pays for his Persian prize and falls into Toxilus' trap, the slave still cannot forbear repeating the ironic phrase *fecisti lucri* again and again,[35] adding insult to impending financial injury, and assuring his greedy victim (lines 712–713):

> Ne hic tibi dies *inluxit lucrificabilis.*
> Nam non emisti hanc, verum fecisti *lucri.*

> I say to you this day will be profuse with profit.
> You haven't bought a maid, you've made a buy — a profit!

Toxilus leaves no verbal trick neglected. His use of *inlucere* reinforces the *adlucere* he employed while tempting the pimp with *Fortuna lucrifera* (line 515). As an ironic *coup de grâce*, when Dordalus finally realizes that he has been bamboozled, he himself unconsciously paraphrases Toxilus' words (lines 780–782):

> Perii, interii. *pessimus hic mi dies* hodie *inluxit* corruptor
> ita me Toxilus perfabricavit itaque meam rem divexavit.
> vehiclum argenti miser *eieci,* neque quam ob rem
> 　　　　　　　　　　　　　　　　*eieci* habeo.

> I'm dead and I'm cursed, why this day is the worst,
> 　　　every pain is profuse and
> 　　　　　　disasters pervade it.
> How that Toxilus tricked me, his stratagems licked me,
> 　　　my capital's looted,
> 　　　　　a ruin he's made it.
> I've just kicked out my cash and what makes my
> 　　　　　　　　　　　　teeth gnash,
> 　　　now I don't have the girl —
> 　　　　who's the reason I paid it!

At this point it will be valuable to turn once again to the prologue of the *Casina*, especially where it encourages the audience to "kick out" their cares: *eicite ex animo curam, atque alienum aes* (line 23). In the speech of Dordalus quoted above, we find the same verb *eicere* (twice, in fact). In the *Persa* a character who cannot follow the holiday rule to set aside thought of gain is punished not only by losing his profit but by "kicking out" his principal as well. What is more, since he himself embodies *cura* and *alienum aes*, Dordalus will be bodily *eiectus*, expelled from the final *komos*. And like many Plautine agelasts he suffers more than financial damage; he is vilified and beaten up. When he appears at Toxilus' party during the finale (lines 824ff), the roisterers insult him, dance around him, and finally punch him (lines 846–847):

> DORDALUS:    Quae haec res est? ei, colapho me icit.
> malum vobis dabo.
> TOXILUS:    At tibi nos dedimus dabimusque etiam!

> DORDALUS:    Now what's going on? Ow — he hit me just
> then!
> Why I'll get you, I'll swat you —
> TOXILUS:    Ah no, we just *got you*, and we'll gladly
> get you again!

And Toxilus speaks in the first person plural, "*all of us* have caused you trouble." It seems to be a universal comic principle that audiences enjoy seeing the agelast attacked by the entire group of revelers.[36] Dordalus, like Malvolio, is the victim of a party of plotters.

On two occasions in the *Persa*, even the pimp is invited to join the dance. When Dordalus first interrupts Toxilus' revels, the slave bids him forget business and register his complaints another day: *iurgium hinc auferas, si sapias* (line 798). But the pimp persists in arguing his case, even when Toxilus' newly freed mistress tries to persuade him (lines 799–801):

> Stultitiast
> cui *bene esse* licet, eum praevorti litibus, posterius istaec
> te magis par agerest.

> No folly could be greater
> To litigate instead of live it up when you have got the
> chance.
> Wait and do this business later.

The girl's argument, that disputation is at odds with celebration, is certainly borne out elsewhere in Plautine comedy. In fact Lysidamus, in the *Casina*, trapped in the forum by a lawsuit, uses the same language: it is *stultitia* to go to business when you can stay (on stage) with pleasure.[37] Still Dordalus cannot give in. In refusing the girl's invitation he growls, "My heart's ablaze," *uritur cor mi* (*Persa* 801). His ruling passion is too strong. But for displaying this rigid attitude Dordalus is then beaten up.

But even after mistreatment, he is once again offered a treat; the courtesan tries to entice him to join the fun (lines 849–851):

LEMNISELENIS: . . . Patrone mi, i intro, amabo, ad cenam.
DORDALUS: Mea Ignavia, tu nunc me inrides?
LEMNISELENIS: Quiane te voco, *bene ut tibi sit?*
DORDALUS: *Nolo mihi bene esse!*

LEMNISELENIS: . . . O master darling, come inside to dinner.
DORDALUS: Worthless wench, you're mocking me!
LEMNISELENIS: I only said, "Come live it up."
DORDALUS: But I don't *want* to live it up!

Dordalus' agelastic *nolo* rings loud, clear, and discordant. *Nolo* was also the churlish reaction of Euclio the miser, who was unable to *bene habere* even at his daughter's wedding, just as the pimp in the *Persa* is too preoccupied with money to *bene esse*.[38] This antagonism to "holiday humor" seems to be implicit in the very name of Shakespeare's notorious agelast, since the attitude of *nolo* may well be described as a display of *mala voglia*. Both the Shakespearean and Plautine spoilsports maintain their ill humor to the very end, and in fact Dordalus' threat *ego pol vos eradicabo* (*Persa* 819) foreshadows Malvolio's equally bitter exit line, "I'll be revenged on the whole pack of you!"[39]

The antipathy in *Twelfth Night* between Malvolio and the holiday forces is typical of a dramatic scheme found very often in Plautus: the agelast versus the revelers. The contest between Pseudolus and Ballio is one of numerous incidents in which the fun-seeker is pitted against the gain-seeker. This same antagonism is presented in the *Persa*, where Dordalus' first thoughts are *quid de argentost?* reflecting an obsessive concern with business that renders him incapable of letting go: *nolo mihi bene esse* (line 851). At the other end of the scale stands Toxilus, whose single concern is precisely *bene esse* (line 30). While Dordalus rejects pleasure and wants money, Toxilus rejects money and wants pleasure. The antithesis of Dordalus' *nolo bene esse* is Toxilus' *iam nolo argentum!* (line 127). This most "un-Roman" utterance expresses the proper festive attitude, which the *Casina* prologue urges upon the audience: kick out your cares, especially financial ones.

The harsh treatment of the man who ignores the call to play is a universal holiday phenomenon. E. K. Chambers in his study of medieval celebrations observes that the people who stay "on the job" are always rudely dealt with. Discussing the "ducking-in-water" customs prominent in many rural festival traditions, he remarks that this practice became "a rough and ready form of punishment . . . against the rustic code of conduct. The churl who *will not stop working*, or will not wear green on the feast-day, must be 'ducked.'"[40] Chambers also notes that the prime victim is very often the miser.[41] This same ganging up against the churl explains why "the whole pack" is against Malvolio, and why so often in Plautus the agelast is attacked en masse. For example, Labrax in the *Rudens*, still harping on his *aurum atque argentum* (line 546), is roughed up by Daemones and his *lorarii* in a wild melee (lines 656ff) as the slave Trachalio comments gleefully (lines 661–662):

> Audio tumultum. opinor leno pugnis pectitur.
> nimis velim improbissimo homini malas edentaverint.

> I hear violent sounds. I think the pimp is being punched
> to pulp.
> And I hope that most unlawful man gets all his teeth
> knocked out.

In *Twelfth Night*, the "exquisite reason" for beating Malvolio is merely that he is "a sort of Puritan."[42] In Plautus, being a *leno* carries the same consequences, and this applies to every member of their agelastic profession. Hence Cappadox in the *Curculio*, a kindly *leno* — if such a thing be imaginable — suffers no less than Dordalus. Cappadox has treated the heroine with respect, as she herself states, *bene et pudice me domi habuit* (*Curculio* 698), but unfortunately he requests that money be paid to him. At this point, Phaedromus the young lover advises the braggart soldier, *collum obstringe homini* (line 707), "squeeze him by the neck."[43] There are, of course, no stage directions in our Roman comedy manuscripts, but it is likely to assume that Cappadox' neck is subjected to more than a little squeezing before he relents —

in the very next line. No pimp would otherwise agree to paying out money from his own pocket. To add insult to injury, Cappadox is further punished by being excluded from the final celebration, which in the *Curculio* is a double dinner, *sororia* (line 660) and *nuptialis* (line 661).

There is a popular notion that in every comic tradition the "harsh father" is a major blocking character. Since Northrop Frye's view that this figure is a sine qua non for the comic formula has gained such widespread acceptance,[44] a brief digression is in order, to demonstrate that the father in Plautus is no agelast. The patriarch who impedes the progress of his son's love affair is certainly a staple figure in Molière, and, perhaps, because the French author is in so many ways indebted to Plautus, critics have deduced, *ex post facto*, that Plautine comedy numbered a "spoilsport father" among its dramatis personae. Or perhaps Ovid's famous description of the typical personalities of New Comedy has been too literally interpreted (*Amores* 1.15.17–18):

> dum fallax servus, *durus pater*, inproba lena
> vivent et meretrix blanda, Menandros erit.

That Ben Jonson, in a polemic mood, rendered these very lines adds further evidence of their influence on interpreters of "the classical tradition" (*Poetaster* I i 59–60):

> Whilst slaves be false, fathers hard, and bawds be whorish,
> Whilst harlots flatter, shall Menander flourish.

But, of course, "Menander" is not "Plautus"; the Roman popular comedy we are studying differed greatly from its Greek predecessors. Terence, on the other hand, may be considered to be in the Menandrian tradition (Julius Caesar hailed him "O fifty percent of [*dimidiate*] Menander!"). In Terence we find a list of characters similar to Ovid's which includes an *iratus senex* (*Heauton* 37). Duckworth translates this somewhat subjectively as "angry *father*," [45] but for Terence this may be justifiable. (Donatus frequently mentions the "irascibility" of Terentian fathers.) But in Plautus, when a *senex* is *iratus*, his anger is directed at the clever slave more often than it is at his son. If a Plautine father does actively oppose his son's love affair, it is usually because the old codger is a *senex amator*, fighting for the same girl. This would hardly make the father *durus*! Actually, most Plautine parents are easygoing, and several even admit that they too were once hot-blooded.[46] And we recall that it is young Pistoclerus' father who *stops* Lydus from railing against his son's high living.[47] Actually, the sternest patriarch in Roman comedy is Demea in Terence's *Adelphoe* (*nimium ipse est durus praeter aequomque et bonum*, "the man is much too harsh, beyond what's good and normal," line 64); no Plautine father is ever so Puritanical.[48]

Since love and *bene esse* are the essential themes of Plautine comedy,[49] it is logical that the agelastic *leno* is the primary blocking character. But there is another antagonist who merits a brief mention: the *miles gloriosus*. In both classical and Renaissance comedy, the swaggering soldier is almost always an impediment to the course of true love (it would not be Plautine to say "the *marriage* of true minds"). Like the *leno*, the soldier is in possession of the girl for whom the clever slave is plotting. While the military man is a blocking character in several Plautine comedies,[50] the *Bacchides*, *Curculio*, *Epidicus*, *Poenulus*, *Truculentus*, and (though he does not appear in person) the *Pseudolus*, he may be studied to best advantage in his most famous incarnation in Roman comedy, Pyrgopolynices, the *Miles Gloriosus*.

The Braggart Soldier has many agelast characteristics, especially greed and vanity. Pyrgopolynices does not give all for love. Quite unlike the true Plautine lover, he does seek

*Das Ende der Kindheit (The end of childhood)*
*Mixed media by Susanne Wawra*

"une femme et une fortune." And it is for this reason, as well as the fact that he "owns" the girl the young man loves, that he suffers so badly in the finale. The soldier is unable to take his mind off the balance sheet. He even thinks of his own (fictitious) exploits as much in terms of ledger as legend. When his parasite Artotrogus reels off the number of men he has supposedly slain on various occasions, the *miles* insists upon knowing the exact amount (lines 46–47):

| PYRGOPOLYNICES: | Quanta istaec hominum summast? |
|---|---|
| ARTOTROGUS: | Septem milia. |
| PYRGOPOLYNICES: | Tantum esse oportet. recte rationem tenes. |

| PYRGOPOLYNICES: | "The total men," your final sum is — |
|---|---|
| ARTOTROGUS: | Seven thousand. |
| PYRGOPOLYNICES: | That's accurate I think. You're good at adding up. |

We are told that Alexander the Great envied Achilles for having a Homer to immortalize his deeds, but Pyrgopolynices, to whom his parasite refers as "Achilles' brother" (line 62), needs a teller, not a bard, to provide the most suitable "accounts." In fact the soldier is happy to have found in his parasite so excellent a "bookkeeper": *recte rationem tenes* (line 47). In discussing this scene, Hanson has made the extremely interesting observation that this "military arithmetic," the totaling of the Braggart's triumphs "has its somewhat embarrassing analogy in the marked desire for numerical precision of official Roman monuments of conquest."[51] War, after all, was a very Roman business.

It is his ruling passion, the Braggart Soldier's pragmatic, mercenary mentality, which proves his downfall. While he is off in the forum negotiating, his antagonists concoct the perfect plot against him, one which appeals to his pride, his passion, and his greed. The plan succeeds largely because the slave Palaestrio cleverly whets the soldier's appetite with materialistic language, much the way Toxilus in the *Persa* entices Dordalus with the promise of *lucrum*. Palaestrio introduces the new love affair to his military master as a *condicio nova et luculenta* (line 952) which could be accurately rendered as "a promising new deal" in the commercial sense. What is more, the slave refers to the ring which the potential mistress has offered the soldier as "the first deposit on a love account": *hunc arrabonem amoris primum a me accipe* (line 957).[52] Pyrgopolynices is further excited by the prospect of being *paid* any amount of money he desires in return for his amorous attention (line 1061). Palaestrio sets the price as a talent of gold, and the soldier, vertiginous with vanity, protests that he is not concerned with making a profit (lines 1063–1064):

PYRGOPOLYNICES:  Non mihi avaritia umquam innatast: satis
                                        habeo divitiarum.
    plus mi auri mille est modiorum Philippi.
PALAESTRIO:                                     Praeter thensauros.


PYRGOPOLYNICES:  Oh I'm not one for greed, I've got all
                                        that I need.
    To be frank, I've got wealth beyond measure,
    Golden coins by the score, by the thousands and more —
PALAESTRIO:                          Not to mention a storehouse
    of treasure!

The soldier is ultimately bamboozled for the very reason that he is so bound to the everyday system of values. In considering his boasts in the passage quoted, we may perhaps recall the *laudatio* of Metellus, in which the making of *pecunia magna* was deemed most praiseworthy.[53] But in Plautus love and lucre are irreconcilable opposites. This is no world for the *miles gloriosus* who, unlike the happy Plautine *adulescens*, does care about such things as dowries.

There is the same poetic justice involved in the soldier's ultimate downfall as in the treatment of Plautus' *leno*-agelasts. Since each of these characters seeks profit, they both end up with a loss. In hopes of greater gain, Pyrgopolynices "kicks out" his current mistress and lavishes upon her all the gold finery he had purchased for her. He is so anxious to get rid of her that he would even resort to force (line 1124), an attitude reminiscent of Dordalus, who "kicks out" a pile of cash (*Persa* 782).[54] The soldier willingly accedes to Palaestrio's suggestion that he "invest" some of his vast riches to get rid of his present sweetheart with dispatch (lines 980ff), a tactic quite similar to that which Toxilus uses on Dordalus when he gets him to pay out good money for the profitable "Persian" girl. In both cases the slaves are inflating the hopes of their victims so that the ultimate realizations will be all the more painful — and comic. This is a familiar scheme to arouse laughter which, by Kant's famous definition, arises from "the sudden transformation of a strained expectation into nothing." [55]

As in the cases of the pimps discussed earlier, the punishment inflicted upon Pyrgopolynices may seem unduly harsh. Like the typical *leno*, the soldier loses both girl and gold and is insulted and beaten as well. Moreover, instead of receiving the reward he expected in return for his sexual services, Pyrgopolynices is forced to pay out still more money to preserve his manhood.[56] But, as even the soldier admits, there is a certain poetic justice to his penalty (lines 1435ff).

The *miles gloriosus* is very much in the mainstream of the Plautine agelasts. Like Dordalus the pimp, he begins as an outsider and ends as an outcast. The play stresses the fact that he is a *foreigner* in Ephesus, just as Dordalus was in Athens.

This explains why, in each case, the agelast is duped so easily; he is not a native, he is in unfamiliar surroundings (and the Braggart Soldier has not been in town long enough to learn that his next-door neighbor does not have a wife). Again, because their attitude is *alien* to the general mood of the play, both agelast-*miles* and agelast-*leno* are ejected, left alone during the finale while all the others make merry.

Whether his preoccupation be military, monetary, or admonitory, the Plautine antagonist to the comic spirit is always beaten by the majority and chased off. Any kind of business is at odds with holiday, and these pragmatic, moralistic "aliens" must go back where they belong. The festive stage is purged of these sober types just as Stichus cleanses himself of "all things foreign" so that he can revel in "the great Athenian way." [57] Because they embody (and defend) everyday Roman obsessions, the Plautine agelasts, like the *curae* mentioned by the prologue to the *Casina*, must be literally kicked out.

There is another Plautine epithet which sums up what the spoilsport in his comedies stands for. It is most vividly expressed in a scene from the *Bacchides* examined at the beginning of this chapter, when Lydus the tutor is taken by Pistoclerus to what the young man considers a pantheon of pleasure, that shrine where he worships (lines 115–116):

> Amor, Voluptas, Venus, Venustas, Gaudium,
> Iocus, Ludus, Sermo, Suavisaviatio.

> Affection, Luxury, Love, Loveliness, Joy,
> Fun, Games, Conversation, and Kissy-kissy-kissy.

The Puritan is shocked, and true to type, makes a hell of heaven, asking his pupil, "do you have dealings with such damned and damaging divinities?" (line 117). The young man defends the sanctity of his pleasure-gods, but the agelast does not even believe they exist (lines 120–123):

LYDUS:   An deus est ullus Suavisaviatio?
PISTOCLERUS:   An non putasti esse umquam? O Lyde, es
*barbarus*!
   quem ego sapere nimio censui plus quam Thalem,
is stultior es *barbaro* poticio.


LYDUS:   Is there such a god as Kissy-kissy-kissy?
PISTOCLERUS:   Don't you think so? Lydus, you're
barbarian!
The man I used to think was wiser than a Thales,
Is stupider than a barbarian baby boy.

By now we are well aware of what Plautus means by "barbarian." In a comic context, this epithet might even describe Cato the Elder, especially if we recall Plutarch's anecdote of how the stern censor reacted when a Roman senator seemed to be worshiping the divinity of "Kissy-kissy-kissy." [58] But Cato's Puritanic antagonism is completely alien to the spirit of comedy, like the antagonism of the Plautine agelasts, who are, in many ways, Catonic caricatures. And so during Plautus' "Athenian revels" they must be banished from the stage for being *barbarus*, that is, for being Roman.

CHAPTER IV·

# From Slavery
# to Freedom

We have thus far dealt with those aspects of Plautine comedy which reflect a "saturnalian overthrow" of the everyday Roman value system. We have seen how traditionally respected qualities like *pietas* and parsimony are mocked in a spirit similar to that of the medieval holidays described by E. K. Chambers, celebrations whose ruling idea was "inversion of status."[1] The subject of this chapter is a far more familiar presentation of the same comic scheme: the ascendancy of slave over master. This reversal is, of course, hardly an innovation with Plautus. It was surely one of the "old gags" to which Xanthias refers in the opening repartee of the *Frogs*. In fact, immediately thereafter, Aristophanic master and man run this very gamut and (several times) exchange roles — with the slave emerging as "the better man." Henri Bergson considered inversion to be the most basic of all comic techniques:

> Picture to yourself certain characters in a certain situation: if you reverse the situation and invert the *rôles*, you obtain a comic scene . . . Thus we laugh at the prisoner at the bar lecturing the magistrate; at a child presuming to teach its parents; in a word, at everything that comes under the heading of "topsy-turvydom" [*monde renversé*].[2]

"Superior" behavior in what is supposed to be an "inferior" character never fails to arouse laughter. The history of stage comedy presents an endless parade of servants smarter than their masters. The reincarnations of Xanthias and Dionysus vary only in name, costume, and — occasionally — sex. In fact when the underling is female, the comic reversal is all the more emphatic, as in Molière's *Le Malade Imaginaire* (I vi):

> ARGAN: Je lui commande absolument de se préparer à prendre le mari que je dis.
> TOINETTE: Et moi, je lui defends absolument d'en faire rien.
> ARGAN: Où est-ce donc que nous sommes? et quelle audace est-ce là à une coquine de servante de parler de la sorte devant son maître?

> ARGAN: I absolutely command her to prepare herself to wed the husband I specify.
> TOINETTE: And *I* absolutely forbid her to do anything of the sort.
> ARGAN: My God, what are we coming to? And what kind of outrage is this when a knavish servant girl speaks out this way in front of her master?

George Meredith would answer Argan's "what are we coming to?" by stating that we had arrived at the perfect comic situation, for the English writer regarded the presentation of a stronger wit in the weaker sex as the basic condition for "true comedy."[3] Satisfying both Bergsonian and Meredithian criteria, Goldsmith creates Kate Hardcastle, a mistress who "stoops to conquer." Marivaux in *Le Jeu de l'Amour et du Hasard* presents a delectable situation in which both a master and a mistress exchange places with their lackeys, just as Molière's young suitors disguised their servants as marquis and viscount to expose the absurd behavior of *Les Précieuses*. In

George Bernard Shaw, we have a modern example of comic inversion on a very sophisticated level. Shavian protagonists frequently succeed in "educating" another character, only to succumb to a superior power which they have helped to create.[4]

But Plautus is, in almost every sense, the most "saturnalian" comic playwright of them all; he turns *everything* topsy-turvy. In one instance even the gods are *déclassés*: [5] almighty Jove and Mercury stoop to become mere actors (*Amphitruo* 152), a group ranked so low in everyday society that they were denied even the basic rights of citizenship. And Mercury not only assumes the face and features of Sosia the slave but subsequently receives the tongue-lashing and threats of more physical lashing that typify the lot of Plautine bondsmen.[6] This irreverent upheaval of social ranks, through a traditional comic motif, has occasioned vehement attacks on Plautus' dramaturgy and his sense of social decorum (as if social decorum were a comic virtue!).

Jean-Jacques Rousseau's angry objection to the inversion of status so frequently presented by Molière serves well to describe the technique in Plautus, who provided the precedent. In his "Lettre à d'Alembert sur les spectacles," Rousseau admits that Molière is a great artist, but at the same time he argues (much as Plato would) that Molière's theater is "une école de vices et de mauvaises moeurs." Here is the essence of Jean-Jacques's complaint:

> Voyez comment, pour multiplier ses plaisanteries, cet homme trouble tout l'ordre de la société; avec quel scandale il renverse tous les rapports les plus sacrés sur lesquels elle est fondée, comment il tourne en dérision les respectables droits des pères sur leurs enfants, des maris sur leurs femmes, des maîtres sur leurs serviteurs! Il fait rire, il est vrai, et n'en devient que plus coupable . . .

Observe how, to multiply his jokes, this man disturbs the entire order of society, how scandalously he inverts all the most sacred relationships on which society is based, how he mocks the well-respected rights of fathers over their children, husbands over their wives, and masters over their slaves. True enough, he does evoke laughter from this technique, but this makes him all the more guilty.[7]

Our first three chapters have already demonstrated how Plautus inverted certain "sacred relationships" on which Roman society was based, but critics throughout the ages have condemned him as most guilty for his indecorous presentation of the relationship between slave and master. It is logical that any society which is based on slavery would make comic use of this significant social distinction, but this motif in Plautus is especially important when we consider how very low the status of slaves was in contemporary Rome.

We are all familiar with Greek arguments for the "natural inferiority" of slaves. To Homer a slave was "half a man"; [8] to Aristotle he is merely "a living tool." [9] Varro's Roman view of a bondsman as *instrumenti genus vocale* [10] seems to echo the Greek philosopher. Indeed the Roman slave was regarded as a mere object, ranked with the inanimate *res mancipi*. The slave had no rights of any sort; his master could torture him, kill him, or dispose of him in any way without the slightest repercussion. A Greek slave, if maltreated, did have some recourse. He might take refuge in a temple and be accorded "due process" if his complaints could be substantiated.[11] Perhaps the most revealing words on the status of slaves in the Rome of Plautus is the famous advice to the Roman farmer by Cato the Elder in *De Agri Cultura* 2:

Boves vetulos . . . plostrum vetus, ferramenta vetera, servum senem, servum morbosum . . . vendat.

When oxen grow old, sell them . . . likewise an old cart, old iron tools, an old slave or a sick slave.

As Cato sees it, slaves not only come after oxen in order of importance but are even considered less valuable than wagons and farm tools. At least Aristotle, in calling the slave an instrument, noted that he took precedence over all other instruments.[12] The far more depreciatory Roman attitude toward slaves must always be borne in mind when we consider how Plautus' bondsmen "troublent tout l'ordre de la société." At the irreverent medieval church holidays an "ass" might chant the mass, and this was of course regarded as a great saturnalian upheaval.[13] But in Plautine comedy, the character who becomes *dominus festi* ranks, according to the normal value system, two steps *below* a beast of burden. Moreover, there is no evidence to indicate that during the celebration of the contemporary Roman Saturnalia slaves ever behaved as audaciously as they do in Plautine comedy.[14] The festivals which Frazer describes in the *Golden Bough* took place centuries later. Those of Plautus' day were more like the genial meal in common described by Accius (quoted above, p. 32). It is commonly accepted that these Roman festivals meant merely a temporary "equality" for the slaves.[15] But equality is a far cry from topsy-turvydom. The Saturnalia enjoyed by Plautus' comic slaves exceeds even the wildness of imperial festivals described by Martial, who saw the capital city at holiday-time transformed into *pilleata Roma*.[16] The Roman festive rule seems to have been similar to the watchwords of the eighteenth-century French rebels who donned their own *pilleus*, crying "liberté, égalité, fraternité." And while the Eternal City wore its collective cap of freedom, *Rome au bonnet rouge* was able to overthrow what Martial refers to as *pallentes curae* and what might — in a festive mood — be translated as "the pale thought of caste."

But among Plautine slaves the "revolution" goes even further than in Martial's Rome. There is *liberté* aplenty, but here the comparison ends. The relationship of master to man is certainly not one of *égalité*, and *fraternité* is in evidence only

# ESCAPE STRATEGIES

John Walters

Y OU WANT TO TAKE A DRIVE, BUT YOU'RE NOT SURE WHERE
your car is parked. It's not out back, so it must be in a nearby
lot. They've hidden it from you. They've done it before,
but each time it gets harder to find. There's only one thing to do.
This time, after you locate it, you will drive it far away—someplace
they'll never think to look.

All right. Time to go. Pull on and tie shoes. Grab jacket. Check
that keys are in your pocket. A quick scan of the hallway for attendants who would stop you from exiting the building. You carefully
close and lock the door; you don't want them taking any more of
your possessions while you're away.

You pass a neighbor entering her room; she gives you a cursory
smile. The thought flits through your mind that you should warn
her about the conspiracy to misplace your car. No time. You've got
to seize the opportunity while the way is clear.

At the end of the hall you are faced with a decision: elevator or among those who triumph and enjoy the final *komos*. Plautine comedy does not break class barriers merely to make every man a "citoyen." Rather, it creates a new — albeit temporary — aristocracy, in which wit, not birth, distinguishes the ruler from the ruled. The extent to which Plautus "ennobles" his clever slaves must be examined in detail to be fully appreciated, for this is the primary theme of all his comedy.[17]

In the *Asinaria*, the scheming slaves Leonida and Libanus have obtained the twenty *minae* needed by their young master to purchase his sweetheart Philaenium. But when the servants encounter young Argyrippus, whose spirits and bank account are now at their lowest ebb, they withhold the financial salvation long enough to demand a reward. It is noteworthy, in light of the argument of Chapter II, that the slaves ask for nothing material; money has no real value to them. The scene itself (one which Fraenkel has singled out as a completely Plautine elaboration) [18] is constructed with almost a ceremonial quality. Leonida begins the festivities by acknowledging the slaves' status in the everyday social scale (lines 650–653):

LEONIDA: Primum omnium servos tuos nos esse non
negamus.
sed tibi si viginti minae argenti proferentur
quo nos vocabis nomine?
ARGYRIPPUS: Libertos.
LEONIDA: Non patronos?
ARGYRIPPUS: Id potius.
LEONIDA: Viginti minae hic insunt in crumina.

LEONIDA: Now first of all, we don't deny we're both of us
your bondsmen.
But if we give you twenty *minae*, all in cash,
By what name will you call us?
ARGYRIPPUS: Freedmen.

LEONIDA:                           Why not *masters?*
ARGYRIPPUS:   All right.
LEONIDA:                   Here are twenty *minae* in a wallet.

The slaves' primary concern is for status, by what name they will be addressed. And it should be noted that they do not request actual manumission. These two servants in the *Asinaria* are a veritable Tweedledum and Tweedledee; their demands are absolutely symmetrical. And the flattery they receive is in a vein similar to that accorded Hamlet's obsequious schoolmates (II ii 33-34):

KING:   Thanks Rosencrantz and gentle Guildenstern.
QUEEN:   Thanks Guildenstern and gentle Rosencrantz.

Both slaves wish to be humbly beseeched not only by their master but by his sweetheart as well (lines 662 and 686):

LEONIDA:   . . . hanc iube petere atque orare mecum.


LEONIDA:   . . . make her flirt and plead with me.

·    ·    ·    ·    ·    ·    ·    ·    ·    ·

LIBANUS:   Nunc istanc tantisper iube petere atque orare
                                                        mecum.


LIBANUS:   Now make her flirt and plead with me for just
                                                a little while.

Each slave requests a great quantity of love epithets, sugared with amorous diminutives.[19] Both, for example, wish to be called the girl's *passerculum* (lines 666 and 694), each receives an *obsecro* from the girl (lines 672 and 688) and is called *patronus* by the master (lines 652-653 and 689). The clever symmetry of this scene is nowhere better in evidence than when the young man turns to Libanus to beg for the sack of money (lines 689–690):

> O Libane, mi patrone, mi trade istuc. magis decorumst
> libertum potius quam patronum onus in via portare.

> O please, Libanus, give me that. It's really far more suitable
> That a servant, not his master, carry loads in public.

By now young Argyrippus knows what his slaves want to hear. Of his own accord he once again acknowledges the inversion of status. In this entire scene, verbs of supplication predominate. Between line 662 and line 699, there are thirteen verbs of "beseeching," notably *orare* (five times) as well as *exorarier*, *obsecrare*, *petere*, and *supplicare*. The enslaving of the master is *summa felicitas* for the Plautine slave.

The rascally servants then shock their master further by requesting a kiss from his sweetheart (lines 668–669):

> LEONIDA:  Prehende auriculis, compara labella cum labellis.
> ARGYRIPPUS:  Ten osculetur, verbero?
> LEONIDA:                    Quam vero indignum visum est?

> LEONIDA (*to the girl*):  O take me by the ears and press
>                                 your little lips to mine.
> ARGYRIPPUS:  What, kiss you, whipping-post?
> LEONIDA (*with mock surprise*):         Does that seem so
>                                               unsuitable?

Naturally Libanus asks for a similar show of affection and meets a similar show of indignation on the part of his master (lines 695–697):

> LIBANUS:  Fac proserpentem bestiam me, duplicem ut ha-
>                                          beam linguam,
> circumda torquem bracchiis, meum collum circumplecte.

ARGYRIPPUS:   Ten complectatur, carnufex?
LIBANUS:                   Quam vero indignus videor?


LIBANUS *(to the girl)*:  O make me like a snaky beast —
                              with double tongue, that is.
Make me a necklace of your arms, and hug me tightly
                                                    too.
ARGYRIPPUS:  What, hug you, gallowsbird?
LIBANUS *(with mock surprise)*:  Do I seem so unsuitable?

It is an artful touch by Plautus that when each servant
makes his request for amorous attention, their master's im-
mediate angry retort contains one of the common epithets
hurled at slaves, *verbero* and *carnufex*, momentary reminders
of "everyday" conditions, when such outrageous behavior
would be harshly punished. But young Argyrippus is quickly
reawakened to the fact that these are saturnalian circumstances, and that his bondsmen have a certain *dignitas* to
preserve (cf. lines 669 and 697).

But a kiss from a courtesan is not itself a great enhance-
ment of status (the finale of the *Stichus* attests to this) so
Leonida and Libanus demand still more deference (lines 670–
671):

LEONIDA:  At qui pol hodie non feres ni genua confricantur.
ARGYRIPPUS:  Quidvis egestas imperat: fricentur. dan quod
                                                        oro?


LEONIDA *(to his master)*:  You'll never get the cash today,
                              unless you rub my knees.
ARGYRIPPUS:  Necessity commands. *(getting on his knees)*
Let them be rubbed. *I beg* . . . please give.

The master's language emphasizes his present subservience:
the situation created by his slave commands *him, imperat.* He

has already referred to Leonida as *imperator* (line 656) and here once again he is beseeching: *dan quod oro?* As usual, Libanus follows his partner's lead and makes a demand still more demeaning (lines 699–702):

LIBANUS: Vehes pol hodie me, si quidem hoc argentum
ferre speres.
ARGYRIPPUS: Ten ego veham?
LIBANUS: Tun hoc feras argentum aliter a me?
ARGYRIPPUS: Perii hercle. si *verum* quidem et *decorum*
erum vehere servom,
inscende.

LIBANUS: You'll carry me today if you expect to get the
cash.
ARGYRIPPUS: I carry you?
LIBANUS: Or else you'll never carry off the cash.
ARGYRIPPUS: I'm dead! Can it be suitable that master carry
slave? (*With a sigh, he bends down.*)
Get on.

Once again the language underscores the sudden inversion.[20] The master explicitly acknowledges that it is "dutiful and proper," *verum quidem et decorum*, to perform what on any ordinary day would be indecorous indeed.[21]

This brace of erstwhile slaves has become the most finicky of masters. Leonida is not pleased with the way Argyrippus has rubbed his knees, it is *tam nequiter* (line 678). Libanus echoes these sentiments in evaluating his master-as-horse, finding him to be a worthless nag, *nequam es* (line 710). In a further twist, Libanus indicates that his master is so bad a piece of horseflesh that he will send him off to work in the mills, *ad pistores dabo* (line 709), an ironic reminder of the plight of the stereotyped comic slave who is so often in dread of being sent *in pistrinum*. But now the servants make the ultimate demand. They have already been "dignified," now they wish to be deified (lines 712–713):

ARGYRIPPUS:  Datisne argentum?
LIBANUS:    Si quidem mihi statuam et aram statuis
atque ut deo mi hic immolas bovem . . .


ARGYRIPPUS (*pleading*): My money —
LIBANUS:    If you establish a statue to me and an altar
And sacrifice an ox to my godhead . . .

As expected, Leonida also asks to be worshiped. The young man does not refuse homage to either one (line 718). And thus, when they have risen from the lowest to the highest possible rank, the slaves are deified — and satisfied. The game is over, as Libanus states it, *satis iam delusum censeo* (line 731).

In the world of Plautus, saturnalian scenes like the one we have just examined are less the exception than the rule or — more appropriately — misrule. The finale of the *Epidicus* may be cited as another case in point. Here old Periphanes has been twice bamboozled by the tricky slave who, unlike the friendly brace of bondsmen in the *Asinaria*, has been his vigorous antagonist throughout the play. And yet after two humiliating defeats at the hands of the wily Epidicus, Periphanes publicly acknowledges that he should beseech his slave: *mi orandum esse intellego* (line 721). In this scene, as in the *Asinaria*, the key word is *orare*. What adds a stunning irony to this climactic moment of the play is the fact that Epidicus is tied up hand and foot and his master must implore permission to loosen the slave's bonds. What better example of Bergson's *monde renversé* theory of the comic? Who, after all, is the prisoner of whom? Epidicus refuses to allow his master even to touch him (line 723) and adds (line 724):

> Numquam hercle hodie, nisi supplicium mihi das, me
> solvi sinam.

> Never will I let you loose my bonds unless you make
> amends.

The old man mistakenly assumes that by "making amends" Epidicus means that he expects some material reward, so the master offers him a new set of clothes, *socci*, *tunica*, *pallium* (line 725), all in addition to *libertas*. Epidicus is not content. Even when Periphanes adds a food subsidy for his newly freed servant, Epidicus' special appetite is still not satisfied (line 728):

EPIDICUS:　Numquam hercle hodie, nisi me *orassis*, solves.
PERIPHANES:　　　　　　　　　　　　　Oro te, Epidice!

EPIDICUS:　Never will you loose my bonds unless you beg.
PERIPHANES (*desperately, falling to his knees*): I beg, I beg!

Like all Plautine clever slaves, Epidicus wants most of all to hear a plaintive *oro te* emanating from his master's lips. Finally he yields to the old man's passionate pleading — but condescendingly (line 730):

> Invitus do hanc veniam tibi.

> Against my will, I'll do it as a favor.

As in the *Asinaria*, the slave's primary concern is for status. Leonida and Libanus asked for nothing material, nor, it should be noted, does Epidicus demand anything beyond a verbal *supplicium* (which might, on any other occasion, be translated as "punishment"!). In direct contrast to the materialistic agelast whose watchword is *dicta non sonant*, the Plautine slave is the essence of the comic spirit. To him, humble words are the highest payment, and only the "sweet nothing" is something of value. This is his richest reward for saturnalian services rendered.

There are two distinct categories of master-man reversals in the comedy of Plautus. The first type is a common circumstance most explicitly described by young Agorastocles in the *Poenulus* (lines 447–448):

> Amor iubet
> me oboedientem esse servo liberum.

> Love commands
> That I, a free man, do the bidding of my slave.

There is an interesting extra dimension to be observed in what seems like the traditional lord-lackey reversal. No Roman could *ever* be made a slave at Rome; in fact, while fathers could have their sons executed, they could never have them enslaved.[22] Evidently, to the Roman mentality this was a fate worse than death. What is more, to be "a slave of love," even metaphorically, was also un-Roman behavior.[23] In the first category of Plautine "enslavings" we find the young men who desperately need the help of their tricky servants and, unlike the imperious masters in the second category, turn in voluntary submission to their bondsmen at the very outset of the play. Included in this group are also the characters who "think young," like Periplectomenus, the "semi-*senex*" in the *Miles Gloriosus*, as well as those would-be youngsters, the *senes amatores*. Typical of the young lovers in this first category is Plesidippus in the *Rudens*, who addresses his own slave in terms which he knows will please the underling (lines 1265–1266):

> Mi anime, mi Trachalio,
> mi liberte, mi patrone potius, immo mi pater!

> My soul, my dear Trachalio,
> O my freedman, no — my master — no no no,
>                    indeed, my father!

There is a special Roman dignity associated with the last epithet the master bestows on his slave. Cicero, in *De Republica* 1.64, talking of the men in whom the citizens put their trust during times of national crisis, says:

> Non eros nec dominos appellabant eos, quibus iuste paruerunt, denique ne reges quidem, sed patriae custodes, sed *patres*, sed deos.

> They did not call the leaders whom they rightfully obeyed either masters or lords, indeed, nor kings either, but they referred to them as "guardians of the fatherland," "fathers," or "gods."

Likewise, the Plautine lover, during a time of internal crisis puts all his faith in the hands of a lowly slave, thereby elevating the servant to the level of civic leader, guardian of his master's state — of mind. Furthermore, as H. J. Rose writes,

> *pater*, the Latin word cognate to "father" and closest akin to it in meaning, signifies not so much him who has begotten a younger person, as him who has *natural authority* over one inferior in age or status.[24]

Thus the youth in the *Rudens* is not only saying, "you are as good as a father to me, Trachalio," but also, "you, Trachalio, enjoy a *natural authority* over me, you are superior in rank." And he means what he says, for later in the play when his slave orders him to follow along, he respectfully replies, *duc me, mi patrone, quo libet* (line 1280).[25]

There are countless instances in the comedies of Plautus when the young "masters" grant similar *patria potestas* to their slaves. Philolaches in the *Mostellaria* makes a declaration of dependence in no uncertain terms: *in tuam custodelam meque et meas spes trado, Tranio* (line 407), "Into your custody all of myself and all of my hopes I now transfer, Tranio." To this statement of self-subjugation, the Plautine clever slave replies (anticipating Beaumarchais's Figaro) that what matters in life is not which man is titularly *patronus* or *cliens*, but which has the talent (lines 408ff). To cite every occasion on which this transfer of authority occurs, would merely be to cite the behavior pattern of every Plautine *adulescens*, the only difference lying in the degree of subservience to which each youth goes. Young Agorastocles in the *Poenulus*, for example, not only offers to change places with his slave, he would even allow Milphio to beat him (lines 145–146):

> Si tibi lubido est aut voluptati, sino:
> suspende, vinci, verbera, auctor sum, sino.

> Please, if it gives you any pleasure, I allow you
> To hang me up, to fetter and flog me, I allow you.[26]

The farcical "old men in love" ape the younger generation in this respect as well. For example, white-haired Lysidamus in the *Casina* speaks in the same vein as the young lover from the *Rudens* quoted above (*Casina* 738–739):

LYSIDAMUS:  Servos sum tuos.
OLYMPIO:                                  Optumest.
LYSIDAMUS:                                              Opsecro te,
  Olympisce mi, *mi pater, mi patrone!*


LYSIDAMUS:  I'm your slave.
OLYMPIO:                                  That's fine.
LYSIDAMUS:                                              I beg of you,
  Olympi-olo, father, master dear!

stairs? The elevator is easier on your hips and knees, but when it opens you're in full view of the receptionist at the front desk.

The stairway, then; slowly and quietly.

A few steps short of the bottom you wait at a point where you can't be seen. When the receptionist goes into the inner office, you cross the lobby and go out through a side exit.

The air is cold and the sky is gray; rain as fine as mist tickles your face. If you remember correctly, the parking lot in question is just beyond that next hill. You attempt to climb over the low iron fence to the garden but can't quite make it. You follow the sidewalk around the building. The fence gives way to a hedge but you can't penetrate that either.

Finally, you come to a gap and push your way through. After traversing a few flowerbeds you reach the base of the slope. Slipping in the mud, you continue upward on hands and knees. No matter that your pants are filthy and wet. Once you reach your car, you'll head for your beachfront cabin, take a hot shower, slip into fresh clothes, and pour yourself a drink.

That's when your captors come for you. They each take one of your arms, pick you up, and escort you back inside, all the while uttering soothing, reassuring words.

But—your car, your car. There was something about your car, and driving on an open highway, and your cabin...

---

"Hello?"

"David? It's Joyce."

"Joyce. Nice to hear from you. How are the holidays going? Are we still getting the families together at your place?"

"Yes, that's still on, but that's not why I'm calling. It's about Dad. He's had another elopement episode."

"Elopement?"

"Wandering off without supervision. I explained it before."

"That's right. So what did he do this time?"

"He somehow gave the attendants the slip, got past a fence and

Once again love commands a free man to obey his bondsman, if indeed Lysidamus' ludicrous infatuation can be compared to the sentiments of the younger Plautine lovers. Here in the *Casina* we have a burlesque of the more common Plautine situation, a sort of comic Pelion piled on Ossa. For after old Lysidamus gives himself to his slave, Olympio quips that he has no need for so worthless a servant: *quid mi opust servo tam nequam* (line 741), an attitude which mirrors that of the haughty brace of slaves in the scene from the *Asinaria* examined earlier in this chapter.[27] It would seem that one cannot act the comic *patronus* without emphasizing the worthlessness of one's servant. This is borne out in Figaro's impudent remark to Count Almaviva in Beaumarchais's *Barber of Seville* (I ii):

> Aux vertus qu'on exige dans un domestique, Votre Excellence connaît-elle beaucoup de maîtres qui fussent dignes d'être valets?

> Considering the talents demanded in a servant, does Your Excellency know many masters who would be worthy of being valets?

Figaro shows some audacity in saying it; Plautine slaves show even more in displaying it.

The *Captivi* is often set apart from (and above) the rest of the Plautine corpus. Lessing extolled it as "das schönste Stück das jemals auf die Bühne gekommen ist" because, unlike the typical Plautine farce, it was a play with a noble theme.[28] Yet in light of our present argument the *Captivi* may be seen to display many typically Plautine features, for its entire plot centers about the exchange of roles between master and man. Despite the protestations of the epilogue that this is no ordinary comedy, but rather one which preaches a higher morality (line 1029), the play abounds in the sort of saturnalian language we have been discussing. If the *Captivi* is at all different from the rest of the plays, it is because of the unusually ironic context in which the commonplace "language of inversion" is spoken. At times there is nothing unique about it at all, as when young Philocrates expresses gratitude to his slave Tyndarus and offers to call him "father": *pol ego, si te audeam, meum patrem nominem* (line 238).

Of course Philocrates' predicament in the *Captivi* is more serious than being "in love and in debt." No mere prisoner of love, he is a prisoner of war, and he lets his slave act as master so that he can escape. In the parting dialogue between the two men who have exchanged roles, Plautus works an ironic variation of what was obviously a familiar theme. It is an inversion of the typical inversion. To convince old Hegio, who is listening carefully to every word, that he, Tyndarus (the slave-disguised-as-master), is indeed master, he speaks to Philocrates (master-disguised-as-slave) in conventional saturnalian language (lines 444–445):

> . . . tu mihi erus nunc es, tu patronus, tu pater,
> tibi commendo spes opesque meas.

> . . . now you're my master, lord, and father,
> Wealth and welfare, all I have, is in your hands.

Except for the special context, these lines are exact echoes of such typically Plautine inversion scenes as *Pseudolus* 119, *Rudens* · 1265–1266 (quoted above, p. 111), and *Mostellaria* 409 (quoted above, p. 113). Thus, if we assume that old Hegio in the *Captivi* was familiar with the motifs of Roman popular comedy (and it is not unusual for Plautine characters to be conscious of theatrical conventions), he would now be certain which youth was the lord and which the lackey. In one form or another, the master-man inversion is ever present in Plautus. It is, in fact, the *trait d'union* between such low farces as the *Pseudolus* and the so-called higher comedies, like the *Captivi*. Even the *Amphitruo*, whose uniqueness is most often stressed by scholars, contains innumerable variations and ironic comments upon the relation of servant to master.[29]

The second type of inversion in Plautus is by far the more significant. Here the slave is not completely in charge at the outset of the play. While his young master may have already transferred *patria potestas* to him, there remains another group of characters, usually including the boy's real father, who do not acknowledge his saturnalian superiority. These leaders (at least they see themselves as such) constitute most of the older generation, all of whom (with the exception of the *genus lenonium*) enjoy a high status in everyday society. Unlike the young masters of the first category, these men are not at all willing to be commanded by their servants and must be forcibly overthrown by the slaves' most powerful weapons, "artful artifice and wily ways" (*facetis fabricis et doctis dolis*, *Miles* 147). This active campaign, the outsmarting of a presumably smarter master, is the subject of the most characteristic and most successful Plautine plots.

The kind of victory paean sung by the lackey who has conquered his lord is epitomized in the ecstatic outburst of Libanus in the *Asinaria* as he rides in triumph, piggyback on his master (line 702):

Sic isti solent superbi subdomari!

Hey — here is how the high and the haughty ought to be
                                       humbled!

The phrase is very similar to the motto of the medieval Feast of Fools, that unique day on the Church calendar when the lowly clerics assumed control of the high ecclesiastical functions. The *baculus* of authority was in the hand of their leader, a *dominus festi* chosen from among the humble subdeacons to lead the devotions. When this "holiday hierarch" came to a particular phrase in the *Magnificat*, the throng of revelers sang it again and again,[30] for it was the theme of their festival (Luke 1.52, R.S.V.):

> Deposuit potentes de sede et exaltavit humiles.

> He hath put down the mighty from their thrones and
> exalted those of low degree.

Chambers notes that in the later Middle Ages the word *deposuit* itself became a generic term for this kind of celebration.[31] Indeed, this is also an appropriate title for the overthrow of the *potentes* by the *humiles* in Plautus.

The Roman playwright always emphasizes the chagrin of the fallen master, who is distressed not because he has lost money (though he usually has) but because he has lost face. Old Theopropides in the *Mostellaria* expresses the general sentiment (lines 1146–1147):

> Iam minoris omnia alia facio prae quam *quibus modis*
> me ludificatust.


> All the rest I rate at nothing. I'm just angered by
> the manner
> He bamboozled me.

Tranio, perpetrator of the many outrages upon his master, is the first to remind him that, being older, he should have been wiser, "a man who's gray on top should not be green inside" (line 1148). Another *senex* who suffers in similar fashion is Nicobulus in the *Bacchides*, who agonizes over the fact that the wiles of Chrysalus have made a wise man foolish, *dolis doctis indoctum* (line 1095). Yet it is precisely this fact that has given the slave so much satisfaction; it seems that Nicobulus was known for his shrewdness. As Chrysalus sings exultingly (lines 642–644):

Erum maiorem meum ut ego hodie lusi lepide, ut ludificatust.
*callidum senem callidis dolis*
compuli et perpuli, mi omnia ut crederet.


How I fooled my older master, fully flimflammed
him today,
Shrewdly tricked a tricky oldster,
Rushed him, crushed him, now he swallows every
word I say.

Near the end of the play, old Nicobulus sings a lengthy song,
bursting with saturnalian embarrassment (lines 1087ff), in
which he confesses that, clever as he is, he has been made to
look *stultissimus* (lines 1099–1101):

Hoc est quo cor peracescit
hoc est demum quod percrucior
me hoc aetatis ludificari
[immo edepol sic ludos factum] [32]
cano capite atque alba barba
miserum me auro esse emunctum.


Here's the one thing that pains me and makes my heart
crack
Here's the one thing that puts my whole soul on the rack:
That a man of my age should be made such a fool
[And the *manner*, by Pollux, of this ridicule!]
With my wise hoary head, my beard eminent gray,
I've been bilked of my gold and made wretched today!

Here in the *Bacchides* the old man needs no Tranio to remind
him of his white hairs; he himself admits he is old enough to
know better. Yet what really pains him is what tortured the
*senex* in the *Mostellaria* as well: the *manner* in which he has

been undone. Like old Theopropides, Nicobulus does not care about the financial loss (lines 1102–1103):

> Perii, hoc servom meum non nauci facere esse ausum!
> atque ego, *si alibi*
> *plus perdiderim*, minus aegre habeam minusque id mihi
> damno ducam.


> I'm debased by my slave, who's so bold to behave
> like I'm nothing. That man's
> so disdainful,
> And it isn't the cost, I would gladly have lost
> even *more* in a manner
> less painful!

But, as we have already seen, the clever slave would not give up this sort of rewarding opportunity for ten times the price.

It is, of course, surefire comic material when an older and wiser *paterfamilias* is overthrown by the lowliest member of his *familia*, especially for the Romans, who, under ordinary circumstances, were renowned for their reverential attitude toward older persons. But, in a *deposuit*, the greater the victim, the greater the pleasure. Thus Plautus makes the inversion of status still more meaningful for his countrymen by presenting as comic butts *senes* who are also *senatores*. Almost every old man in his comedies enjoys some sort of social or political rank and is esteemed by the public at large; hence public disgrace is all the more painful. In the *Casina*, for example, Cleostrata spies her wayward husband's accomplice in mischief and exclaims (line 536):

> Sed eccum egreditur senati columen, praesidium popli.

> Here he comes, Crown of the Senate, Great Protector of
> the People.

Yet this bulwark of the state is quickly twisted around the
finger of a mere housewife and cannot even negotiate a simple
invitation to clear the way for his friend's amorous rendezvous. It is a ludicrous prelude to the fooling of Lysidamus,
who, it should be remembered, is at this moment in the forum
arguing a case.

Again, in the *Epidicus* the clever slave acknowledges the
high status of his two elderly antagonists, while at the same
time boasting that he will conquer this formidable duo "who
are known as Crowns of the Senate" (line 189). Fraenkel
suggests that *columen senati*, used here as well as in the quotation above from the *Casina*, was actually a semiofficial title in
early Rome.[33] But whether the epithet is official, unofficial, or
even a dramatic fabrication, the intent of the playwright is
clear: to stress the lofty rank of the comic victim. In the
*Asinaria* also, old Demaenetus is said to be a leading adviser
in the senate as well as to his clients (line 871); Demipho in
the *Mercator*, if we may take his word for it, is a *vir spectatus*
(line 319).[34] Hegio in the *Captivi* is not only rich, with con-
nections in the government, but is known throughout the city
as *senex doctus* (line 787). What is more, the reaction of this
old fellow when he realizes that he has been bamboozled is
couched in the most common Plautine saturnalian language
(*Captivi* 781–787):

> Quanto in pectore hanc rem meo magis voluto
> tanto mi aegritudo auctior est in animo.
> ad illum modum *sublitum os* esse mi hodie!
>      neque id perspicere quivi.
> quod cum scibitur, tum per urbem inridebor.
> cum extemplo ad forum advenero, omnes loquentur:
> "hic illest senex doctus quoi *verba data* sunt."

> The more I consider the matter inside myself
> The more I get angrier, pained and beside myself.

> The manner in which I was flimflammed, the way
> I couldn't perceive when they led me astray!
> O when this is known I'll be mocked through the city,
> When I reach the forum the whole world will say:
> "That clever old chap was bamboozled today!"

Hegio's chagrin is exactly like that of the old codgers in the *Mostellaria* and the *Bacchides*, providing further evidence that the play itself is more typically Plautine than critics like Lessing would have us believe.[35]

That Plautus constantly emphasizes the stature of the *senex* victim is also noted by Duckworth, who calls attention to the irony of such *redende Namen* as Theopropides, "son of prophecy"; Nicobulus, "conquering in counsel"; and Periphanes, "notable." [36] The last named, the old man in the *Epidicus*, is still another renowned statesman subjected to public humiliation [37] (lines 5 1 7, 5 2 1): [38]

> Quid nunc? qui in tantis positus sum sententiis
> ei sic data esse verba praesenti palam!

> What now for me — so often spokesman for the senate —
> I've been bamboozled both in person and in public!

But despite his disgrace, Periphanes has some small consolation: he can derive some *Schadenfreude* from the overthrow of his colleague Apoecides, who is even more respected than he in matters of statecraft (lines 5 2 2–5 2 4):

> Atque me minoris facio prae illo, qui omnium
> legum atque iurum fictor, conditor cluet;
> is etiam sese sapere memorat.

> But I'm not half as fooled as he — who's famous as
> A Framer of Laws and Legislation, Founding Father,
> And always boasting of his shrewdness, too.

Periphanes' satisfaction is justified, for in an earlier scene we have watched old Apoecides praising his own cleverness.[39] But how much consolation can there be after both a prominent senator and a "Framer of Laws and Legislation" have been flimflammed by an insignificant servant?

Moreover, old Periphanes' downfall is not yet complete. This respected statesman will soon be forced to kneel and beseech his slave Epidicus for permission to free him.[40] In this second category of master-man reversals in Plautus, the forcible inversion, the reduction of the master to an abject position of supplication is even more important (and satisfying) than in the case of those who willingly surrender their natural authority. In both situations, however, the slaves delight in the sound of *orare* emanating from their masters' lips. Thus Chrysalus in the *Bacchides* states quite plainly that his scheme is aimed at making old Nicobulus beg: *orabis me quidem ultro ut auferam* (line 825). The master does indeed have to beseech his slave to accept money, a predicament similar to the finale of the *Epidicus*. And Chrysalus proves to be just as obstinate as Epidicus, refusing to take the sack of gold, even when Nicobulus pleads abjectly (line 1063). Finally, in much the same spirit as Epidicus' condescension (to *allow* his master to untie him), Chrysalus consents, accepting the gold as a favor to his master: *cedo, si necesse est* (line 1066).

The master-as-suppliant is thus an extremely important feature of the Plautine comic finale. Simo at the end of the *Pseudolus* can lament that he has become a *supplex* (1319), and even in the last scene of the *Mostellaria*, with Theopropides still fuming at Tranio, indulgence is begged on behalf of the slave (who himself remains impudent and totally unrepentant). In the final thirty lines of the play, many verbs of supplication are employed: *orare* (twice), *exorare* (twice), and *quaeso* (four times). And while Tranio continues to act defiantly, Theopropides begs Callimidates *not* to beg: *nolo ores . . nolo inquam ores* (line 1176). Clearly the saturnalian overthrow of solid citizens, senators in particular, had a very special appeal to the Roman audience.

The leading senator was certainly the most esteemed member of Roman society. The only other person likely to enjoy anything approaching the respect given the *princeps senatus* would have been the military hero. More often than not (Coriolanus being a noteworthy exception), the same man would have owned both these distinctions, especially since, as Polybius (6.19) tells us, no Roman could hold political office until he had served ten years in the army. And it would be no exaggeration to describe Rome at the time our playwright flourished as a nation of soldiers; the country was engaged in constant hostilities, not only with Carthage, but in the East as well. In fact, Plautus' career spans a period in which his country knew no respite whatever from war. If we take a highly conservative estimate of 220 B.C. for his first comedy and allow an equally conservative 190 B.C. as the date of his last (the *didascalia* accurately places the *Pseudolus* at 191 B.C.), we find the Romans engaged in five major conflicts: the Second Illyrian War (220–219 B.C.), the Second Punic War (218–201 B.C.), the First Macedonian War (215–205 B.C.), the Second Macedonian War (200–196 B.C.), and the War against Antiochus III (192–189).[41] These were the campaigns that forged the greatness of Rome and proved her military mettle. And yet the warriors who tread the Plautine boards are un-Roman in the extreme.[42] But then their very un-Romanness was surely the guiding comic principle behind their characterization. As mentioned earlier, Freud pointed out that the prime targets of comedy are precisely those figures or institutions which command the most respect in ordinary life.[43]

It would, of course, be a gross distortion (not to say a

a hedge, and was crawling up a hill when they found him. He was looking for his damned car again."

"But you took that away months ago, didn't you?"

"Of course I did. He still doesn't realize it. I explain it, and then he forgets it almost immediately."

David sighed audibly.

"They want to move him to the memory care section," Joyce said. "They say it's for his protection. They can't watch him closely enough where he is now. During the next episode, he might accidentally do something to injure or kill himself. Can you help me with the furniture and personal effects?"

"When?"

"Tomorrow."

"Damn."

"They'd do it tonight if they could. As it is, they asked me to come out and stay with him so he doesn't try to sneak off again. It's impossible for me. Can you?"

"No, I can't. Look Joyce, I love him but you have to understand that..."

"I *do* understand. Can you at least make it tomorrow?"

Another sigh. "Yes, of course. What time?"

---

You stare at the mute shadow images that bubble up on the TV screen as you ruminate. That car represents much more than transportation. You envision yourself out on a drive with no particular destination in mind. As usual, you stick to the back roads and the old unused highways. You revel in the sense of movement, the cool wind flowing through the partially open driver's window, the towering evergreens interspersed with young alders and tangled undergrowth, the scattered farms and cabins, the occasional glimpse of wildlife such as bald eagles in flight.

And you recall another snippet. This time you are without a car. You stand by the roadside, thumb out, pack at your feet, and you await forward motion in the form of a proffered ride. You have no idea who pointless argument) to state that Plautus "invented" the *miles gloriosus*. We find such types not only in Greek New Comedy, but, mutatis mutandis, in many of the Aristophanic *alazon* types as well (e.g., General Lamachos in the *Acharnians*). And yet, as Hanson aptly points out, we must appreciate the fact that the frequent appearance of the vainglorious soldier in his comedies reveals a Plautine predilection, not merely an accident of his sources.[44] And surely Plautus preferred it because his audience loved it.

The Roman playwright does not indulge in personal satire of the Aristophanic kind; there are no *ad hominem* attacks on any particular general.[45] His soldiers, like his statesmen, are merely authoritarian types; and, like his comic senators who contrast so sharply with the real bulwarks of the Roman state, the military characters embody the Roman ideal turned topsy-turvy. One scholar goes as far as to say that Plautus is subverting the noble concept of *dulce et decorum est pro patria mori*.[46] But suffice it to note that Romans of Plautus' age explicitly forbade any sort of lying about military valor, a sin of which all his stage soldiers are egregiously guilty.[47]

The saturnalian overthrow of Pyrgopolynices, the *Miles Gloriosus* himself, is perhaps the most stunning *deposuit* in all Plautus. It is not really of vital importance whether the soldier is "Greek" (as T. B. L. Webster argues)[48] or "Roman" (as Hanson has more recently stated);[49] the basic fact that he is a military *leader* is what is important for the comic effect.[50] There are undeniably Roman touches to the soldier's characterization, but this is the least we should expect from a playwright creating Roman entertainment. The soldier's boast that he is descended from Venus (a claim with which he is later taunted) may well reflect, as Hanson argues, the contemporary fascination with the Aeneas legend,[51] whose first appearance in Latin literature coincides almost exactly with the introduction of drama to Rome, right after the First Punic

War. Moreover, Naevius, the first poet to put the new legend
into epic form, was also the chief playwright of the age before
Plautus. And it may well be worth noting that in the *Miles
Gloriosus* Plautus makes one of his rare topical allusions —
and it is to the poet Naevius.[52] But there is no need to press
this sort of inquiry further; let us merely acknowledge that
military men enjoyed great respect and high status among
Plautus' countrymen and that the comic author takes full
advantage of this attitude to arouse laughter.[53]

In the opening scene, the playwright establishes the "leadership qualities" of his *miles gloriosus*, or at least allows the
soldier to give vent to claims of fantastical exploits. Among
other things, Pyrgopolynices "admits" that he has defeated an
army whose *imperator summus* was the grandson of Neptune,
puffed away legions with a single breath, and done other epic
feats (lines 13–18). His parasite Artotrogus suggests that the
*miles'* qualities surpass even those of the Roman god of war
(lines 11–12):

> . . . Mars haud ausit dicere
> neque aequiperare suas virtutes ad tuas.

> . . . why, Mars himself would hardly dare
> To claim his powers were the equal of your own.

The soldier is, of course, painted with the broadest, most
farcical strokes, and his more fabulous feats are merely fabri-
cations inspired by his parasite's hunger (*offae monent*, line
49). Still, Pyrgopolynices is an officer of enough importance
to be doing business with King Seleucus of Syria, who, at least
according to the soldier, has "very urgently begged him" (*me
opere oravit maxumo*, line 75) to sign up mercenaries. At the
end of the first scene, that brief but brilliant exposure of the
soldier's towering *alazoneia*, he struts off to the forum. Consistent with his overblown view of himself-as-leader are his

final words to his attendants. He addresses them as if they were the retinue of a king or prince, "follow, flunky followers," *sequimini, satellites* (line 78).

But, as the plot progresses, this great leader is gradually transformed into a lowly follower, and finally to a cowardly suppliant. After a while his own lackey leads him by the nose, and the inversion is underscored in Plautus' language. At the beginning of the play, Palaestrio, the brilliant slave-strategist, is already in command of the opposition forces. The confident manner in which he gives orders to old Periplectomenus, as well as to young Pleusicles, his former master, is a fine example of the first type of saturnalian reversal we have described, the willing transfer of authority from lord to lackey. In one scene, the slave sends the old man scurrying off to the forum to do his bidding (hire women for his scheme), and then turns to Pleusicles (lines 805–806):

> PALAESTRIO:   Ergo adcura, sed propere opus est! nunc tu
>                                       ausculta, Pleusicles.
> PLEUSICLES:   Tibi sum oboediens.

> PALAESTRIO (*calling off to the old man*):   Hurry, go, we
>      need 'em right away. (*to the young man*) Now listen,
>                                            Pleusicles —
> PLEUSICLES:   I'm at your service.

The *adulescens'* eager subservience to Palaestrio is typical of those Plautine youths who are prompted by love to enslave themselves to their slaves. It takes a good deal more effort on Palaestrio's part to make the words here spoken so willingly by Pleusicles come out of the mouth of his military master. But by playing up to the soldier's vanity, lust, and especially his avarice, Palaestrio gradually induces Pyrgopolynices into asking *him* what to do in every situation.[54] The soldier even "surrenders his ears" to listen to his slave's ideas (line 954).

Sooner or later Plautine masters all obey their servants, and Pyrgopolynices unwittingly echoes the young master's earlier (willing) submission to Palaestrio when he answers his slave's command to "hurry up, go inside," with a compliant *tibi sum oboediens* (line 1129).[55]

By the end of the play, the capitulation is complete, a topsy-turvydom which Plautus emphasizes by playing on the word *sequor*. The maid Milphidippa appears and "whets the soldier's appetite for love" (line 1006), whereupon the *miles* begs Palaestrio to speak to her and begin amorous negotiations on his behalf. The slave does so, and leads his master across the stage just as this great leader had earlier (line 78) directed his minions with a regal *sequimini, satellites* (line 1009):

PALAESTRIO:  Sequere hac me ergo.
PYRGOPOLYNICES:  Pedisequos tibi sum.

PALAESTRIO:  All right, follow me.
PYRGOPOLYNICES:  I'll be your follower.

Now the eminent general not only tags dutifully after the footsteps of his own slave, *pedes sequitur*, but as he does so he unconsciously admits[56] that he has been transformed into a *pedisequus*, a lackey, the meanest of menials.[57]

Nor does Plautus stop at such a subtle *déclassement*. The leaders overthrown in his plays are always embarrassed in public as well. This holds true for the *Miles Gloriosus*, whose special disgrace is even more ignominious than that which Plautus' boastful senators suffer. At the end of the play, Pyrgopolynices must confess that he is a craven coward and then beg for mercy. His plaintive *obsecro hercle* sets the tone for the final humiliating scene, and it is repeated four times in the last forty lines. Indeed the appropriate retort to this so-called hero who begs "by Hercules," is Periplectomenus' *nequiquam hercle obsecras* (line 1396), "by Hercules, your begging isn't worth a thing." [58]

Throughout their history, the Romans prided themselves on being unexcelled soldiers and statesmen. It is these very qualities that Aeneas' father Anchises (*Aeneid* 6.847ff) eulogizes as "the Roman arts" (lines 851–853):

> Tu regere imperio populos, Romane, memento;
> hae tibi erunt artes: pacique imponere morem
> parcere subiectis, et debellare superbos.

> Remember, O Roman, you are destined to govern nations;
> these shall be your arts: to affirm law and order with peace,
> to spare the conquered, and to beat down the proud.

Throughout Anchises' speech may be noted a firm emphasis on authority and domination, even when it is by peaceful means. And yet on the Plautine stage the Romans watched authoritarian figures mocked and defeated *domi militiaeque*. The dignified suffer indignities, the leaders are abjectly led.

But there is another characteristic to be noted in the Plautine saturnalia. For each merry *deposuit*, there is a corresponding *exaltavit*. The mighty are overthrown and the humble are elevated, leaping proudly onto the temporarily unoccupied pedestals; many even feel at home perched on the holy altars. Lords of misrule, the slaves themselves become (for the time being) soldiers and statesmen of the highest rank. We have already seen how often the other characters in the plays spontaneously attribute qualities of leadership (and titles) to the clever servants. Old Periplectomenus in the *Miles* must hurry to the "senate" called by the bondsman Palaestrio, lest they vote in his absence (lines 592–595). Clearly, Palaestrio is the *princeps senatus*, who both introduces and enforces the legislation; Periplectomenus and his young master Pleusicles barely have the opportunity to say "aye." [59] Still other Plautine slaves are more explicit in claiming to possess whole "senates of wisdom" within themselves; and the senate metaphor itself adds a particularly Roman touch to what was probably βουλή in the Greek original, which might easily have been rendered by Plautus with a less specific *consilium*; cf. *Epidicus* 158–159:

> EPIDICUS: . . . Ego de re argentaria
> iam senatum convocabo in corde consiliarium.

> EPIDICUS: . . . As for budget problems, I
> Now will summon a serious senate assembly inside my
> interior soul.

or *Mostellaria* 687–688:

> TRANIO: . . . Huc concessero
> dum mihi senatum consili in cor convoco.

> TRANIO: . . . I'll step aside
> And summon a senate assembly inside my inner soul.

And though they often praise themselves as statesmen, the slaves take an even greater pride in being *military* leaders.[60] In fact, as in the case of Epidicus' cerebral synod, the slave-senators usually vote a declaration of war: "I urge this course of action: an assault on the old man's citadel" (*Epidicus* 163). There are countless instances in Plautus where the slave plays commander in chief, perhaps the most memorable being Chrysalus' comparison of himself with the legendary Trojan Lord of Men, Agamemnon (*Bacchides* 944ff). Fraenkel has noted a significant similarity between Chrysalus' language (line 1071ff) and the triumphal tablet of the Roman general T. Sempronius Gracchus.[61] Thus to the eyes (and ears) of Plautus' audience, Chrysalus was a conqueror at once Homeric and Roman. The slave himself would not consider this an exaggeration at all; in fact, since he claims superiority not only in generalship but in counterintelligence, he proceeds to boast that he is not only Agamemnon, but Ulysses as well (*Bacchides* 941, 949–950).

Since various legends on the Homeric heroes were enjoying great popularity in Rome, thanks especially to the tragic playwrights,[62] it is not unusual that many Plautine similes allude to exploits of the Trojan War. For example, the strategy of Pseudolus, like that of Chrysalus, is compared to the wiles of Ulysses (*Pseudolus* 1063 and 1244). In fact, although Ilium is not always mentioned specifically, as in *Miles* 1025 ("what's your method for storming our Troy here?"), the slaves' rebellious actions are very often referred to as storming a city or citadel, as in Epidicus' declaration of war, *senem oppugnare* (line 163) quoted above, Chrysalus' plan to *erum expugnare* (*Bacchides* 929), and the use of similar terms to describe Pseudolus' campaign against Ballio (*Pseudolus* 585ff; 761ff).[63]

The slaves not only compare themselves to Homeric heroes, sometimes to the latter's disadvantage, as in *Pseudolus* 1244, but allude to historical generals as well. Witness, for example, Tranio's praise of his own exploits (*Mostellaria* 775–777):

Alexandrum magnum atque Agathoclem aiunt maximas
duo res gessisse: quid mihi fiet tertio
qui solus facio facinora immortalia?

They say that Alexander and Agathocles
Both did great things. But how about *me* as a third —
Who solo does so many memorable deeds?

The lowly servant puts himself on a par with two great Hellenistic heroes, each renowned for wisdom as well as generalship. Alexander was a portentous name; for, as Pierre Grimal notes, the entire world, Carthaginian no less than Roman, was at this time "obsessed" by the memory of Alexander.[64] And Agathocles of Syracuse was the only Hellenistic ruler among the western Greeks to have assumed the title *king*. Thus Tranio's boast is indeed regal — nay, imperial. And if the slave seem overbold, it should be noted that in the *Pseudolus* old Simo predicts that the clever servant will *surpass* all the feats of this same Agathocles, if he can make his plans work (lines 531–532). Pseudolus succeeds brilliantly, thereby dwarfing the achievements of the Sicilian king. The slaves are always thinking on a grand scale. Just as their heads contain entire senates, their mental military maneuvers are also epic in scope. Pseudolus controls whole legions (lines 586 and 761) and Palaestrio in the *Miles* proudly refers to his own armies, composed of specifically Roman divisions.[65]

In brief, the Plautine *dominus festi* insists as much upon the *exaltavit* as upon the *deposuit* of the saturnalian process. We have already mentioned the frequency with which slaves are addressed as masters. To review but a few examples: the function of *magister* is attributed to Epidicus (line 592), Tranio (*Mostellaria* 33), and Pseudolus (lines 932–933). Many of the menials are called *patronus* and even *pater* by the men who are supposed to be their masters.[66] We have already discussed the slave-senators and slave-generals. To add but a few instances in the latter category, Pseudolus is called *dux* early in the play (line 447) although his exploits earn him rapid promotions (e.g., line 1244). Chrysalus (*Bacchides* 759), Leonida (*Asinaria* 656), and Palaestrio (*Miles* 1160) are *imperatores*, while both Tranio and Chrysalus are later on ranked with the greatest commanders in chief who ever lived.

The prospect of kingship is also attractive to the lord of the festival.[67] Gripus in the *Rudens* dreams of being considered *apud reges rex* (line 931), although he lacks the regal wit to make his dream come true.[68] Pseudolus, of course, claims to surpass *regi Agathocli* (line 532). And, if *rex* was an ennobling (albeit horribly un-Roman) title, how much more so would be the epithet "king of kings." Sceparnio in the *Rudens* refers to himself as *basilicus* (line 431), an adjective which seems to have been used exclusively by Plautus, and which clearly carried the aura of the great Alexander, who had crowned himself βασιλεύς after the death of Darius of Persia.[69] Tranio, as cited earlier, mentions Alexander by name, but there may also be an allusion to the conquering emperor in Pseudolus' haughty stance described as *statum vide hominis . . . quam basilicum* (line 458), "look at that fellow's stance . . . so king-of-kingsly." Even when Toxilus proposes to live it up *basilice* (*Persa* 29 and 31; and again, line 806) he may well have in mind some of the luxurious *Persici apparatus* of the eastern monarchs.[70]

But the *exaltavit* of the Plautine slave does not even stop at "the sweet fruition of an earthly crown," however great the crown may be. Some of the more audacious servants wish not merely coronation but deification. And if the title "king" would have aroused Roman hostilities under ordinary circumstances, the notion of a mortal becoming a god was — at this time — even more abhorrent and un-Roman. For, while Alexander the Great had already sown some of the seeds of the ruler cult throughout the Greek world, the sort of Roman deification that began with Julius Caesar and became standard procedure during the empire was totally unthinkable in the Rome of Plautus' day; it was, as Lily Ross Taylor states, "*foreign* to the very nature of early Roman religion." [71] And yet the Plautine slave aspires even to Olympian heights, or at least to appear godlike in his master's estimation. The references to the slaves' divinity may be subtle, as in the *Bacchides*, where the two young men stand in despair, unable to find a

33

33

ISBN 978-0-9997137-0-9
Library of Congress Control Number: 2017963084

**Fiction, Nonfiction, and Art Editors**
Lantz Arroyo
Nicholas Hurd
Sarah Lopez
Joaquin Fernandez

**Poetry Editor**
Erin Mathieu

**Interior Layout & Design**
Lantz Arroyo

**Cover Concept & Design**
Sarah Lopez

Printed and published in Brooklyn, New York by Radix Media.

Radix Media
522 Bergen Street
Brooklyn, New York 11217

**radixmedia.org**

might stop or where you might end up, but it doesn't matter. You are free to go whithersoever you will, wherever the road takes you.

A third recollection: you're typing, putting one word after another, and the sensation is almost like being on the road because you're venturing forth to an unknown destination...

Abruptly your perceptions return to your present predicament. The air smells stale; you have the tickle of an urge to pee; you develop a momentary spark of interest in the program that's on. You consider opening the window, going to the bathroom, and turning up the volume on the TV. The transient thoughts vanish and you end up doing none of these things.

---

An ambulance pulled up outside the entrance while they waited, and two attendants carefully removed a gurney from the interior. The woman on the gurney looked withered and light as down on a breeze. Her sparse frizzy white hair surrounded her head like a halo. She stared upward with a vacant expression, neither smiling nor frowning, as they wheeled her off into the interior.

"Hello. My name is Leonard Dutton. I oversee the memory care facility here." Dressed in a short-sleeved dress shirt and slacks but no jacket, he was slim, middle-aged, and somber-faced. "Let me give you a tour of the unit while the nurse practitioner speaks with your father."

As Joyce and David followed him down a wide hallway, they passed old people sitting in wheelchairs, propping themselves up with walkers, and ambling along under their own energy. Most of the residents gave them a smile and a nod.

They arrived at a closed door with a thick panel of glass at eye level.

"This door is always locked," said Dutton. "On either side, you have to enter a code to get it open. It consists of the corner numbers entered clockwise: one, three, nine, seven. As you can see, above the keypad is a seemingly unrelated message with the code reminder embedded in it. The decryption seems obvious, but no resident has ever cracked the code."

"My father could well be the first," said Joyce.

> All the gods in heaven, not to mention twelve
> immortals more,
> Now do battle by my side and aid me as my aides-de-camp!

Epidicus not only has all the hosts of heaven but even has a dozen more divinities in his army, Titans no doubt, as would befit these rebellious, saturnalian circumstances. It should also be noted that the clever slaves in Plautus can get away with the most extravagant claims of divinity (not to mention other virtues), whereas the anti-comic figures who make similar claims are always punished for this verbal *hubris*. The readiest example is that of Pyrgopolynices' having his boasts of being "grandson of Venus" hurled painfully back at him (*Miles* 1413, 1421). Chrysalus can freely boast that a golden statue should be raised to his divinity (*Bacchides* 640); [74] the symmetrical demands for statues and divine worship on the part of the slaves in the *Asinaria* have already been discussed. [75] And there are several instances in which the clever slaves suggest that they have the power of gods, as for example Pseudolus' boast (lines 109–110):

> Scis tu quidem hercle, mea si commovi sacra,
> quo pacto et quantas soleam turbellas dare.

> Can you imagine when I start my sacred service
> The quantity of wondrous whirlwinds I'll arouse?

He appears to be equating himself with Aeolus, powerful lord of the winds who figures prominently in Roman as well as Greek epic, [76] and his subsequent actions justify his high-sounding claim. Moreover, this sort of braggadocio seems to have become part of the standard vocabulary of the scheming slave throughout the history of comedy. Take, for example, Figaro's echo of Pseudolus' vaunt:

> par la force de mon art, je vais, d'un seul coup de baguette,

endormir la vigilance, éveiller l'amour, égarer la jalousie, fourvoyer l'intrigue, et renverser tous les obstacles.[77]

with the power of my talent, with one stroke of my magic wand, I'll put vigilance to sleep, wake up love, thwart jealousy, get control of the plot and turn topsy-turvy all the obstacles in our path.[78]

No boast is too extravagant, for his wit enables him to perform the impossible, the miraculous. Is it any wonder that such characters think of themselves as heaven-blest? Drunk with his own success, Ben Jonson's Mosca can rhapsodize:

> O! Your Parasite
> Is a most precious thing dropt from above,
> Not bred 'mongst clods and clot-poules here on earth.[79]

Molière's Scapin, another distinguished member of the brotherhood of scheming servants, reflects Mosca's attitude exactly:

> . . . il y a peu de choses qui me soient impossibles, quand je m'en veux mêler. J'ai sans doute reçu du Ciel un génie assez beau pour toutes les fabriques . . . et je puis dire sans vanité qu'on n'a guère vu d'homme qui fût plus habile ouvrier de ressorts et d'intrigues, qui aît acquis plus de gloire que moi dans ce noble métier.[80]

There are very few things I can't do when I put my mind to it. I think Heaven has blessed me with a sort of genius for inventing ploys . . . And I can say without vanity that we've seen few artists more talented than I am when it comes to machinations, and few who have achieved more glory than I in this noble profession.

Plautus' fondness for the "divinely clever" servant seems to have influenced the entire later history of stage comedy.

In the Roman playwright's dramatic saturnalia, those who enjoy authority and respect in the ordinary Roman world are unseated and ridiculed, while the lowliest members of society mount to their pedestals. The humble are in fact exalted far above any conceivable everyday status, since both kingship and personal deification were shockingly un-Roman concepts. Still, the clever slave excels as soldier and statesman, monarch, oriental potentate, and even god. Whatever the circumstances, these menials never humble themselves before anyone. They are conquering heroes who, like Pseudolus, can cry *vae victis* to their humiliated old master (line 1317), echoing the famous words of the Gaulish leader who had captured Rome and denied all mercy to the vanquished Romans.[81] Plautine slaves even breathe freely in rarefied Olympian air. They feel quite comfortable, as does Tranio in the *Mostellaria*, seated on a holy altar, and speaking his mind *de divinis locis* (line 1104).

CHAPTER V ·

# From Freedom
# to Slavery

The previous chapter analyzed the Plautine saturnalia in which distinguished members of society are unseated by their own slaves, who then subject their erstwhile masters to all manner of indignities. The behavior of the "exalted slave" is impudent, to say the least, more than justifying the epithet *scelerum caput* ("fount of impiety") by which he is so often addressed.[1] *Scelus*, we recall, is the antithesis of *pietas*.[2] Under normal circumstances, the slaves' rogueries would occasion the harshest punishment, and yet, strangely enough, the Plautine protagonists suffer no penalties whatever. Stranger still, the threat of painful retribution is omnipresent; the servants frame their boldest schemes in the shadow of the pillory — and the gallows. The cleverest of slaves is always aware of what an infinite variety of tortures he risks in his pursuit of mischief. The uncommonly large number of references to the punishment of slaves is a significant Plautine characteristic, without real precedent in New Comedy and virtually absent in the plays of Terence.[3] As this chapter will demonstrate, the threat-of-punishment motif, or more accurately, a special practice of *non*-punishment, provides the key to a general understanding of Plautus' holiday humor.

We have already discussed the lowly position of slaves on the everyday Roman scale and the fact that they could be beaten or killed at the slightest whim of their masters. Tortures were many and varied, including not only whippings but also the breaking of bones or the amputation of a limb.[4] Moreover, the slave's offense need not have been very serious to earn him a beating or even execution. Plutarch relates that Cato the Elder had his cooks flogged for preparing a dinner which failed to please him.[5] In imperial times, Petronius tells how one of Trimalchio's slaves was crucified for having cursed his master.[6] Juvenal describes a wife blithely sending a servant to the cross merely because she is of a humor to do so.[7]

But the most elaborate catalogue of slave discomforts is to be found in Plautus himself. Besides the countless references to the standard whipping instruments like *virgae* (rods) and *stimuli* (goads), his comedies display a vocabulary of tortures which, for color, variety, and inventiveness, is matched only (appropriately enough) by his Rabelaisian rosters of trickeries. Plautus mentions an astounding number of torture devices, including iron chains, hot tar, burning clothes, restraining collars, the rack, the pillory, and the mill.[8] The fact that his bondsmen are so frequently referred to as *verbero* ("flog-worthy"), *mastigia* ("whip-worthy"), and *furcifer* ("gallowsbird") is an additional reminder of what retribution usually awaits a misbehaving slave. (These allusions are far too numerous to cite, but it may be worth noting that there is a high incidence of these "torture titles" in, of all plays, the *Captivi.*)[9] Of course these epithets are also hurled at random by characters in Menander and Terence — not to mention Aristophanes.[10] The important difference in the case of Plautus, however, is that, by any standards, his slaves are egregiously "whip-worthy."

Slave-beating is surely as old as comedy itself, and the bondsman complaining of the lashes on his back was already a stock figure by the time of Aristophanes. In the *Peace* 743–744, the Greek poet expresses his annoyance that this hack-

neyed stereotype appears so frequently on the comic stage.
Yet Aristophanes himself presents this characterization, in the
*prologos* to the *Knights*, for example, and in Bdelycleon's servant Xanthias, a lackey piteously moaning that he has been
beaten black and blue (*Wasps* 1292–1296). Almost every
Plautine slave has been treated like Xanthias at one time or
another, but most of them (at least the clever ones) view the
experience lightheartedly. In a comic way, the purple stripes
on his back distinguish the Plautine slave much as the purple
border on his toga distinguished the Roman senator. Whiplash
marks seem to have been an essential feature in the characterization of a slave in Roman popular comedy. Plautus even
jokes over this convention when Sosia encounters Mercury
in the *Amphitruo*. Mercury is dressed like Sosia, and tries to
convince the befuddled bondsman that he, Mercury, is really
Amphitryon's slave. Sosia is amazed at the likeness between
himself and the man who confronts him (lines 443–446):

> Itidem habet petasum ac vestitum: tam consimilest
> atque ego;
> sura, pes, statura, tonsus, oculi, nasum vel labra,
> malae, mentum, barba, collus: totus. quid verbis opust?
> *si tergum cicatricosum*, nihil hoc similist similius.

> Absolutely similar: his hat, his clothes, he's so like me!
> Calf and foot, his height and haircut, eyes and nose and
> lips as well.
> Cheeks and chin and beard and neck — why everything.
> What need of words?
> If he's got a back of scars, no likeness could be more alike!

All that is needed for a final *anagnorisis* is the set of scars
which testify to his past behavior. Unheroic Sosia may lose
his identity with the same evidence used by heroic Odysseus
to regain his.

Sosia's comment demonstrates a basic truth. By Plautine standards, a slave is "he who gets whipped." In fact most of the allusions in Plautus are more distinctive than Sosia's vague reference to past punishments, and their presence has far more thematic significance than what are superficially regarded as similar instances in Aristophanes. Even when a whipping constitutes the basis of an Aristophanic scene, as with Dionysus and Xanthias in the *Frogs*, the setting is fantastic and remote. But in Plautus the references are usually very specific and very detailed, deliberately to remind the audience of the practice of ordinary Roman life. Torture is mentioned so often in Plautus that it may well be called an obsession — on the part of the playwright as well as of his characters.[11] Furthermore, a host of scholars, among them the great historian Theodore Mommsen, distinguish a special "Roman severity" in the punishments described. In fact, Mommsen believes that the mistreatment mentioned by Plautine slaves mirrors some of the actual policies of Cato the Elder.[12]

Judged by the standards of contemporary Rome, Plautus' slaves truly merit the dire penalties with which they are menaced. If Cato whipped his cooks for ruining dinner, what would be adequate recompense for the rogueries of a Tranio, a Pseudolus, or an Epidicus, who not only subject their masters to incredible public embarrassment, but remain impudent and unrepentant to the very last? It would be too easy to dismiss this question merely by remarking that comedy by definition has a happy ending and that it is therefore perfectly proper for Pseudolus to escape crucifixion and exit arm in arm with his master at the play's conclusion. After all, Aristotle describes a similar scene which would arouse "comic pleasure," one in which Orestes would not kill Aegisthus and the two would stroll amicably offstage.[13] But "happy endings" and immunity from punishment are not identical phenomena. In the comedy of Ben Jonson, to cite an extreme example, all ends well and "happily" (for society), but the rogues do not escape retribution for their rogueries. In fact, the judgment meted out at the end of *Volpone* is particularly severe: Mosca the clever servant will be whipped and sent to the galleys (the Renaissance equivalent of *in pistrinum*), and Volpone, because he has feigned illness, must lie in prison, "till thou b'est sicke and lame indeed." [14]

Especially since the spectator had the harsh example of everyday practice with which he could compare the actions he saw on the comic stage, the amazing immunity of the Plautine slave must be regarded as more than merely a "happy ending" device. For Plautus abounds in threats; tortures are enumerated with minute specificity — and then never carried out. This aspect of his plays has always puzzled scholars. Professor Duckworth, for example, can offer no explanation for the freedom of Plautus' bondsman, except that it "bears little relation to reality":

> No respectable householder in Greece or Rome would have countenanced such activity and the spectators were well aware of the fact. Slaves guilty of lying, cheating or stealing would have been whipped or imprisoned, or condemned to hard labor. [15]

Of course, one of my major arguments has been that Plautine comedy may be viewed as "real Roman life" turned topsy-turvy. It had great appeal precisely because the audience was well aware of the ordinary practices of Roman society. Furthermore, few critics have noticed that even the characters within the plays are themselves cognizant of the real-life situation. By harping, as they do repeatedly, on the beatings that they intend to inflict or hope to avoid, they are acknowledging the everyday standards of right and wrong.

As might well be expected, the slaves are most preoccupied with punishment; what distinguishes the clever from the

unclever is their attitude toward this prospect. Messenio in the
*Menaechmi* is an example of the good and fearful slave who
sees his situation in its proper real-life perspective. He sings a
song in praise of the obedient servant who wisely guards his
master's interests even while the master is absent. Those who
act otherwise (and here he might cite any of Plautus' brilliant
slave characters) will inevitably suffer for their misdeeds
(lines 973–977):

> Recordetur id,
> > qui nihili sunt, quid eis preti
> detur ab suis eris, ignavis, improbis viris:
> > verbera compedes
> > molae, lassitudo fames frigus durum,
> > > haec pretia sunt ignaviae.
> id ego male malum metuo; propterea bonum esse
> > certumst potius quam malum.

> His masters will reward them,
> > > let the worthless slaves be told,
> The lowly lazy louts get whips and chains,
> And millstones, great fatigue, starvation, freezing cold,
> The price for all their misbehavior's — pains.
> I therefore fully fear this fate and very gladly
> > Remain determined to be good —
> > > so I won't end up badly.

Messenio displays an outlook diametrically opposed to that of
the typical Plautine slave-hero, when he states, "I do whatever
I think is best for my shoulder blades" (line 985). This attitude is echoed by certain other slaves in Plautus; in fact, the
playwright must have taken some delight in depicting craven
bondsmen, since he often has them express their fear in song.[16]
This type of character provides an excellent foil for the ma-
chinating slave who rates his back at nothing. Molière follows
Plautus' example by contrasting Scapin's bold attitude to that

of his fellow servant Sylvestre, a chap who trembles at the very thought of "un nuage de coups de bâton qui crèvera sur mes épaules." [17] On the other hand, Scapin shows the mettle of a Plautine *servus callidus* when he takes "onto his back" the responsibility for the *fourberies* he is about to commit:

> SYLVESTRE: . . . tu vas courir risque de t'attirer une venue de coups de bâton.
> SCAPIN: Hé bien! C'est au dépens de mon dos, et non pas du tien.
> SYLVESTRE: Il est vrai que tu es maître de tes épaules . . .[18]

> SYLVESTRE: You'll be running the risk of a harvest of blows with a stick.
> SCAPIN: So what? I'm risking my own back, not yours!
> SYLVESTRE: That's true. You're master of your shoulder blades.

Scapin's words are not only Plautine in attitude, they are Plautine in origin, being a direct translation of Tranio's reply to the "good slave" Grumio: *mei tergi facio haec* (*Mostellaria* 37). All the clever slaves in Plautus echo this philosophy in much the same terms. As Epidicus says to his young master, "as long as I please you, I don't care a straw about my back" (line 348). Pseudolus, when threatened with dire revenge, can reply calmly: *quid minitare? habeo tergum* (line 1325), "Why threaten me? It's my own back." Libanus in the *Asinaria* knows what gainful reward his mischief may bring him, and yet he can say lightheartedly, "I have my own back and won't borrow anyone else's" (line 319), expressing a state of mind exactly like that of Chrysalus when he learns his master is out buying lashes to punish him: *si illi sunt virgae ruri, at mihi tergum domist* (*Bacchides* 365), "his rods are in the country, but my back's at home."

Dutton proffered the trace of a smile. "We're aware of his abilities. We'll keep an eye on him." He pulled the door open. "After fifteen seconds a cautionary alarm goes off at the attendants' desk, so you have to enter and close the door promptly." After they did, Dutton gave the door a tug. "Check that it's closed and latched and that no residents are near the door to grab it before you move on. The security code is reversed when you leave: seven, nine, three, one. If you forget, it's written there above the door."

Just inside, a door to the right revealed a dining area with parallel rectangular tables. Several women sat at one silently chewing food. At another sat a man in a wheelchair; with a trembling hand, he absent-mindedly used a fork to fumble around with the food on his plate.

"That's Mr. Beck," said Dutton. "He's the only other male resident in the facility right now. Your father will be eating with him."

The entry hallway opened out into a spacious common room with couches, armchairs, a television, and a few tables stacked with board games. Along both sides were the doors to the private quarters.

A slim, middle-aged woman in a light green pantsuit stood behind the desk at the attendants' station.

"This is Wendy. She recently transferred here, and she knows your father from the other section—although he may not remember her. These are Brad Couragger's children."

Wendy shook Joyce's and then David's hand. "We'll take good care of your dad," she said.

"This room on the right is where he'll be moved initially," said Dutton. "He'll be able to stay here until another spot opens up in a week or two, but unfortunately his insurance doesn't cover a fully private room like this."

To the left, as they entered, was a bathroom. Farther in were a tiny kitchenette with sink and fridge, and a narrow living area with a twin bed. The ground floor window looked out onto an asphalt roadway; beyond were thick woods.

"There's no space for his double bed," said Joyce. "He won't like it."

"He'll have to adjust," said David. "We can put his favorite chair here next to the bed and his TV on a table over there."

Dutton next took them to a room a few doors farther on that had

Scholars have been puzzled by the Plautine slave's willingness to risk his shoulder blades for the sake of mischief. Philippe Legrand offered one explanation: "The fact that the slaves in Roman comedy scorn the floggings they are threatened by . . . shows their degraded state." [19] This statement is misleading on two counts. First of all, he should be saying "Plautine" and not "Roman" comedy, since this attitude toward beatings is not at all characteristic of Terence.[20] Secondly, the slave's disdainful attitude shows his *exalted* state; he can scorn the punishment because in every comedy he manages to elude it. Not that Legrand has overlooked this; in fact it is another feature of Plautine comedy which distresses him. Discussing the double-dealings of Epidicus, he remarks that "such misdeeds call for punishment." [21] Of Pseudolus' behavior, he states: "His impudence goes too far, and I think that a master . . . would have replied to such impertinent talk with a whip." [22] But the most significant single feature of Plautine comedy is the very fact that the lowly slaves who are so readily tortured and beaten in real life can go "too far" with impunity. The license to go "too far" is the essence of both the comic and the festival spirit. The most obvious (and most valid) reply to those who wonder why Plautus' rogues go unpunished is quite simply that the spectators wished it so. As Northrop Frye describes it, the comic resolution always comes "from the audience's side of the stage." [23] Or, as John Gay justifies the last-minute reprieve of the rogue Macheath, "all this we must do, to comply with the taste of the town." [24]

We have already observed that part of the special pleasure which the Roman spectator derived from watching a rascally Pseudolus go unpunished was due, to a great extent, to his awareness of what would happen under ordinary circumstances. And the slaves themselves enjoy the same awareness that the present circumstances are very special. Every bondsman, from moral Messenio to tricky Tranio, knows his catalogue of tortures the way a Roman child knew his alphabet (in each case the lesson was doubtless instilled by the hickory stick). Witness, for example, Libanus' victorious shout in the *Asinaria* (lines 545–551):

Perfidiae laudes gratiasque habemus merito magnas
quom nostris sychophantiis, dolis astutiisque
[scapularum confidentia, virtute ulmorum freti] [25]
advorsum stetimus lamminas, crucesque compedesque
nervos, catenas, carceres, numellas, pedicas, boias
inductoresque acerrumos gnarosque nostri tergi!


We give our great and grateful thanks to Holy Trickery,
For by our shrewdness, wiles, deceits, and clever
machinations,
[Our shoulders bold, displaying courage in the face
of rods,]
We've just defied hot-iron tortures, crucifixion, chains,
Strappadoes, fetters, dungeons, locking, stocking, manacles,
And harsh persuasive whippers well acquainted with
our backs!

Beyond the Rabelaisian review of punishments for which it is frequently quoted, this passage offers a great deal toward understanding the peculiar character of the Plautine clever slave. To begin with, Libanus spews forth this comic catalogue merely to stress what pains he and his comrade Leonida have *eluded* by their "wiles, deceits, and machinations." Wit seems to be a magic armor which protects the clever slave, although he realizes that the circumstances which permit him to escape scot-free are exceptional. Libanus states in no uncertain terms that the whippers whom he and his friend have today avoided are, from previous encounters, well acquainted with their shoulder blades, *gnarosque nostri tergi* (line 551). Theirs is a

pleasure not unlike that which Lucretius extols in the proem
to Book 2: knowing what trouble you do *not* have.[26]

The brace of bondsmen proceed to enumerate their previous villainies and — this should be especially noted — the
sound thrashings to which these villainies have inevitably led.
Leonida begins by praising his fellow slave's "noble achievements . . . at home and in the field" (lines 558–559), a
phrase which almost certainly had special Roman reverberations.[27] The achievements include (lines 561–565):

> Ubi fidentem fraudaveris, ubi ero infidelis fueris
> ubi verbis conceptis sciens libenter periuraris,
> ubi parietes perfoderis, in furto ubi sis prehensus,
> ubi saepe causam dixeris pendens adversus octo
> artutos, audacis viros, valentis virgatores.

> You fooled a faithful friend and were unfaithful to
>                             your master,
> You spoke a pack of perjuries on purpose — just for fun.
> You tunneled through a wall, got caught red-handed
>                             in a theft.
> You often offered your excuses hanging upside down
> Before eight well-built, bold and brawny, birch-rod
>                             beating brutes.

Consistent with the Tweedledum-Tweedledee behavior of
these two scurrilous servants, Libanus in turn recites the many
misdeeds of Leonida, all similar to his own, and which also
resulted in the slave's being caught and beaten, again by eight
sturdy whippers (lines 566–574). The offenses of both slaves
represent the standard rogueries of Plautine comedy: lying,
cheating, tricking their masters, and, in the case of Libanus,
digging through the wall of a house (line 563), a wild caper
which parallels precisely what the clever Palaestrio does in the

*Miles Gloriosus.* The entire first phase of the *Miles* depends upon Palaestrio's scheme, as he himself explains in the prologue (lines 138–143):

> Itaque ego paravi hic intus magnas machinas
> qui amantis una inter se facerem convenas.
> nam unum conclave, concubinae quod dedit
> miles, quo nemo nisi eapse inferret pedem,
> in eo conclavi ego *perfodi parietem,*
> qua commeatus clam esset hinc huc mulieri.

> Now here within I've started mighty machinations
> To make it easy for the lovers' visitations.
> The soldier gave the girl a bedroom of her own —
> No one but she can enter it, it's hers alone.
> So in this bedroom I have tunneled through the wall,
> Right to the other house — in secret — she can crawl.

*La machine est trouvée.* No doubt the audience was already smiling in anticipation of the comic confusions Palaestrio's tunnel would create. Surely no spectator would say, "Oh no, that is an illegal action which could bring dire retribution, a whipping or worse." And yet Leonida's remarks in the *Asinaria* demonstrate that Palaestrio's device is indeed an unlawful and punishable offense. On another occasion Libanus was soundly beaten for the same action that earns Palaestrio nothing but admiration. From this curious double standard, we discover that the immunity of the Plautine slave is very special: the rascal is merely absolved from what he does *during the play*, that is, during his reign of misrule. All the torture talk serves as a deliberate foil to emphasize what will *not* happen during today's comedy.

A familiar routine in Plautus is a snappy vaudevillian exchange between two slaves who have not seen each other for some time. The answer to "Where have you been all this

while?" is always some variation of "I have been beaten up."
The meeting between Toxilus and Sagaristio at the opening of
the *Persa* is typical of this gambit. Sagaristio has just returned
from a painful year *in pistrino*, to which he alludes lightheartedly (in Paul Nixon's clever rendering): "I have been Minister
Extrairondinary and Plentyblowtentiary at the — mills." [28]
And yet Sagaristio is anxious to undertake a wild bit of mischief that might well send him back for more.

There is a similar exchange at the beginning of the *Asinaria*,
when Leonida and Libanus plan an escapade which might well
start them "cruising for crucifixion" (line 314); nonetheless,
their enthusiasm is undiminished. At the outset of the *Epidicus*,
the protagonist reveals that during the interval in which he has
not seen Thesprio, his fellow slave, his back has been subjected
to many beatings (lines 17–18). This does not, however, deter
Epidicus from setting in motion a double deception, at the risk
of still greater punishment. In fact, midway through the play,
it does seem as if Epidicus will suffer dreadfully; after his first
scheme fails, he states sadly that even the Olympian gods could
not save him *ex cruciatu* (lines 610 ff). But his outlook is still
in sharp contrast with that of such craven slaves as Sceledrus
in the *Miles Gloriosus*,[29] who take to their heels at the merest
hint of trouble (lines 582–583):

> Nam iam aliquo *aufugiam* et me occultabo aliquot dies
> dum haec consilescunt turbae, atque irae leniunt.

> I'll run off somewhere, hide myself a day or two
> Till this commotion quiets, and the shouting stops.

The very *turbae* which Sceledrus fears are the same sort of
commotions his clever counterparts take pride, not in fleeing,
but in stirring up.

But Epidicus, in the face of what seems more certain (and

more painful) disaster, remains unafraid, resolved to face up to (and outface) his master (lines 664–665):

*Non fugio*, domi adesse certumst. neque ille haud
                                              obiciet mihi
pedibus sese provocatum. abeo intro, nimis longum loquor.


I won't run off, that's firm. I'll stay right here.
    They'll never say that
Master made me sprint. I'll go inside. I talk too much.

The Plautine clever slave recognizes potential punishment as the price for present pleasure. To epitomize his philosophy (*Asinaria* 324):

Fortiter malum qui patitur, idem post potitur bonum.

Grin and bear the ills, then later you can grin —
    and bear the thrills.

Rarely do these rascals pause for reflection, and, when they do, they only become more resolute. Having sent old Nicobulus to Ephesus on a wild goose chase (*Bacchides* 329–357), Chrysalus has freed the stage for revels. But there will be a *limit* to this revelry. Nicobulus, like every father in comedy, is bound to return. Chrysalus knows that his triumph will be short-lived, and so at the same moment when he joyfully shouts *quas ego turbas dabo* ("I'll stir up such commotions!") he succumbs for a moment to reality (lines 358–362):

Sed quid futurumst, cum hoc senex resciverit,
cum se excucurrisse illuc frustra sciverit
nosque aurum abusos? *quid mihi fiet postea?*
credo hercle adveniens nomen mutabit mihi
facietque extemplo Crucisalum me ex Chrysalo.

But what will happen when the old man finds me out?
And he discovers that he's raced around in vain
And we've destroyed his cash? What will become of me?
I think when he returns, he'll change my name a bit:
I'll be ex-Chrysalus — excruciatingly.

Later in the play, when his scheme is in full swing, he once again acknowledges his culpability directly to the audience (lines 1055–1057):

Edepol qui me esse dicat cruciatu malo
dignum, ne ego cum illo pignus haud ausim dare;
tantas turbellas facio!

By Pollux, anyone who'd say that I deserve
Titanic tortures — (*smiles*) I won't contradict the man.
What storms I'm stirring up!

And yet, what is most ironic, he immediately receives not chastisement but reward. In the "saturnalian scene" examined in the previous chapter, old Nicobulus begs his slave to accept a bag of gold (lines 1059ff).[30] Chrysalus' confessions have merely served to emphasize the contrast between Roman and Plautine retribution. To employ the slave's own puns, on any ordinary day, Chrysalus would be "chrysified" (line 362), but today he makes good a more pleasant play on his name, *opus est chryso Chrysalo* (line 240), "golden boy needs gold."[31] This is strange justice indeed, when a slave who has earned welts is offered wealth, and then must be humbly begged to accept it!

We find a similar disregard for punishment in the *Persa*, where Sagaristio, fresh from a year at the mills, agrees to spend the money with which his master has entrusted him, all to help his fellow slave free a courtesan: "They'll whack my back, but I don't care!" (*tux tax erit tergo meo, non curo!*

line 264). But then he wavers, conceding that it is sometimes
a virtue to consider the consequences (line 267). Like Chrysalus in the scene from the *Bacchides* discussed above, he thinks
briefly of what will happen when his master discovers
the mischief (lines 268–271):

> *Quid faciet mihi?*
> verberibus caedi iusserit, compedes impingi? vapulet,
> ne sibi me credat supplicem fore: vae illi, nil iam mihi novi
> offerre potest quin sim peritus.

> What will he do to me?
> Command that I be lashed and gashed and thrown in
> chains? To hell with him!
> Don't let him think I'll grovel. He can croak. There's
> nothing new
> That he can do to me — I'm too experienced.

Every Plautine slave is aware — in detail — of what risks he
is running; he has an "experienced back." Yet his attitude, if
he is an *architectus doli*, a builder of schemes, is always a
festive *non curo!* We have already acknowledged that the
torture speech *in general* is a feature common to all ancient
comedy. Even in mild Terence, bondsmen think of whip-
pings-to-come. In the *Phormio*, for example, Geta expresses
his worry of what may befall him, should his own complicity
with the wily Phormio be brought to his master's attention
(lines 248–251):

> Meditata mihi sunt omnia mea incommoda, erus si redierit:
> molendum usque in pistrino, vapulandum,
> habendae compedes,
> opus ruri faciendum. horum nil quicquam accidet
> animo novom.
> quidquid praeter spem eveniet, omne id deputabo esse
> in lucro.[32]

Within my mind, I have rehearsed what pains will come
    if master does:
The grinding-at-the-mill-to-be, the blows-to-be,
    the chains-to-be,
And sweating on the farm. And *none* of these will come
    as something *new* to me.
What happens less than what I fear, I'll call it all
    a welcome gift.

Compared to that of his Plautine predecessors, Geta's catalogue is mild, in both *verba* and *verbera*; but milder still is his "rebellion." Like many of the Plautine schemers we have discussed, he knows that blows may come; he has been bad before, and beaten. But he *cares*; he is worried about physical pain. He does not dismiss his future flogging with scorn. Conspicuously absent is that singular attitude of the Plautine slave, his *non curo!* Indeed, it is the blithe disregard for punishment that characterizes Plautus' great slave characters. And if this were not in itself remarkable, the following surely is: while none of Plautus' rogues expects less than the punishment to which he is accustomed, in fact they all go scot-free. They enjoy an impunity to which they — no less than their audience — are completely unaccustomed.

The many vivid "torture passages" in Plautus have given rise to strange theories concerning both the playwright and the world he presents.[33] Perhaps the most extreme is that of P. S. Dunkin, who sees the merry Plautine slave as "a man driven to cunning by ill-treatment."[34] While Dunkin is not the only critic to overlook the fact that no slave is ever ill-treated during a comedy, he must be taxed with naïveté for concluding that the slave in Plautus is "the victim of an oppressive capitalistic system."[35] For, as demonstrated in the previous chapter, at the very heart of the Plautine comic scheme is the victimization of the ruling class by the lowly slave. And while the slaves concede that punishment awaits them, they also insist that they will be bloody but unbowed; they will never humble themselves and be a *supplex* before their master, as Sagaristio most emphatically states (*Persa* 270, quoted above). On the contrary, it is the master who becomes the *supplex*, as does old Simo in the *Pseudolus* (line 1319), and it is the bondsman, mixing harshness and hauteur, who refuses all mercy to "the vanquished victim" (line 1317).

While not all views are so radical as Dunkin's, the notion still persists that Plautine slaves are generally beaten in retribution for their misdeeds. Even Bernard Knox distinguishes a whole class of slaves in Roman comedy which is "punished with blows or a stint at the mill." [36] Although Knox is arguing that it is usually the unclever slave who receives the blows, he does not cite a single example of a Plautine servant being punished while the play is on. Now and then, a bondsman may feel a punch or two, but never in payment for roguery. For example, Mercury cuffs Sosia in their famous encounter in the *Amphitruo* (lines 153ff). Here the verb *vapulare* ("to be knocked around") appears seven times, and Amphitryon's slow-witted servant is indeed pounded, but for reasons completely beyond his control. And unlike his cleverer confrères, Sosia takes the blows in a cowardly manner.

In the *Casina*, there is a boxing match between the bondsmen of the husband and wife (lines 404ff). The husband's slave is "punished" merely because he is not a very good fighter. Chalinus, the wife's slave, is the same chap who ultimately masquerades as "Casina the bride" and beats up the husband himself, Lysidamus the *senex amator* (lines 937ff). This is the only instance in Plautus where a slave gets to injure his master physically in the way Scapin beats Géronte. But in Molière's comedy the drubbing takes place on stage, whereas in Plautus we merely receive a vivid description of the assault from the astonished old man. In the *Poenulus*, it does seem as if young Agorastocles cuffs his slave Milphio for daring to indulge in amorous badinage with his sweetheart two single beds side by side. "This is the type of room your father is supposed to stay in, considering his insurance status. He and Mr. Beck would share."

"It'll never work,"said Joyce. "My father won't put up with it. He'll make life hell for his roommate and the staff."

"We're aware of that," said Dutton. "Mr. Beck is the same way. That's why we're going to go with an alternative. It's a semi-private room with separate bedrooms but common kitchenette and bathroom. Come, I'll show you that next."

---

Snippets of your past life come to you as you sit and ruminate while shadow images chase themselves across the screen. They are clear and sharply focused as if you are reliving them. Some concern the travels of your youth: the fascinating landscapes, the intimidating cities, the diverse people, the exhilarating danger, and the liberating freedom. Some evoke your family life as you and your wife raised your children: the challenges, the intimacies, and the pratfalls. Then there are the glimpses of past professional experiences: in some you sit before a keyboard with full concentration, absorbed in the task at hand; in others you stand at a podium facing an audience eager to hear what you have to say.

That's it: you have an appointment. You knew there was something that you have to do. If you're not on your way soon you'll be late.

You stand and jiggle the keys in your pocket. They must be the car keys. But where is the car? Ah, yes. For some reason they've hidden it from you and you have to find it.

You start for your room door but hesitate. It's cracked open and you can see the green-clad attendant at the desk. You recall that for some reason they don't want you to go outside and look for your car. The first step is to elude them. It's a game, like when you would sneak out of your mother's house after she had grounded you, to meet up with your friends.

For an indeterminate amount of time you stand waiting just inside your room. Although the precise reason why it is imperative to exit the (lines 381ff). But the absence of stage directions prevents us from knowing how earnestly the master is striking at his man, and it is not unlikely that in actual performance Milphio would dodge the blows, for this scene affords the opportunity for many *lazzi* of this kind. In any event, Agorastocles' rage cannot be taken too seriously, since — in true saturnalian fashion — he is about to beseech his slave for assistance (lines 421–422).[37] Clearly none of these incidents involve retribution for misbehavior. For during a Plautine comedy, no slave, be he subtle as Pseudolus or stupid as Sceledrus, ever feels a whip, and none is sent *in pistrinum*.

There is one possible exception, and it is ironic in the extreme. The single "clever slave" who may indeed suffer for his wiles is, in fact, no slave at all. This exceptional instance is, of course, that of Tyndarus in the *Captivi*, a play which is in so many ways an inversion of the typical Plautine inversion. Here, for once, the dire threats seem to be carried out, although the text leaves some doubt as to what hardships Tyndarus actually does experience. When old Hegio realizes that Tyndarus has bamboozled him (and, as noted earlier, his language is that of the typical Plautine butt) [38] his thoughts turn immediately to revenge, and he calls for whippers to put chains on the malefactor (line 659). Like the typical Plautine slave, albeit in somewhat less audacious tones, Tyndarus denies nothing. He is proud to have undone Hegio by his *fallaciis* and *astutia* (lines 678–679). In this respect, his pride is like that of Tranio in the *Mostellaria* (line 1147). Old Hegio insists that Tyndarus will suffer *cruciatu maxumo* (line 681). There is nothing unusual about the ensuing catalogue of tortures except the ironic context in which they are spoken (lines 721–726):

> Ducite
> ubi ponderosas crassas capiat compedes
> inde ibis porro in latomias lapidarias

ibi quom alii octonos lapides effodiunt, nisi
cotidiano sesquiopus confeceris,
Sescentoplago nomen indetur tibi.

                              Take him away
Where he'll be joined to mighty massive metal manacles
(*to Tyndarus*)
Then you'll be rushed into the roughest rocky quarry
Where others have to dig eight rocks a day. But you —
Unless you break that daily quota by a half,
We'll see to it your name is changed to Lashius-Gashius.

Hegio's threat in line 726 reminds us of the slave Chrysalus'
fear that his own name will be altered by "Chrysifixion"
(*Bacchides* 362). But here in the *Captivi* it is not clear
whether or not Tyndarus suffers a painful change of name.
He is immediately dragged off to have irons placed on him,
but the text does not indicate how much time elapses between
this exit and the moment young Philocrates returns to set him
free.[39]

If young Tyndarus has endured any pains, the *Captivi*
would then be the only play of Plautus in which the *astutia*
and *fallacia* we have seen on stage are actually punished. But
of course Tyndarus is finally discovered to be freeborn, and
what Hegio damned as punishable trickery is now seen in its
proper light as the praiseworthy action of a noble heart. In
general, however, we may say that the Plautine slave, no
matter how outrageous his offense, never suffers for his rascality; at the play's end, he is always forgiven. Amnesty is
automatic, even where, but a few seconds from the end,
punishment seems a certainty. The following exchange is
typical (*Pseudolus* 1329–1330):

PSEUDOLUS:  Quid nunc? numquid iratus es aut mihi aut
                    filio propter has res, Simo?
SIMO:                                              Nil profecto.

PSEUDOLUS: All right Simo, are you angry with me or your son because of our ploys?

SIMO:                                                          Not at all.

It is also characteristic that the master's pardon is expressed in the fewest possible words, spoken without the slightest emotion. This contrasts sharply with earlier moments of the play, especially when the master is hell-bent on punishing the malefactors. As, for example, Nicobulus in the *Bacchides*, incensed, embarrassed, and not to be swayed from revenge (lines 1183–1184):

> Quadringentis Philippis filius me et
> Chrysalus circumduxerunt
> quem quidem ego ut non excruciem
> alterum tantum auri non meream.

> Four hundred Philippi they've swindled from me
> My son and his slave, but they won't go scot-free.
> If Chrysalus isn't now racked full of pain,
> Then I deserve to be swindled again!

Offers of appeasement — even financial restitution — have no effect (line 1187):

> Minime, nolo, nil moror, sine sic.
>     malo illos *ulcisci* ambo!

> No no no, not at all, I don't care, let me be.
> The two of those boys will get vengeance from me!

Yet, after a few sweet words from one of the Bacchis girls, Nicobulus relents and makes no further mention of punishment. It may be argued that this play is not typical, that the old man in the *Bacchides* is being offered something in return for his pardon (or at least feminine wiles are at work); but the reaction of Nicobulus *is* typical, even if the circumstances are not. To demonstrate this, let us examine the most outrageous case of non-punishment, that of Tranio in the *Mostellaria*.

Of all the elders in Plautus, Theopropides best deserves the description *senex iratus*. He is justifiably enraged at the embarrassment his slave has caused him and is determined to have his revenge. But, since Tranio's own impudence intensifies in direct proportion to his master's indignation, it looks very likely that he will suffer not merely a whipping, but crucifixion as well. At line 1064, Theopropides enters with a gang of slaves to clap handcuffs on Tranio. (The ambush and capture of an unruly slave seems to have been a familiar scene on the comic stage.) [40] But Tranio anticipates his master's assault, and leaps onto a nearby altar, thereby enjoying immunity for as long as he can stay there.

When the slave haughtily refuses to descend from his "holy place" (lines 1103ff), the old man threatens to surround the altar with flames (lines 1114–1116):

THEOPROPIDES: Iam iubebo ignem et sarmenta, carnifex, circumdari.
TRANIO: Ne faxis, nam elixus esse quam assus soleo suavior.
THEOPROPIDES: Exempla edepol faciam ego in te.
TRANIO: Quia placeo exemplum expetis?

THEOPROPIDES: Now I'll see you're bundled up by fire and kindling, gallowsbird!
TRANIO (*smiling*): Don't do that. I taste much sweeter boiled, instead of grilled and broiled.
THEOPROPIDES: I'll make you an example —
TRANIO (*smiling*): Thanks, you think that I'm exemplary!

Young Callimidates begs the old man to forgive and forget and to join in the traditional comic finale, the dinner party. Theopropides sternly refuses, and Tranio hardly helps mat-

ters by making an audacious saturnalian suggestion: he offers
to take his master's place at table. The response is predictable
(lines 1132–1133):

THEOPROPIDES:  Verbero, etiam inrides?
TRANIO:               Quian me pro te ire ad cenam autumo?
THEOPROPIDES:  Non enim ibis. ego ferare faxo, *ut meruisti,*
                                                    *in crucem.*


THEOPROPIDES:  Whipping-post, you mock me still?
TRANIO:                    Because I'd go to dine for you?
THEOPROPIDES:  No — you'll go where you deserve. I'll see
                                to it you reach the cross!

Only if Tranio is punished will the old man's dignity be
repaired. And yet the slave is determined that this dignity not
be repaired, and seeks only to exacerbate his master's discomfort (lines 1146–1147):

THEOPROPIDES:  Iam minoris omnia alia facio prae quam
                                                    quibus modis
     me ludificatust.
TRANIO:      Bene hercle factum, et factum gaudeo!


THEOPROPIDES:  All the rest I rate at nothing. I'm just
                                                    angered
                    by the manner
     He bamboozled me.
TRANIO:      Well-done it was — and I rejoice in it!

Savoring his triumph, Tranio claims that his exploits surpass
everything ever seen on the comic stage (lines 1149ff). Callimidates must silence the slave so that he can plead the cause
of the young lover Philolaches. To the suit for filial pardon,
the old man readily accedes; youth must have its fling (line

1157) and Plautine fathers are generally indulgent parents. But he still intends to hang up Tranio, lash him and gash him: "By Hercules, if I live, he dies" (line 1168). Like old Nicobulus in the *Bacchides* (who would also have preferred to lose more money in a less demeaning way), Theopropides is intent on answering crime with punishment (lines 1170–1171):

> Aliud quidvis impetrari perferam a me facilius
> quam ut non ego istum *pro suis factis pessumis*
>                             pessum premam.

> I'll give in on anything, on *anything* except for this.
> I'll repay the wretch, for every dirty deed
>         I'll make him bleed.

The finale of the *Mostellaria* suffers from a characteristically Plautine weakness in dramatic technique: the playwright's tendency to repeat the essential idea of a scene too often (the Mercury-Sosia *agon* in the *Amphitruo* is the classic instance). In the *Mostellaria*, Callimidates' persistent requests for a general amnesty, *gratia cuncta*, are met by the old man with a persistent refusal to forgive Tranio. But just when it seems that an impossible impasse has been reached, the slave himself offers the single argument that can satisfy his master's thirst for revenge (lines 1178–1179):

> Quid gravaris? quasi non *cras* iam commeream aliam noxiam
> ibi utrumque, et hoc et illud, poteris ulcisci probe.

> Stop complaining. Don't you think I'll earn myself
>         new pains tomorrow?
> Then you'll get me — double vengeance — you can
>         pay me two-for-one!

To this the old man replies, in the penultimate line of the play, *age abi, abi impune*, and then turns to the Roman audience to request applause (lines 1180–1181). After endless wrangling and what seems implacable ire, the old man simply looks at Tranio, says, "Go on, scot-free," and the comedy is over.

The end of the *Mostellaria* bears a very close resemblance to the finale of Molière's *Fourberies de Scapin*, where Géronte is resolved to wreak dire vengeance on his rascally servant: "C'est un coquin que je veux pendre." [41] Scapin then enters, pretending to be mortally wounded, and requests a pardon so that he can die in peace. Actually, like Tranio, Scapin wants to add still further to his master's discomfort, and does so by referring endlessly to "les malheureux coups de bâton," the escapade in which he duped Géronte and severely drubbed him. [42] Despite his pose of humility, Scapin is actually vaunting his "témérité bien grande," much in the vein of Tranio's *factum gaudeo*. When Géronte sees through this dodge, he gives his servant a qualified amnesty: "I forgive you . . . if you die." It now appears that Scapin will be completely unable to escape his master's punishment. [43] But then Argante steps in, like Callimidates in the *Mostellaria*, who proposes a *gratia cuncta*, and asks Géronte to proclaim a pardon "sans condition." At this point the old man who, but a moment earlier, was bent on hanging Scapin accedes with a monosyllabic "soit." Then everyone goes to dinner.

When evaluated for dramatic technique, the pardons granted by both Theopropides and Géronte seem equally unmotivated. Both appear to be caprices on the part of the playwrights merely to bring their comedies to a swift and happy ending. Molière received much criticism for this sort of mechanical, facile resolution, but there seems little doubt that the Frenchman is following a precedent he had seen time and again in Plautus. And yet what is mere convention in Molière has deeper meaning in Plautus. The angry French fathers relent simply because Molière wants to tidy things up, whereas the Plautine fathers do have a *reason*, a plausible motivation for overlooking the current misdeeds of the clever slave.

In the *Mostellaria*, it is Tranio himself who provides old Theopropides with the clinching argument (line 1178): "Don't you think I'll earn myself new pains tomorrow?" *Tomorrow* is the significant word that makes all the difference, for then the ordinary rules of crime and punishment will be in force and when Tranio steps out of line he will be dealt with *ut meruisti*. Tomorrow Theopropides will again enjoy his unquestioned *patria potestas* (over his son as well as his slave), and Tranio will be back at the very bottom of the social scale. Tomorrow the rascally slave will not perch majestically on the altar, a pose which both suggests his temporary "divinity" and serves as a vivid reminder that today is, in every sense, a holiday.[44]

It is interesting to contrast the brevity of Theopropides' absolution of Tranio, *abi impune* (and Géronte's still briefer "soit"), with the behavior of the clever slaves when they play at being condescending masters. How much more haughty and reluctant is Chrysalus' phraseology when he gives in to Nicobulus' pleas: *cedo si necesse est* (*Bacchides* 1066), or Epidicus' reply when his own master asks him for pardon (lines 728–731):

PERIPHANES:                            Oro te, Epidice,
   *mihi ut ignoscas*, siquid imprudens culpa peccavi mea.
   at ob eam rem liber esto.

EPIDICUS:                    Invitus do hanc veniam tibi
   nisi necessitate cogar. solve sane, si lubet.

PERIPHANES:       Epidicus, I beg of you —
   Please forgive whatever wrongs I've done you — I'm
                                       to blame.
   And because of this — be free.

EPIDICUS (*magnanimously*): Against my will, I'll let you
do it,
Owing to the circumstances. Free me, if it makes you
happy.

This is the proper tone for a reconciliation between master
and man. Here we find supplication, *oro te*, pleas for pardon,
*mihi ut ignoscas*, and an abject confession of guilt: *imprudens
culpa peccavi mea*. There is, of course, but one inconsistency:
the master is beseeching the slave. Traditionally, comedies
end on a note of forgiveness and reconciliation, whether it
be Menander's *Arbitration* or Shakespeare's *Tempest*. But in
Plautus, the reconciliation has a special topsy-turvy aspect,
and is therefore all the more comic.[45]

But not every character on the Plautine stage enjoys the
clever slave's immunity from punishment. There *are* blows
struck in retribution for misdeeds, and sometimes they are
delivered right before the audience's eyes. To cite three significant examples: Labrax in the *Rudens* is clubbed by two
burly *lorarii*, who are appropriately called Turbalio ("com-
motion-maker") and Sparax ("mangler"). The waggish slave
Trachalio is perhaps punning on these names when he listens
to the offstage assault on Labrax and quips, "I hear a com-
motion, I think the pimp's being pounded to pulp" (line 661).
Another pimp, Dordalus, is punched and pinched by all the
revelers during the finale of the *Persa*. In the *Miles Gloriosus*,
the soldier is badly beaten onstage by the household slaves
of Periplectomenus. His anguished cries leave no doubt that
he is being cudgeled with a vengeance (cf. lines 1406 and
1424).

What is important to note in the above examples is the
fact that these characters are being — in a special sense —
justly punished. Labrax the pimp has lied and cheated and
desecrated the shrine of Venus (*advorsum ius legesque*, line

643). Even Pyrgopolynices, at the height of his distress, can admit that he deserves the severe treatment he has received: *iure factum iudico* (line 1435), "I judge the verdict just." Yet we have earlier seen how many Plautine characters act quite as "unlawfully" as Labrax and Pyrgopolynices, and go off scot-free. This apparent inconsistency in Plautus has puzzled many, including Legrand, who notes that, while pimps, swaggerers, and the like are so often punished and derided, "slaves guilty of all sorts of rascality are usually pardoned or forgotten . . . contrary to justice." [46]

But far from being "contrary to justice," this unusual double standard is consistent with the special Plautine "holiday code." Dordalus, Labrax, the soldier, and others like them are all of the same breed: agelasts, antagonists to the comic spirit, described in Chapter III. These are the churls who work while the whole world plays and are therefore infringing upon the rule of the day. And the "holiday justice" presented by Plautus is similar to the "ducking-in-water" customs which are part of the rustic festival tradition described by Chambers, and related in an earlier chapter of this book to the punishment of the spoilsport in comedy.[47] In fact, the Plautine agelast suffers retribution for his crime against nature: obstructing, or refusing to join, the festivities.

We have already remarked that, by Roman definition, a slave was "he who gets whipped." In Plautine comedy, the rule holds true, but in a topsy-turvy sense. Since only the agelasts are whipped, *they* must be regarded as the slaves. For as Northrop Frye describes these characters, they are in "some kind of mental bondage . . . slaves to a predictable self-imposed pattern of behavior." [48] Paradoxically enough, it is the slave who enjoys the most freedom in Plautus, including freedom from all sorts of everyday punishment.

One of the *Paradoxa Stoicorum* dealt with by Cicero best articulates the "saturnalian philosophy" in Plautus: ὅτι μόνος building and drive off in your car has slipped out of your conscious-ness, the resolution remains. Finally the attendant turns and crosses to the opposite side of the desk and begins writing in a ledger with her back to you. Opening the door just enough to slide through, you head up the hallway and pause at a point inside the dining room entrance where you can watch the locked exit door.

Time passes.

An attendant approaches the door and enters the code onto the keypad, but you are unable to discern the numbers. Before you are able to hurry forward, the door closes and relocks.

Time passes.

Another attendant enters with a resident. She takes the time to be sure the door is secure before she moves on.

Time passes.

At some point you become discouraged and frustrated and, though your resolve to escape is as strong as ever, you wander off to discover another egress to the outside.

Slowly, you shuffle around, inspecting the dining room and com-mon areas, entering the living quarters of other residents, studying the floors, walls, ceilings, doors, and windows for a way out.

With a flash of insight the solution occurs to you: the window. You return to your own room and close the door. It should be easy. After all, you're on the ground floor.

As you slide open the window you feel a hint of the cool free air of beyond. After six inches the panel stops and won't glide any farther.

You look closer.

They've attached a small metal plug onto the frame, which arrests the window's motion. It should be simple enough to remove. You need a screwdriver or perhaps a hammer and chisel. Where have you put your tools? You search the kitchenette cupboards, the cabinet under the sink, and the bathroom shelves.

While you're in the bathroom your mind blanks out. You try to recollect why you have gone in there. After a contemplative moment, you unzip your fly, take a leak, and return to sit down in the chair beside your bed.

Shadow images chase themselves across the TV screen.

ὁ σοφὸς ἐλεύθερος, καὶ πᾶς ἄφρων δοῦλος, "Only the wise man is a free man, and every fool is a slave." [49] Horace bases a saturnalian dialogue of his own (*Satires* 2.7) on this same notion: Davus the slave ultimately proves that he is "freer" than Horace his master. (Horace's satire actually contains a great many Plautine elements.) [50] In the plays of Plautus, this paradox is never explicitly stated, but it is demonstrated time and again. The playwright has created a world in which "only the shrewd are free." For σοφία can indeed be rendered as "shrewdness" (not necessarily exalted "wisdom"), a quality in which, Herodotus tells us, the *Greeks* always took pride.[51] The epilogue of the *Epidicus* provides another variation on the saturnalian paradox; the clever slave is singled out for special admiration (lines 732–733):

> Hic is homo est qui libertatem malitia invenit sua.
> plaudite et valete . . .

> Here's a man who won his freedom, making good
>                                            by acting bad.[52]
> Now applaud and all go home.

This is the pattern for all of Plautine comedy and Epidicus himself is unique in only one respect. Unlike the typical clever slave, he wins his freedom permanently, not merely for twenty-four hours.

One of the essential features of a Plautine slave's saturnalia is the very knowledge that his liberty is limited, that tomorrow he *will* be a slave again. For, contrary to a widely held notion, the clever slave does not even desire manumission. While Epidicus is freed, it should be noted that he himself does not request the manumission. He has merely asked his master for a *supplicium* (line 724); *libertas* is spontaneously offered by old Periphanes (line 726).[53] Of the handful of slaves who are set free in the course of the comedies, only Epidicus is "shrewd." The others are "dumb and loyal" like Messenio in the *Menaechmi* and do not earn their liberty by force of wit.

In the *Rudens*, a play of reconciliation so unusual that even the pimp is invited to the final dinner, two slaves are set free, but more because of the spirit of the play than their own esprit. The rustic Gripus wins his freedom by sheer luck; he finds the trunk containing the articles which identify the girl Palaestra.[54] Old Daemones is so overjoyed at discovering his long lost daughter that he promises to obtain freedom for the slave Trachalio and then give him the girl Ampelisca in marriage (lines 1212–1220). This last feature assuredly marks the finale of the *Rudens* as unique. As a general rule, Plautine characters prefer love without marriage, *komos* without *gamos*. For Plautus the words of Shakespeare's Don Armado, "the catastrophe is a nuptial," represent not merely a pun but a philosophy.[55]

It is also noteworthy that in two instances where a tricky slave is offered freedom he is not excited by the offer. This attitude, Livy tells us, is most *un-Roman* [56] (still another aspect of the alien "*pergraecari* behavior" which the Plautine slave displays). Palaestrio in the *Miles* has arranged an elaborate scheme by which his master can escape to Athens with his sweetheart. Young Pleusicles is overwhelmed with gratitude (lines 1193–1195):

PLEUSICLES:                     Atque ubi illo veneris
    triduom servire numquam te, quin liber sis, sinam.
PALAESTRIO:  Abi cito atque orna te.


PLEUSICLES:                        Back in Athens
   You won't be a slave for three days longer, there I'll
                                  free you —

PALAESTRIO (*waving him off*): Quickly now, and dress
                 yourself.

The prospect of manumission makes no impression whatever
on Palaestrio; his only concern is to trick the soldier. Likewise,
when Milphio in the *Poenulus* is beseeched by Agorastocles
for aid, *per tuam libertatem* (line 420), he hurries his master
offstage to hire the witnesses needed for his scheme to swindle
the pimp. As he exits, Agorastocles tries once again to offer
liberty to his slave (lines 428–430):

AGORASTOCLES: Egone, egone, si istuc lepide ecfexis —
MILPHIO:                            I modo.
AGORASTOCLES: Ut non ego te hodie —
MILPHIO:                 Abi modo.
AGORASTOCLES:          — emittam manu —
MILPHIO: I modo.
AGORASTOCLES: Non hercle meream —
MILPHIO:         Oh —
AGORASTOCLES:           Vah —
MILPHIO:                  Abi modo!


AGORASTOCLES: I tell you if you really work this ploy —
MILPHIO:                       Be off!
AGORASTOCLES: I promise you today —
MILPHIO:            Be off!
AGORASTOCLES:         I'll grant you freedom.
MILPHIO: Be off!
AGORASTOCLES: By Hercules, if I —
MILPHIO:              Oh please —
AGORASTOCLES:                 But —
MILPHIO (*an imperious shout*):        Off!

The true Plautine slave refuses emancipation. How else but
as a slave could he revel in a saturnalia? He would rather take

a liberty than receive it. Like Pseudolus, he aims merely to *act* "freely" (lines 1286–1288):

SIMO:    Sed quid hoc? quo modo? quid video ego?
PSEUDOLUS:    Cum corona ebrium Pseudolum tuom.
SIMO:    *Libere* hercle hoc quidem. sed vide statum.

SIMO:    What's this? Can it be? What do I see?
PSEUDOLUS:    Pseudolus, your drunken slave, wearing a
wreath.
SIMO:    "High" and mighty, thanks to wine. Such haughty
posture!

It might well be argued that the slaves themselves want the misrule to be temporary, that they do not wish all the days to be "playing holidays." The farthest thing from their minds is actual manumission. Their attitude might be compared to that of Chekhov's Firs, the servant in *The Cherry Orchard* who had once been a serf:

FIRS:    It was the same before the misfortune; the owl
hooted and the samovar kept singing.
GAYEV:    What misfortune?
FIRS:    Before they gave us freedom.[57]

The "Liberation Festival" which the Plautine slave celebrates is precisely like the *eleutheria* of Stichus: *hunc diem unum* (line 421), and, as Stichus' master is quick to remind him, *only* today (lines 424, 435). It is celebrated, like the *eleutheria* of Toxilus in the *Persa* (lines 28ff), with the full awareness that this period of *bene esse* is strictly limited and that the liberties the slave is taking (robbery, trickery) are, according to the rule book, punishable ones (*Persa* 263–264):

Nunc et amico prosperabo et genio meo multa bona faciam
diu quo bene erit, die uno absolvam: tux tax tergo erit
meo, non curo!

Now I'll help a friend and do my soul a few good turns.
                                        We'll *live* —
In a single day, we'll burn it all. They'll whack my back,
                                        but I don't care!

In Toxilus' desire to bring joy *genio meo*, we are reminded
of the rustic holidays of a pristine past which Horace praises
in *Epistles* 2.1, where the farmers honor the *genium memorem
brevis aevi*, "the spirit which is so aware of the shortness of
life" (line 144). The focus on *now*, on *today*, is at the very
heart of the holiday spirit. *Di doman' non c'è certezza!*

The essential characteristic, not merely of holiday but of
"play" in general as defined by Johann Huizinga, is that it is
different from every day and strictly limited in time.[58] Every
celebrant realizes that what is happening is uncommon and
unreal, and that he is experiencing a temporary anarchy that
implies order. As C. L. Barber expresses it, "In the actual
celebration of customary misrule, the control of the disruptive
motives which the festivity expresses is achieved by the
group's recognition of the place of the whole business within
the larger rhythm of their continuing social life." [59]
The epilogue of a play, aside from its usual plea for
applause, also serves to dispel the illusion which the actors
have created, to escort the audience back to reality. Sometimes
the words are as direct as those of Prospero at the conclusion
of the masque he and Ariel have produced:

> Our revels now are ended. These our actors,
> As I foretold you, were all spirits and
> Are melted into air, into thin air.[60]

Although less explicitly, the final lines of the *Cistellaria* [61]
express similar sentiments to the Roman audience (lines 782–
787):

Ne expectetis, spectatores, dum illi huc ad vos exeant;
nemo exibit, omnes intus conficient *negotium*.
ubi id erit factum, ornamenta ponent; postidea loci
qui deliquit vapulabit, qui non deliquit bibet.
nunc quod ad vos, spectatores, relicuom relinquitur,
*more maiorum*, date plausum postrema in comoedia.


Don't you wait, my dear spectators,
                    for the actors to come out.
They'll all stay inside, they have
                    their own affairs to go about.
After that's completed and they
                    doff their costumes, then I think
"Malef-actors" will be beaten,
                    those who've acted well will drink.
Now spectators, please excuse me,
                    what remains remains with you,
In the manner of your ancestors,
                    applaud us please — our play is through.


The comedy has ended. All thoughts, even of those within
the dressing rooms, must turn to *negotium*, the very antithesis
of holiday. Costumes must be shed, especially the pallium,
and, along with the Greek clothing, the license to Greek-it-up.
What is most important is the strong reminder that everyday
rules will once again be in force; "malef-actors" *will* be
whipped (line 785). Even the spectators must now behave
according to the time-honored traditions, *more maiorum*.[62]
And with this sobering thought, they leave the play and
return to their own *negotium*: the business of being Roman.

# Appendix: Problems in Plautus

## Why Plautus Chose *Amphitruo*

*Amphitruo* is Plautus' strangest — and most enduring — play. It seems never to have been out of favor. According to Arnobius and Prudentius, it was still being successfully produced during the late Empire. It has been readapted in every age. Harold Pinter's *The Lover* (1963) stands in a long line of theatrical variations by such diverse authors as Vital de Blois, Camoëns, Molière, Dryden and Kleist. When Giraudoux called his version *Amphitryon 38* he was surely underestimating the number of adaptations that preceded his own.[1]

The play has also been a favorite with the critics, who have spared no effort in trying to unearth Plautus' source for this "tragicomic" admixture of mythology and mirth. It would seem that no ancient author has been denied credit for having inspired the Roman playwright. The *honorandi* include Aeschylus, Sophocles, Euripides (cf. *non ventus fuit, verum Alcumena Euripidi* — *Rud.* 86), Ion of Chios, Archippus, Plato Comicus, Epicharmus, Rhinthon of Tarentum, with further candidates waiting in the wings.[2]

But the present essay will not be yet another attempt at *Quellenforschung*. Nor will it discuss the nature of "Middle Comedy," of which this play is said to be the unique Roman example. Indeed, the entire "genre" may have existed only in the imagination of Apuleius, who first coined the term in the second century A.D. (*Florida* 3:16).[3] There have already been examinations of the parallels between the use of myth in Plautus and in the satyr plays as well as on the *phlyax* vases of

South Italy.[4] Thus, at the risk of seeming antiintellectual, this essay will concentrate on what the author believes to be the essential argument: what aspects of Plautus' *Amphitruo* caught the Romans' interest — and fancy? Why did they keep producing it? Why did later authors continually adapt it?

Notwithstanding the majority of critical opinion, I do not believe we are dealing with an atypical comedy. The tone and purpose of the play are not that far removed from the same author's extremely farcical *Casina*. In fact, the *Amphitruo* is even more Plautine — and more Roman. And if one wished to compare it to another comic author it would be more appropriate to adduce Feydeau than Philemon.

For the play is essentially about adultery — which has been a fundamental comic theme from the moment that marriage became a fundamental social constraint. Freud defines the targets of wit (*die Angriffsobjekte*) as "institutions and their representatives, moral or religious injunctions or other deeply-held views that enjoy so much respect that resistance to them can be made only under the mask of a joke, and indeed a joke hidden by a facade."[5] Moreover, Freud reminds us that since marriage has always been invested with a rigorous morality, it has inevitably been the target of cynical humor.

We recall the oldest joke on record — made by the quasi-mythical Susarion of Megara — a quip about wives in the *nec tecum nec sine te* vein (Kock 1.3):

> Though women be an evil, yet there's still
> No way I know to live without such ill.

Many Aristophanic comedies conclude with a joyous — and illicit — *gamos*. At the end of the *Acharnians* (lines 1220–1221), Dikaiopolis staggers in with a courtesan on each arm leaving the audience in no doubt as to what he intends: "I'm lewd, in the mood, and I'm aching to get screwed!"

We find similar scenes in *The Knights* and *The Wasps*. *The*

*Peace* and *The Birds* conclude with what anthropologists call a ritual or sacred marriage — *hieros gamos*. The latter deserves particular attention because the hero is going to bed with *paredros Dios* (line 1753), the "companion of Zeus." This is almost a topsy-turvy version of the *Amphitruo* theme.

In the *agon* of *The Clouds* (lines 1076ff), Dishonest Logic argues that life is not worth living unless one can indulge in the joys of drinking and adultery. In fact, he suggests that lovers should take their inspiration from Jove, who is an ingenious source of techniques of feminine conquest.[6] And again in *The Birds* (lines 793ff) the chorus suggests that one of the advantages of having wings is being able to fly to the bed of a woman whose husband is still seated in the theater. Clearly adultery was a popular theme in Attic comedy.

What can we say of Plautus' *Amphitruo*? We can begin by noting that, *consensu omnium*, it is one of his latest comedies.[7] This means that the playwright had already perfected his meters and methods and had reached a point where he might allow himself a bit of experimentation. At the same time he was clever enough not to go too far from the formula which had long brought him unparalleled success. We will therefore concentrate on the Plautine elements of the comedy.

There is no need to discuss what Della Corte calls "la commedia dei 'simillimi,'"[8] nor to emphasize the way in which Plautus has varied his favorite theme — that of the relationship between master and slave. Others have already dealt with the parodies of Ennian poetry and the neatness of the play's structure (despite the sloppiness of some of the individual scenes). Space limitation will also not permit a discussion of the "dream" elements which both fascinated and influenced Shakespeare. Our attention will be limited to determining what the play is *about*.

It is *not* about the birth of Hercules, despite the ingenious thesis of Zeph Stewart who notes the parallels between Plautus' comedy and Euripides' *Bacchae*.[9] Indeed, the criti-

"He got this one from Nepal, didn't he?" David said, lifting a small, framed painting down from its hook on the wall.

"Yes," said Joyce. "It's Tibetan."

David surrounded the piece of art with bubble wrap and taped it securely.

"He collected these soapstone animals on various trips to Delhi," Joyce said as she crumpled tissue around them and carefully arranged them in a box.

"There's stuff from all over the world," David said. "Are you sure he won't want any of it?"

Joyce shook her head. "He's got a few things down there, but Mr. Dutton said not to bring the valuable pieces. Evidently residents wander in and out of each other's rooms, and they have a habit of picking up and taking whatever appeals to them."

They continued packing in silence. David emptied the desk drawers. Joyce pulled clothes from the closet and chest of drawers, sorting them into two bags: one for donating and one for disposal.

"And now the books," David said.

"Yes, the books."

David knelt down in front of the shelf with an empty box. Joyce sat on the bed, whose sheets and pillowcases had been relegated to the throw-away bag.

"Look," said David. "His original Ballantine Books set of *The Lord of the Rings*. His grandmother gave him this, right? I'll never forget his description of the first time he read *The Fellowship of the Rings*. He had no idea what to expect. He was all alone in his room, and he became so absorbed in it that he lost touch with his environment. They're all worn out now; he's read them many times. And here's *Dune*, and *Lord of Light*, and *Stranger in a Strange Land*."

"All his inspirations."

"Yes. *On the Road*, which got him traveling. *Walden*, from his isolation phase. *The Gulag Archipelago*, from his period of social consciousness."

David continued to pack the books one by one while Joyce watched and they shared reminiscences.

cal point of departure is to recognize that the Plautine play is at once close to the Euripidean and at the same time completely unlike it. The tragic playwright gives us a serious epiphany, a violent act of revenge, a potent affirmation of the divinity of Dionysus and a vindication of the honor of Semele. By contrast, the *Amphitruo* presents nothing more elevated than an act of adultery and the joys of Alcmena's body. A close reading will show us that Plautus' interests are in fact limited to sex and cuckoldry.

The prologue, spoken by Mercury, is, as always in Plautus, a *captatio benevolentiae*. And there is no more effective way to capture a Roman ear and entice them to keep still than the sound of money. The Romans must listen:

> Vt vos in vostris voltis mercimoniis
> emundis vendundisque me laetum lucris
> adficere atque adiuvare in rebus omnibus
> et ut res rationesque vostrorum omnium
> bene expedire voltis peregrique et domi
> bonoque atque amplo auctare perpetuo lucro. . . .
>
> (lines 1–6)

> If you would have me benefit your businesses
> Your buying and your selling and your profiting
> To further you and foster all of your affairs
> And have me see your dealings and the deals you make
> At home and overseas turn out successfully
> And have me help your profit be perpetual. . . .

Indeed, the first fourteen verses teem with financial language: *lucrum* and *res* (in the sense of business affairs) each appears four times and there are at least eight other monetary references, including *mercimonium* and *ratio*. Plautus knew his audience. And the Roman character hardly changed between his own day and that of Tacitus, who remarked *ego facilius crediderim naturam margaritis deesse quam nobis avaritiam* (*Agricola* 12.6): "I would more easily believe that quality was lacking in [sc. British] pearls than avarice in the Romans." [10]

Mercury proposes to give us the *argumentum . . . huius tragoediae* (lines 50–51). Too many critics have failed to notice that this was merely a comic aside and unfortunately have taken it all too seriously, thus wanting to transform Plautus' comedy into an innovative *tragico(co)moedia* (line 59).[11] But unlike Terentian prologues, those of Plautus contained nothing more elevated or literary than *ridicula res* (*Asinaria*, line 14). And what is more important to note is that, whether by Mercury or Jove, during the entire action of the play the *Amphitruo* is referred to as a *comoedia* (cf. lines 88, 868).

The prologue tells us not to be amazed that "gods" appear dressed as actors:[12]

> Mirari nolim vos quapropter Iuppiter
> nunc histriones curet; ne miremini:
> ipse hanc acturust Iuppiter comoediam.
> > (lines 86–88)

> I would not have you wonder why great Jupiter
> Now cares for thespians. No, wonder not—
> For Jove himself intends to play this comedy.

This same ironic tone of *ne miremini* is used elsewhere by Plautus to exculpate — or at least explain — the behavior of slave characters who are behaving *à la grecque*:

> Atque id ne vos miremini, homines servolos
> potare, amare atque ad cenam condicere:
> licet haec Athenis nobis.
> > (*Stichus*, lines 446–448)

> Don't be surprised that lowly little slaves like us
> Can drink, make love, and ask our friends to supper.
> At Athens we're allowed to do this sort of thing.

Once again, this is all tongue in cheek. It is highly unlikely that Mercury was wearing buskins.

As expected of a prologue, he explains the situation. Amphitryon is off at war as a *praefectus legionibus* (line 100) and in the meantime "you know what sort of man my father Jove is" (line 104), *quantus amator siet* (line 106):

> Is amare occepit Alcumenam clam virum
> usuramque eiius corporis cepit sibi,
> et gravidam fecit is eam compressu suo.
>
> (lines 107–109)

> Now he began — without her husband knowing it —
> To take a heavy interest in her wealth of charms
> And his embraces made the lady swell with child.

Has there ever been a more explicit expression of male chauvinism than *usura corporis*, " 'interest' in her body?" [13] And this phrase would surely have a mercantile connotation to the Roman ear. In any case, these are the terms in which the situation is presented and they are repeated almost verbatim at the end by Jupiter himself:

> Primum omnium Alcumenae usuram corporis
> cepi, et concubitu gravidam feci filio.
>
> (lines 1135–1136)

> Now first I took an interest in her body's charms
> And sweetly sleeping with her swelled her with a son.

And in the course of the comedy, Alcmena is mentioned twice as *uxor usuraria*, first by Mercury (line 498), then by

Jove (lines 980–981). This is not merely the language of a Lothario but of a sexual embezzler.

In the prologue — the longest in any of Plautus' plays — Mercury emphasizes his father's *cubare* (lines 112, 132) almost as if to inure us against feelings of tenderness or affection in this amorous relationship. Referring casually to the most famous aspect of the myth, he tells us that Jupiter has lengthened the night for the sake of *voluptas* (line 114). Mercury seems to take vicarious pleasure in his father's success: *cubat complexus cuius cupiens maxume est* (line 132), "he lies embracing her who is his heated heart's desire." And what a strange bit of *Schadenfreude* — that Alcmena thinks she is with her husband when in reality *cum moecho est* (line 135), "she is with her adulterer."

The lengthy prologue is followed by the longest scene in any Plautine play: the confrontation between Mercury and a slave whose name is still used in the French theater for a double or an understudy — Sosia. Did Plautus create this character? Very likely, because he seems to take such joy in the scene (and at several points, e.g., lines 305, 384, makes what seem to be purely Roman puns). Pascal observed that laughter was inspired by the similarity of two otherwise uncomic faces, thus essentially inspiring Bergson's *Le rire*.[14] Indeed, here we see, as Shakespeare might put it, Sosia "outfaced" and obliged to repudiate his own identity.

Without examining every aspect of this lengthy scene, let us nonetheless recall Sosia's remarks on the longness of the night:

> Ubi sunt isti scortatores qui soli inviti cubant?
> haec nox scita est exercendo scorto conducto male.
> (lines 287–288)

> Where are you, wanton wenchers who can't stand to
> sleep alone?
> Here's the night to make a pricey prostitute worthwhile.

To which the eavesdropping Mercury responds:

> Meu' pater nunc pro huius verbis recte et sapienter facit,
> qui complexus cum Alcumena cubat amans, animo
> > > opsequens.
> > > (lines 289–290)

Father's being very wise — he's doing just precisely that:
Lying with and loving Alcumena to his heart's content.

Once again, the carnality of it all is emphasized. It would seem that Mercury considers Alcmena a mere prostitute — except that Jupiter does not even pay her for his *usura corporis*.

We are already at line 462 when Sosia disappears. This would be almost halfway through a normal Plautine comedy. And what has happened up until this moment? Nothing more than *Iuppiter cubat*.

Once again Mercury pronounces a prologue, this one slightly more "Euripidean" than the first, although he again dwells on what is happening in the room between Alcmena and Jupiter, who is "embracing" her (*amplexarier*, line 465) in complete sensual abandonment (*satietatem capiet*, line 472). At this point we are apprised of Alcmena's double pregnancy and the imminent *turbae* in Amphitryon's household. But Mercury assures us all will end well, with a single parturition (lines 477ff). And he adds almost parenthetically, *nemo id probro / profecto ducet Alcumenae* (lines 492–493), "no one will consider Alcmena to have sinned." Hardly the greatest gift a god could grant a mortal. Most important, in contrast to Euripidean practice, the birth of Hercules is not specifically announced *at all*.[15]

At this moment, Jupiter enters with his *uxor usuraria* (line 498) and laments that his duties as *summus imperator* (line 504) oblige him to return to the army. The irony is hardly veiled (*nimis hic scitust sycophanta*, "what a shrewd imper-

sonator he is," as Mercury says in praise of his father's performance [line 506]). This solemn declaration by a military
leader would surely have touched a sensitive chord in Roman
hearts. Because this *Amphitruo subditivos* (line 497) (again
the words of Mercury) is exactly the opposite of Regulus,
that most Roman of Romans (cf. Horace, *Odes* 3.5). Moreover, Jove hints at a certain clandestinity when he gives Alcmena the golden trophy which he — that is Amphitryon —
has won: *clanculum abii: a legione operam hanc surrupui tibi*
(line 523), "surreptitiously I stole away to give this secret
little gift to you." [16]

Finally, left alone on the stage, Jupiter "liberates" the night
(line 546). In delaying the sunrise, he has realized the traditional lovers' fantasy: one thinks of Ovid's *Amores* 1.3.40,
*lente, currite noctis equi,* and the words of John Donne:
"Busy old fool, unruly sun . . . must to thy motions lovers'
seasons run?"

And now we pass from the dream of a lover to the night-
mare of a husband. The real Amphitryon enters, followed by
Sosia who is in the midst of an identity crisis, not to say
schizophrenia: *sum profecto et hic et illic* (line 594) "I'm
here — but I'm *there*, too!" Amphitryon insists that what his
slave has seen was *in somnis Sosiam* (line 621) while the
slave continues to maintain that what he saw was *vigilans . . .
vigilantem* (lines 623–624). At this point, Alcmena enters singing of . . . the joys of love. *Voluptas,* she repeats three times
(lines 635, 637, 641), *parumper datast* (line 638).[17] But, as a
kind of compensation for the lack of *vir,* she can at least share
in his *virtus,* celebrated in a song (lines 643ff) which concludes as follows:

> Virtus praemium est optumum;
> virtus omnibus rebus anteit profecto:
> libertas, salus, vita, res et parentes, patria et prognati
> tutantur, servantur:

virtus omnia in sese habet, omnia adsunt
bona quem penest virtus.

(lines 648–653)

The greatest prize of all is virtue;
Of all things 'tis best — must ne'er desert you.
Freedom, health, one's life, one's business, parents,
fatherland and children are preserved and kept.
He who'd be in everything adept
Must first have virtue.

She is without any doubt, as J. A. Hanson observed, the greatest incarnation of *pietas* on the Roman stage.[18] Yet this still cannot help her husband.

Amphitryon addresses his wife in words that, as we will see later, are as much a Roman *laudatio* as a Greek salutation. He refers to her in phrases like *quam omnium Thebis vir unam esse optumam diiudicat* (line 677), "the woman whose husband judged her to be unique — the very finest in all Thebes." But having barely seen him off, she is confused to have him once again appear before her. The household *turba* has already been stirred up, leading her to suspect that she is being put to the test (lines 688–689).

Amphitryon himself considers her behavior to be pure *deliramenta* (line 696) or the fantasy of a daydream (*quaene vigilans somniat?* [line 697]). But Alcmena insists she is awake and aware. Indeed, she has seen her husband, *immo vigilans vigilantem* (line 726). And when Amphitryon maintains that he spent the preceding night on board his ship, she retorts: *immo mecum cenavisti et mecum cubuisti* (line 735), "no, indeed, you dined with me and after you reclined with me." Though she may represent a paragon of reserved and humble Roman femininity — whose virtues traditionally include *sedatus cupido* (line 840)—Alcmena nonetheless is made of flesh and blood and can appreciate the conjugal joys.

She reminds her increasingly anguished husband of their conversation the previous night about his military triumphs (lines 745ff). She insists that he gave her the golden trophy which he had captured from the enemy (lines 760ff).

Amphitryon is still obstinate: *neque edepol dedi neque dixi* (line 762). We recall the protests of Menaechmus I to his wife (regarding the stolen *palla*):

> Per Iovem deosque omnis adiuro, uxor (satin hoc
> est tibi?)
> non dedisse.
>
> (*Men.*, lines 655–656)[19]

> By Jove and all the gods, I swear—is that enough for
> you, dear wife?
> No, I didn't *give it to her.*

Even when Alcmena displays the golden trophy to prove that Amphitryon was there the evening before, Sosia several times insists that his master gave it to her secretly, *clanculum* (line 795), *dedisti . . . clanculum* (line 797).

At this point Amphitryon begins to interrogate his wife about the events of the preceding night. And Alcmena is anything but reticent about the physical details: *lavisti. . . . accubuisti. . . . cenavisti mecum, ego accubui simul* (lines 802–804), "You washed. . . . Reclined. . . . We dined together and reclined together." Again we are reminded of the *Menaechmi* where the joys of sex are similarly emphasized:

> Prandi, potavi, scortum accubui
>
> (line 476)
> I've wined, I've dined, I've concubined.

> Potavi atque accubui scortum
>
> (line 1142)[20]
> I've wined and concubined.

Flabbergasted, Amphitryon cannot help but ask:

AMPHITRYON: In eodem lecto?
ALCMENA:                           In eodem.
                                                    (line 805)

AMPHITRYON: In the same bed?
ALCMENA:                           In the very same.

And again:

AMPHITRYON: Ubi tu cubuisti?
ALCMENA:            In eodem lecto tecum una in cubiculo.
                                                    (line 808)


AMPHITRYON: Where did you sleep?
ALCMENA:                  In the bedroom and in bed with you,
                                                    of course.

Amphitryon is shattered by it all. Someone in his absence has tainted with *vitium* the *pudicitia* of his wife (line 811). Alcmena's heartfelt protest is useless; Amphitryon is offended that she does not even attempt to lie (line 819).

Alcmena swears by Jove and Juno, *quam me vereri et metuere est par maxume* (line 832), "whom I should most revere and dread" (an ironic echo of Mercury's ironic quip in the prologue [line 23]). And once more she insists that no other mortal has *touched her body* (lines 833–834). Then she pronounces (lines 839ff) the famous words that describe the ideal Roman *matrona* (herself in this case), which include a dowry of — among other virtues — *pudicitia, pudor, sedatus cupido* and *pietas*, the last both to the gods and to the family.[21] But nothing can convince the outraged husband; he marches off to fetch his *cognatus* Naucrates to act as arbitrator. The possibility of divorce looms (line 852).[22]

When the confused and troubled mortals leave the stage, Jupiter once more returns. He himself announces as if in a prologue *ego sum ille Amphitruo . . . qui interdum fio Iuppiter quando lubet"* (lines 861, 864), "Now I play Amphitryon . . . and when I'm in the mood, turn into Jupiter again." He has come to reassure the audience that they are still watching a comedy (line 868). But in the meanwhile he will continue the intrigue by masquerading as Amphitryon (*adsimulare*, line 874) to create a *frustratio maxuma* (line 875) in the household.

We encounter the term *frustratio* elsewhere in Plautus, at the farcical conclusion of the *Mostellaria*, when the slave Tranio harshly abuses the bamboozled *senex* Theopropides and boasts that his own trickery could provide the playwrights Philemon and Diphilus with *optumae frustrationes* (line 1151) for their own comedies. Do we not perhaps sense a gratuitous cruelty in Jupiter's behavior? A schemer as well as a seducer? Is this the "divine comedy" of Plautus?

It is true that Jupiter promises to reveal everything to Alcmena and Amphitryon at the end and that he constantly protests her innocence (lines 869, 872, 895). She will be awarded at the end with a painless double birth (line 879). Once again, that is all. There is no mention of Hercules.

The virtuous Alcmena is too disconcerted to be easily placated. She comes out of the house, already prepared for divorce. Like Caesar's wife, she must be above suspicion. In one sense she reminds us of Boccaccio's *paziente Griselda* — albeit the latter's sufferings end less joyously.[23] Jupiter-Amphitryon cannot find sufficient excuses for her, even invoking Jove to curse him (that is, Amphitryon, [line 934]). At this point, *pietas* obliges her to bless him instead.

Yet again, we find Jupiter alone on the stage and observe what Pelion of complications he places upon the Ossa of the preceding intrigues. To begin with, he boasts about his trickery like an arrogant Plautine *servus callidus*. Then he

The shelf was nearly empty when David said, "Here are a few of his."

"Damn," Joyce said.

"I know," David said. "Do you want these?"

"I have them all. More than one copy of most of them."

"Me too," David said. After a pause he continued: "That was the worst part, wasn't it? When he stopped writing. He vowed he never would. He kept doing it even when he always repeated himself and his vocabulary became infantile. And then he came to a point where..."

"Do we have to talk about it?"

"No. No, of course not."

---

You have been sitting in your chair watching the silent TV for an indeterminate amount of time when you suddenly snap out of your abstract reverie and realize you are supposed to be somewhere to do something.

You stand up and look around, first at the TV and then outside the window at the asphalt road and the woods on the other side. You hesitate. What was it you had been planning to do?

Your attention turns to a small box of personal items on the counter next to the kitchenette sink. There are notebooks, pens, and other odds and ends. You pull out a book, a slim paperback with a flamboyant cover of abstract images that suggest dragons, and a castle, and an alien or fantasy landscape. This is important. Something about it enthralls you and compels you to... What? The thought drifts away. You reach out and grasp for it with what remains of whoever you were, but it dissipates and disappears.

You sit back down in your chair and resume watching TV.

calls Mercury and adds this ingenious new invention to the traditional myth: he commands his *subparasitus* (cf. lines 515, 993) to keep all troublemakers away from the house because he wishes — yet another time — to take to bed his *uxor usuraria* (lines 980–981).

If the audience is not yet persuaded that Plautus' comedy emphasizes the carnal, this further episode should dispel all doubts. For the principal characteristic of the classical myth of Amphitryon is that Jove paid a single visit to Alcmena and on this one occasion had lengthened the night.[24] This does not suit the Greek Zeus very well, for that divinity usually takes unusual forms — swan, bull, golden rain — for his visitations. But here we find the opposite: a sensual Roman who takes perverse pleasure in repeatedly cuckolding another.

For this argument we need not discuss other details of the comedy, neither the cruel and grossly farcical dousing that Amphitryon receives when he returns home[25] (compare *Lysistrata*, lines 381ff), nor the unexpected change of tone in the final "act." [26] Here the description of the birth of Hercules — even though the name of the divine neonate is never mentioned in the entire comedy — is quite Euripidean. Suffice it to note the role of Jupiter in the dénouement. First, the maidservant Bromia describes a voice heard during Alcmena's giving birth:

AMPHITRUO: Quis homo?
BROMIA:                    Summus imperator divom atque
                                    hominum Iuppiter.
        Is se dixit cum Alcumena clam consuetum
                                    cubitibus.
                                    (lines 1121–1122)

AMPHITRUO: What man?
BROMIA:                    Supreme commander of all men
                                    and gods, great Jove.

He proclaims he's slept in secret with Alcmena,
making love.

But for a moment the great god of Olympus displays a
minimum of tact and style. In the finale when he appears *ex
machina* he informs the audience and the stupefied husband
for the nth time:

Primum omnium Alcumenae usuram corporis
cepi, et concubitu gravidam feci filio.

(lines 1135–1136)

Now first I took an interest in her body's charms
and making love I made the body swell with child.

Is it, in fact, "all's well that ends well," as Jove has prom-
ised? He commands the couple to continue their life together
according to their *antiqua gratia* (line 1141), and then simply
turns and leaves the stage: *ego in caelum migro* (line 1143),
"I'm off to heaven."

Jupiter's exit comes but a few verses from the end of the
play. What conclusion can we draw from it? It is significant
that Alcmena's thoughts are not mentioned at all. Amphitryon, having just heard the "good news," exclaims:

Pol me hau paenitet,
si licet boni dimidium mihi dividere cum Iove.
Abi domum.

(lines 1124–1126)

Why, by Pollux, I'm not sad at
Having been allowed to share my property with Jove
himself.[27]
Go home.

What would have been the reaction of the Roman audience?
One can reply with another question: What did the Italian

audience think at the end of Macchiavelli's *Mandragola,* when
the cuckolded Messer Niccia says:

> Andronne anch'io in casa a mettermi e' panni buoni. Faro
> levare e lavare la donna, e farolla venire alla Chiesa ad en-
> trare in santo. Io vorrei che voi e Callimaco fussi la, e che
> noi parlassimo al frate per ringraziarlo, e ristorallo del bene
> che ci ha fatto.
>
> (V.2)

> I too will go back home and dress up in my finest clothes.
> I'll have my wife get up and wash, then go to Church and
> have her motherhood be blessed. And I want you [the
> clever slave] and Callimaco [*adulescens*] present too, so
> we can speak to the friar, thank him and reward him for
> the good he has done for us.

There is little or no doubt that we have here a similar type
of irony. The reader may object that, although Macchiavelli
was cynical about religion, did not the Romans honor Jupiter
Optimus Maximus in all seriousness, perhaps at the very
*ludi* during which this comedy was produced? [28] The answer
is . . . no. That is to say, not really as an anthropomorphic
divinity. The Romans, as scholars of history and religion inform us, remained at heart intransigent animists. In fact,
scepticism came to Rome almost simultaneously with anthro-
pomorphism. Many learned opinions can be adduced to
substantiate this, but perhaps the words of Kurt Latte will
suffice:

> The entire rationalistic criticism of mythology from the ethi-
> cal standpoint, which in Greece since the time of Xenoph-
> anes had destroyed Homer's divinities, here [in Rome]
> entered a society that had only just begun to combine their
> divinities with these [Greek] gods.[29]

In this regard, ancient Rome was quite different from its Latin neighbors. See for example Bayet [30] as well as Grenier, who argue that the Plautine comedy is itself a proof of the fact that the Roman aristocracy sympathized with the contemporary religious scepticism.[31] To this we can add the famous comment of *doctissimus* Varro cited by Augustine (*Civ. Dei* 6.2) that Roman religion was condemned to destroy itself *civium negligentia*. Let us not forget that Ennius, Plautus' younger — and more esteemed — contemporary, translated into Latin the *Hiera Anagraphe* of Euhemerus — a work that calls into question the "divinity" of the gods. And Fowler argues that

> of the two great literary figures of the age . . . , Ennius and Plautus, we know beyond all doubt that they taught the ignorant Roman of their day not only to be indifferent to his deities, but to laugh at them.[32]

Bearing this in mind, one may ask whether the Roman of Plautus' time would take any satisfaction in sharing his own wife *cum Jove*. In this view at least, his only reward would be a crown of . . . horns.

And what can we say about the comic effect? As noted earlier, Freud described the targets of comedy as the most *revered* institutions. The Romans' reverence for chastity was far greater than the moderns could possibly imagine.

Whatever their morality was in fact, the Greeks of the fifth century B.C. could at least laugh at theatrical adultery with great freedom. We have already mentioned the *gamoi* of Aristophanes, but we should also recall that even the Greek playwright's women make jokes about having lovers (cf. *Lysistrata*, lines 107, 212–213; *Thesmophoriazusae*, lines 395ff et passim; *Ecclesiazusae*, lines 225, 522). And in Fragment 187 of his comedy *Daedalus* we find the playful repartee stating that a lover is as necessary to every woman as a desert to every meal.

But note the moral contrast between Aristophanes and Plautus. There is not a single Roman comedy which celebrates an extraconjugal *gamos*. Compare two husbands — Menaechmus and Philocleon; and two conclusions: the *Acharnians* and the *Asinaria*. The difference is clear and emphatic. Plautine husbands dream of adultery; they even — like Menaechmus I — go so far as to plan it. But they *never* succeed in their schemes. In fact, the only adultery that is consummated on the Roman stage in all of Roman comedy is in the *Amphitruo*.

It is fruitless to argue that Jupiter is a "god" and he has "forced" Alcmena (cf. *mea vi subactast facere* [line 1143]), for but a few moments earlier, Mercury was praising his father's flirtation, encouraging all men (*homines*) to follow this example for obtaining pleasure (lines 995ff).[33] Thus, however we look at it, Alcmena has been compromised and Amphitryon cuckolded. There is no way around these facts.

The Romans surpassed the Greeks in their reverence for chastity. A Roman matron was praised for being *univira* (the actual term is, of course, of the classical era). This meant that "chaste" widows were not supposed to remarry.[34] Consider the following epitaph from the time of Accius (170–86 B.C.):

> H]aec quae me faato praecessit, corpore casto
>   c]oniunxs una meo praedita amans animo
> f]ido fida viro veixsit, studio parili qum
>   nulla in avaritie cessit ab officio.[35]

> This woman who preceded me in death
>   Was loving, chaste, and of my heart possessed,
> Repaying love with love and faith with faith;
>   No greed in her put duty to the test.

This Roman concept, that is a single relationship with a single man for every woman, was so important that Horace felt impelled to endow the empress Livia with this epithet even though in reality she did not merit it (cf. *Odes* 3.14.5). And Gordon Williams emphasizes the fact that "there is nothing in Greek to correspond to this ideal."[36]

The Romans severely punished every violation of feminine chastity. We are told of a so-called "law of Romulus according to which a wife was condemned to death if she was found to have cheated on her husband or drunk wine.[37]

For all their obsessive qualms about the fidelity of their wives, the Roman husbands practiced the well-known "double standard." We recall what Valerius Maximus says of the mother of *Cornelia, mater Gracchorum* in his chapter *de fide uxorum erga maritos* (7.1): the woman so respected her husband, Scipio Africanus the Elder, that she not only calmly accepted his relationship with a young female slave, but after her husband's death went as far as to honor the girl by freeing her.

With this perspective, let us re-examine the *mores* and the *tempora* of Plautus' audience. In everyday life, the men *could* "play the rake," but they never consummate adultery on the stage. Menaechmus I may dream about it, but it is his twin brother, a bachelor, who succeeds in *scortum accumbere*. And the single extramarital *accumbere* in all of Roman comedy occurs . . . in the *Amphitruo*. What can we say about these Roman values? In a true comedy they would be turned topsy-turvy, for this is what Bergson defines as a *monde renversé* — the comic situation par excellence.[38] This is why the playwright insists — almost beyond the limits of good taste — on the *usura corporis* of Alcmena.

In 1970, J. N. Hough published a brief but stimulating article in which he studied a certain acoustical effect in the comedy under discussion:[39] the sound *cucu*, which suggested *cuculus* (cuckoo). This aural pun is heard distinctly in several portions of the dialogue, for example *complexus cum Alcumena cubat* (line 290). Hough traces the repetition of these syllables throughout the comedy, pointing out their culmination in the "explanation" of Jupiter as related by the maid-servant: *cum Alcumena clam consuetum cubitibus* (line 1122).

It is a persuasive theory, and Hough concludes, "such a joke would not be unworthy of the writer with the *latranti nomine* (*Cas.* 34) who would make . . . [a drunken young man] deny his condition with *mammamadere* (*Mostellaria* 331)"[40] *Cucu* is indeed the note which resounds across the entire comedy and which finds its diapason in "cuckoldry." One might well describe the Plautine Amphitryon with Rostand's play on words — *ridicoculisé*. This may seem to be a bitter theme for comedy, but it is nonetheless a perennial one.[41] One thinks once again of the *Mandragola*:

LIGURIO: Non perdiam piu tempo qui. Io voglio essere el capitano, e ordinare l'esercito per la giornata. Al destro corno sia preposto Callimaco, al sinistro io, intra le due corna stara qui el dottore. Siro fia retroguardo, per dare sussidio a quella banda che inclinassi. El nome sia San Cucu.

NICIA: Chi e San Cucu?

LIGURIO: E' il piu onorato santo che sia in Francia.

(IV.9)

LIGURIO: No more wasting time here. I want to be the captain and lead the army for today. Callimaco will be in the right "co-horn" and I on the left co-horn. In the middle will be Dr. Nicia. Siro will bring up the rear, to lift any member that weakens. The password will be "San Cucu."

NICIA: Who is San Cucu?

LIGURIO: Why, he's the most revered saint in all of France.

But of course the "saint" is not honored merely in France but wherever there is monogamy. Shakespeare testifies to his universality in a delightful song:

The cuckoo then, on every tree,
Mocks married men; for thus sings he,

                                        Cuckoo;

Cuckoo, cuckoo; O, word of fear,
Unpleasing to a married ear!
                        (*Love's Labour's Lost*, V.ii.887–891)

As I have hoped to demonstrate, the reigning divinity in the *Amphitruo* of Plautus under whose aegis the comedy was presented is not Jupiter Optimus Maximus, but . . . San Cucu.

## Is the *Captivi* Plautine?

Just as the *Amphitruo* has always been set apart from the Plautine corpus, the *Captivi* is most often set "above" it. Lessing's rhapsodic judgment that this was "the most beautiful play ever to come upon the stage," has, even in our own day, continued to distort critical appraisal. The lodestone for panegyrics is the scene in which a slave displays *ingenium liberale* by offering to exchange places with his master after they have both been captured in battle. This noble sacrifice enables his master to go free. It has traditionally been viewed as inhabiting a special province on the frontier of tragedy; both the old man Hegio and the "slave" Tyndarus have been praised as tragic figures. Even articles of relatively recent date have not totally abandoned the somber approach.[1]

This misreading is based in part on an overliteral interpretation of a casual remark by the Prologue (personified) that if he would merely allow warriors to take the stage, "this comic enterprise would quickly become a tragedy" (lines 60–62). But from what we are able to intuit, the Romans generally disliked the serious genre. This is evident, for instance, from Mercury's quip in the *Amphitruo* prologue.[2] And even the term "tragedy" itself had a different connotation for an ancient audience than it does for us today.[3]

The Prologue's statement that this play is not *ut ceterae* (line 55) has also been adduced as evidence for the *Captivi*'s "high seriousness"; its language is pure and none of the Roman comic stereotypes will appear in it:

> Hic neque peiiurus leno est nec meretrix mala
> neque miles gloriosus.
>
> (lines 57–58)

> There'll be no lying pimp or scheming prostitute
> Or braggart soldier.

But the lines most often cited to support the claims for the *Captivi*'s uniqueness are from the epilogue:

> Spectatores, ad pudicos mores facta haec fabula est,
> neque in hac subigitationes sunt neque ulla amatio
> nec pueri suppositio nec argenti circumductio,
> neque ubi amans adulescens scortum liberet clam suom
> patrem.
> Huius modi paucas poetae reperiunt comoedias,
> ubi boni meliores fiant.
>
> (lines 1029–1034)

> Folks, this play was played to foster chaste morality,
> You'll find in it no vulgar titillations or cheap love affairs.
> Absent too are children interchanged and cash
> bamboozlements
> Nor have we seen lovers freeing sluts behind their fathers'
> backs.
> Playwrights find few comedies as lofty and as noble-toned
> Where the people who are good become yet better.

While it is ludicrous even to imagine any audience taking Aristophanes seriously when he made similar statements,[4] too many scholars have accepted Plautus' own sanctimonious self-praise at face value. The *Captivi* epilogue is perhaps the biggest joke the playwright ever worked on his admirers. We shall scrutinize these verses in their proper place. For the moment, let us try to establish what in the *Captivi* is in fact *ut ceterae*.

We know from Terence's sad experience with the *Hecyra* that the beginning of a Roman comedy had to capture the interest of a rowdy Roman audience or the play would not even have a hearing. Plautus, well-versed in *operis artificum scaenicorum*, was already too much of an old pro to make such a cardinal error.[5] So his Prologue — which will have a lot of exposition to dole out — begins by warming up the crowd with some silly banter:

> Hos quos videtis stare hic captivos duos,
> illi quia astant, hi stant ambo, non sedent.
>
> > (lines 1–2)

> Those people standing there are captives — both of them;
> They're standing there because — they aren't sitting
> > > down.

There is no joke like an old joke: Plautus jests in a similar vein at *Miles Gloriosus*, line 1260 and *Menaechmi*, line 3.

Abuse of the spectators was another tried and true comic device;[6] hence the Prologue's banter with an imaginary heckler who alleges he cannot hear the actor:

> > > Accedito.
> si non ubi sedeas locus est, est ubi ambules,
> quando histrionem cogis mendicarier.
> Ego me tua caussa, ne erres, non rupturu' sum.
> > > (lines 11–14)[7]

*Ken, Anna Schott's childhood friend*

> Come closer, sir.
> If you can't find a seat at least there's room to walk;
> If not you'll make a beggary of my performance.
> Because of you I'm not about to bust my chords.

He then flatters the playgoers in the expensive seats (lines 15–16).

In short, there is plenty of traditional Roman humor at the outset of this "unique" play. But there is more: line 5 contains some intriguing information. Pointing to Tyndarus, the announcer reveals that he is "serving in slavery to his own father." This situation (restated for emphasis in line 21) would have a startling impact. For although Roman fathers held *ius vitae necisque* over their children, they were forbidden to enslave them. And it has long been argued that what was normally prohibited in everyday life was precisely what appealed to the Roman holiday spirit.

Interspersed with the levity is the necessary explanation of who is who, how Eleans Philocrates and Tyndarus have been captured in a battle with the Aetolians, that Hegio's son has been taken by their side, that the old man has been buying up prisoners to ransom him, and so forth. But the most important fact is that master and man on stage have exchanged identities as a trick to gain freedom for Philocrates.

If they were not already engaged by the Prologue, the audience would react with delighted expectation at the phrase *confixerunt dolum*, a signal that a typical comedy was about to be enacted. Trickery was a favorite Roman theme, and continued to beguile the Romans' descendants.[8]

Indeed, the Prologue repeats the words *dolum* and *fallacia* twice (lines 35, 47; and 40, 46 respectively). And for good measure Plautus emphasizes the stupidity of all the participants in today's merriment. Within seven lines (44–50) we find the adjectives *inprudens*, *insciens*, *inscientes* and *ignorans*. This is a recipe for irony and — according to theorists as diverse as Hobbes and Baudelaire — the essence of comic delight: when the audience feels superior to the characters onstage and can say inwardly, "What fools these mortals be." Or as the Latin playwright here puts it, *homunculi quanti sunt* (line 51).

Sufficient exposition having been supplied, sufficient gags having titillated the spectators for the errors and trickery to follow, Plautus then makes the curious statement that this play will *differ* from the Romans' standard fare — with no off-color, unrepeatable lines, and none of the usual comic stereotypes (lines 55–58, see above, p. 192). But these characters were precisely the ones that the Romans enjoyed most! They were the most colorful dramatis personae of the traditional amatory plot. Is the playwright not working against his own best interests?

Yes, but only if one assumes that the audience would be taking the Prologue seriously. Though no one believed similar claims by Aristophanes (e.g., *Clouds* 537ff), too many have taken Plautus at his word, arguing that he is trumpeting the morality of his play. But these are people who sit in libraries, not theaters. The Latin playwright is merely teasing his audience.

To prove this, we need look no further than the very first scene of the play. Only eleven lines after the audience is told that there will be no *meretrix mala* in the piece, on walks a parasite — a decidedly un-Roman figure — whose first words are:

Iuventus nomen indidit 'Scorto' mihi.

(line 69)[9]

The youth have given me the name of "Prostitute."

Much criticism has been raised to the very presence of Ergasilus in the *Captivi:* he allegedly lowers the tone, spoils the mood, is extraneous to the plot. Yet, there are answers to all these objections. First of all, were we to remove Ergasilus completely, we would be left with a play shorter than all but one other extant comedy. Of course, this argument can be countered by Viljoen's opinion that Plautus abbreviated his Greek original to engraft this parasite for "comic relief." [10] Leach, on the other hand, sees him as a parodic foil for the actions of the captives and Hegio — as well as a bridge between the Greek and Roman worlds.[11]

But is there not a simpler reason for the inclusion of Ergasilus? The *edax parasitus* was a much appreciated stock persona of Roman comedy (cf. Ter. *Eun.* 35ff). He is clearly Plautus' favorite character in the piece, since his speeches have been expanded and embellished with what all acknowledge to be Plautus' original touches:[12] puns on his nickname (lines 69ff), the elaborated similes that Fraenkel singled out as especially *plautinisch*[13] — parasites as mice (line 78), snails (line 80), dogs (line 86), his references to the canines as *Molossici odiossici* and *incommodestici* (lines 86–87) are all comic coinages, as is his description of Hegio's now-empty house as *aedes lamentariae* (line 96), "house of lacrimosity." His speech abounds in topical allusions, from mentions of local sites like the Porta Trigemina (line 90), to the Romans' favorite real-life activity: commerce. Most conspicuous is his complaint at the lack of "business" for parasites because of *res prolatae*, "dealings have been postponed" — a formulaic phrase repeated no fewer than four times in eight lines (78–85).

Few would argue that he was in the Greek original, but there is no need to posit a second Hellenistic source and claim *contaminatio*.[14] One need look no further than the *Menaechmi* for Plautus' inspiration. Indeed, he seems to be working over some of the same gags that must have been successful in the mouth of Peniculus.

Ergasilus' primary purpose is to arouse laughter and the only justification for his long monologue is the fact that he reiterates the salient facts of what is to come: that old Hegio has been buying up enemy prisoners to find one of sufficient rank to ransom his son. His speech serves as a secondary prologue and prepares us for the appearance of the *senex*.

Despite the levity of the play thus far, we are disposed to meet in Hegio a saddened, desperate parent — with at least the dignity of Daemones in the *Rudens*, if not Alcumena in the *Amphitruo*. But, in fact, critics have read into Hegio strongly differing traits. While Lejay took the extreme position that the old man was "un imbécile," [15] a greater number of critics have erred to the opposite extreme, seeing him as a tragic hero.[16] Neither conclusion is particularly fruitful, since Plautus' many dramaturgical talents do not include consistency of characterization. That is Menander's forte; Plautus has the *vis comica*.

Hegio may be a bereft and grieving father, but he is also an extraordinarily witty one. And the situation has a touch of comic reversal: the vivid paratragic expressions of grief are uttered by the parasite, *Ego, qui tuo maerore maceror / macesco, consenesco et tabesco miser; / ossa atque pellis sum misera — macritudine* (lines 133–135), "I waste and wilt in woe for you . . . becoming skin and bone. . . ." And the comforting phrase *habe bonum animum*, "stiff upper lip" is spoken twice — not *to* the parent but *by* him — to the parasite (lines 152, 167).

Moreover, the scene also contains an extended Plautine metaphorical comic gamut. For after Ergasilus laments that since Hegio's son has been *captus*, his own *edendi exercitus* has been disbanded (line 153), Hegio — temporarily forgetting his mourning — launches into an elaborate series of gastronomic puns on possible regiments in the parasite's army:

> Multis et multigeneribus opus est tibi
> militibus: primumdum opus est Pistorensibus;
> eorum sunt aliquot genera Pistorensium:
> opu' Panicis est, opu' Placentinis quoque;

opu' Turdetanis, opust Ficedulensibus;
iam maritumi omnes milites opu' sunt tibi.

(lines 159–164)

Freely translated:

You'll need soldiers of all sorts and every flavor
And most important you'll be needing trenchermen:
The many kinds of trenchermen who can dig in:
First saucy Bolognesi to spice up the flanks;
Then Parmesans who have a mighty veal for biting;
A regiment from Turkey and Bavarians to cream them;
We'll also need Crustaceans to provide the shells for us.

The plot is only briefly alluded to (lines 168–170) before
Ergasilus gets himself invited to dinner by Hegio. It is his
birthday (line 174),[17] and in accepting, he "sells" himself to
the old man in Roman commercial language, *quasi fundum*,
"like real estate," to which Hegio puns *profundum vendis tu
quidem*, "you mean like meal of state" (lines 181–182).[18] We
need not cite further examples to prove that the scene is full
of snappy patter, not lamentation. The audience is surely in
a buoyant mood as Hegio exits to visit the prisoners at his
brother's house.

The two captives now take the stage and, quickly stepping
out of their guard's earshot, conclude plans for their *fallacia* —
to trick Hegio into setting free the master-disguised-as-slave.
Philocrates warns his former servant to take utmost care:

Nam doli non doli sunt, ni<si> astu colas,
sed malum maxumum, si id palam provenit.
Nam si erus mihi es tu atque ego me tuom esse servom
adsimulo,
tamen viso opust, cauto est opus, ut hoc sobrie sineque
arbitris

accurate agatur, docte et diligenter;
tanta incepta res est: hau somniculose hoc
agendum est.

(lines 222–228)

For tricks will not be tricks unless you're very shrewd.
We risk titanic tortures if the plan's made plain.
Now you're pretending to be master, I portray the slave.
But care is needed, caution's needed, there must be no
witnesses

Action accurate, wily and wise;
So much underway, don't close your eyes:
Good acting's needed!

This is the imperious prolixity of the typical Plautine clever slave (cf. Palaestrio in *Miles Gloriosus*, lines 597ff). Tyndarus, for his part, urges his master not to forget him. For even people who are *boni*, once they achieve their ends, *ex bonis pessumi et fraudulentissumi / fiunt* (line 235), "those who once were good become the worst and most dishonest." [19] Philocrates declares his desperate dependence on Tyndarus' successful masquerade. He looks up to his slave: *pol ego si te audeam, meum patrem nominem* (line 238), "by Pollux, if I dared I'd call you father dear." Plautus has often used similar language in his more typical saturnalian reversals of master and man.[20]

With all hopes in the hands of his bondsman, Philocrates pleads that Tyndarus will *memoriter meminisse, inest spes nobis in hac astutia* (line 250). Thus, what is usually metaphorical in Plautus has in this play become a dramatic reality. Slave and master have literally exchanged roles. Have we thus far seen anything atypical enough to segregate the *Captivi* from the rest of the corpus?

Continuing in the traditional comic vein, old Hegio reappears, setting himself up to be duped by emphasizing how clevely he will avoid being *captus:*

> Qui cavet ne decipiatur vix cavet quom etiam cavet;
> etiam quom cavisse ratus est saepe is cautor captus est.
> (lines 255–256)

> He who's cautious 'gainst deception cannot act too
> cautiously;
> Even cautious folk sometimes get caught despite their
> cautiousness.

Given the circumstances, is there not an obvious comic irony in Philocrates' response when Hegio tells him that his own son is a prisoner of war on the other side: *captus est?* (line 262).

Indeed, the play's title *Captivi* has a wonderfully ambiguous resonance throughout the action, playing on the double meaning of *capio,* "take prisoner" or "take in." According to Bergson's classic definition of comedy as being a *monde renversé,* we might well epitomize this plot as *captor captus.*[21] As Hegio takes Philocrates aside to question him, a gleeful Tyndarus addresses the audience:

> Nunc senex est in tostrina, nunc iam cultros adtinet.
> Ne id quidem, involucre inicere, voluit, vestem ut ne
> inquinet.
> Sed utrum strictimne attonsurum dicam esse an per
> pectinem
> nescio; verum, si frugist, usque admutilabit probe.
> (lines 266–269)

> Now the oldster's in the barber chair, and we've got
> scissors ready.
> We don't even want to put a towel on — lest he get
> somewhat soiled.
> I don't know — should he be clippered short — or
> merely combed a bit?

> Actually, if we succeed, the man should be expertly
> shorn.

The vocabulary is from Plautus' rich storehouse of synonyms for bamboozlement and similar to speeches in several other comedies.[22]

With Tyndarus standing apart and commenting chorus-like, there follows a dialogue between Hegio and Philocrates about the wealth and status of his "master." There is much jesting here that is totally superfluous to furthering the action. A plausible dramatic explanation for the young man describing his own father as a miser to rival Euclio (cf. lines 286ff and *Aulularia*, lines 302ff) has yet to be put forth. The only approximate justification might be the Roman delight in such characterizations.[23] Furthermore, once Hegio has expressed willingness to exchange his prisoner for his own son's freedom — and nothing else — there is really no necessity for the masquerade at all. But just like the slave in *Poenulus* who already has all the money he needs for his master's love affair, he continues with his trickery merely for the sake of playing the game.

The farewell scene between the reversed master and man has often been praised for the noble sentiments expressed by both prisoners. Their display of *ingenium liberale* brings old Hegio to tears (lines 418ff). But of course, their speeches teem with "Euripidean" as well as saturnalian irony.[24] Tyndarus cannot forbear instructing his "slave" to urge Philocrates' father to *free* his faithful slave (line 408), that is, Tyndarus himself. At the end of the piece, this quip will be seen to have a further ironic dimension.

Tyndarus concludes his orders to Philocrates with the humble plea:

> Tu hoc age. tu mihi erus nunc es, tu patronus, tu
> pater,

tibi commendo spes opesque meas.

> (lines 444–445)

Do this please. You're now my master, you're my
patron — father, too!
In your hands I've given all my hopes and all my
worldly goods.

This has been said before in many Plautine saturnalian situations,[25] but here is a new twist: the reversal reversed. The slave-playing-the-master enslaves himself to the master-playing-the-slave. Surely Plautus is sporting with the familiar stage motif, and his audience would not fail to appreciate the novelty.

As Philocrates exits to freedom, the parasite enters to make another of his allegedly extraneous appearances. He has had a bad time in the forum, and his lament is not unlike Menaechmus' in a similar situation (*Menaechmi*, lines 596ff). They have both missed out on a gourmet meal. Ergasilus has tried to latch on to a host but he has encountered a lack of appreciation for witty parasites. All in all, there has never been a day *ieiuniosiorem neque magis ecfertum fame* (line 466), "more full of fasting and stuffed with starvation." His monologue is long and full of Roman references. And in addition to keeping the groundlings laughing at the account of his misadventures, it concludes with a casual remark that will later actually serve a dramatic purpose:[26]

nunc ibo ad portum hinc: est illic mi una spes
cenatica

> (line 496)

Now I'll seek the harbor as my final shining-dining
hope.

This will put Ergasilus in the best position to spot the returning Philocrates and play the *servus currens*.

But first the comedy's central feature must be played out: the bamboozlement of the oldster. Plautus artfully sets up his victim by making him return to the stage inflated with self-congratulation, swollen with *alazoneia*. His triumphant song is not unlike the self-satisfied boast of the *Miles Gloriosus* (lines 947ff) as he is about to be set up for a fall:

> Quid es suaviu' quam bene rem gerere
> bono publico, sicut ego feci heri, quom
> emi hosce homines: ubi quisque vident,
> eunt obviam gratulanturque eam rem.
> Ita me miserum restitando retinendo[que] lassum reddiderunt:
> uix ex gratulando miser iam eminebam.

> (lines 498–504)

> What is sweeter than when business goes your
> way
> And you also serve the state — as I did yesterday
> When I bought up those men. Today whoever
> spies me
> Rushes up to me to eulogize me
> They detain me and delay me — it's such tiring stuff
> I barely 'scaped their praises — for I'd had enough.

But he has brought along another prisoner, Aristophontes, who claims to be a good friend of Philocrates. As they enter his house, Tyndarus rushes onstage in a panic — his ruse will be discovered and there is no escape. Lines 516ff abound in the language of trickery. But no scheme he could come up with could possibly save him now:

> Neque iam Salus servare, si volt, me potest, nec copia est,
> nisi si aliquam corde machinor astutiam.

# GETTING IT DOWN

Anna Schott

K EN MOVED INTO MY PARENTS' HOUSE IN 1977, WHEN I WAS
four years old. He must have been about eighteen. His own
parents, back in Georgia, had kicked him out after he told
them he was gay. He moved to California and enrolled as a writing
student at the small college where my father was a professor. He was
one of the brightest students at the college and a brilliant writer. It
was an unusual school in some ways—where students and teachers
often became friends. My father brought Ken home one day to
meet the family, and not long afterward, he moved in. He lived in
the spare room downstairs until he graduated.

I remember him at first as being full of fun—almost wild, unlike
other adults, and more like me. We were too alike; in our wildness
we indulged every impulse. It was exhilarating, but as a little kid I
couldn't self-regulate, and Ken didn't regulate me at all. I remember
how I would prance naked in front of him, begging him to chase
me, which he did—tackling me to the ground and tickling me until

Quam, malum? Quid machiner? Quid comminiscar? Maxumas
nugas, ineptiam incipisse. Haereo.

(lines 529–532)

Not even Safety herself could protect me — there's no way
she'd find,
Unless I concoct a new trick in my own tricky mind.
What, damn it? How can I dream up a scheme to escape this
bad luck?
No, it's futile and useless to try: I am stuck!

Tyndarus' *atrox astutia* (line 538) — to try to persuade
Hegio that Aristophontes is *homo rabiosus* — provides the most
farcical moment in the play. It, too, has echoes of the
*Menaechmi*,[27] and the actor playing Tyndarus would surely
have an opportunity to display a tour de force of comic
frenzy, as he tries to discredit the man who threatens to expose his scheme. He must thrust and parry, jest and pun, all
the while vainly trying to convince Hegio that Aristophontes
is insane.

This is also the *longest* scene in the play (lines 533–750),
offering yet more evidence that Plautus' target is the funny
bone, not the heartstrings. But at last the game is up, and
Tyndarus' role switch becomes clear to Hegio. Now the old
man speaks ruefully in the tones — and typical language —
of the Plautine *deceptus senex*:

Tum igitur ego deruncinatus, deartuatus sum miser
huius scelesti techinis, qui me ut lubitum est ductavit dolis.

(lines 641–642; cf. 671–674)

I've been cheated then, torn into pieces, what a wretch
I am!
He bamboozled me — the rogue with all his trickery and
wily wiles.

Then:

> Verba mihi data esse video.
>> (line 651)

> Now I see I've been bamboozled.

And finally:

> Satin med illi hodie scelesti *capti* ceperunt dolo?
> illic servom se adsimulabat, hic sese autem liberum.
> Nuculeum amisi, reliqui pigneri putamina.
> Ita mihi stolido susum vorsum os sublevere offuciis.
>> (653–656)

> Haven't those two rogues just captured my good
>> sense with guile?
> One pretended to be bondsman and the other claimed
>> that he was free.
> Now I've lost the nut and I've been left with just an
>> empty shell.
> That's the way they've smeared my stupid face with
>> egg — fool that I am!

Once again, the word *capti* reminds us of the ambiguity of the play's title. And the language resembles that of the *senes decepti* in the more "traditional" Plautine comedies.[28] Similarly, Tyndarus acts the typical impertinent, carefree slave. As Hegio berates him for his *scelestae falsidicae fallaciae* (line 671; cf. also 674), the trapped slave speaks *confidenter* (line 664) and proudly admits all his roguery:

> Fateor omnia
> facta esse ita ut <tu> dicis, et fallaciis
> abiisse eum aps te mea opera atque astutia.
>> (lines 677–679)

> I confess
> It's all been as you say and he's escaped from here
> All thanks to my most cunning cleverness and fancy
> tricks!

This is reminiscent of the cheeky Tranio in the *Mostellaria*, as is the old man's reply, *ego te exemplis excruciaro pessumis* (line 691; cf. *Mostellaria*, line 1116), "I'll put you through exemplary tortures."

But at the conclusion of the scene, Tyndarus expresses motives for his actions that are undeniably loftier than those of the usual Plautine tricksters: he is proud to have "served and saved" his master (line 707 et passim). This example of fidelity does not impress the furious old man, who orders Tyndarus clapped into *crassas compedis* (lines 722, 734) and sent off to suffer hard labor in the stone quarries.[29]

Before departing, however, Tyndarus has had the opportunity to deliver a few noble speeches, which critics have often quoted to perpetuate the Lessing-inspired, eulogistic attitude towards the play. He expresses a brave, philosophical[30] acceptance of death and what one might call an "Achillean" heroic belief in the enduring glory of good deeds: *Qui per virtutem periit, at non interit*" (line 690), "He who dies for virtue, does not perish utterly," perhaps the most-quoted line in the play.

But, as often in Plautus, one must be aware of the context in which these words are spoken. In the *Bacchides* (lines 816–817), the celebrated "He whom the gods love dies young," is actually pronounced by a cheeky *servus callidus*.[31] Donatus argued that lofty statements placed in the mouth of slaves became, ipso facto, ridiculous (*ad Phorm.* 138). Still, it would be a distortion to argue that Tyndarus' remarks fall neatly into that category, since he will soon be discovered to be a free man — hence his display of *ingenium liberale*.

The moment Tyndarus is dragged off (line 750 hints at

possible slapstick), Hegio delivers a sixteen-line speech, the first half (lines 750–757) essentially a repetition of the chagrin he has expressed before, concluding with his resolution, *satis sum semel deceptus* (*capio* again!).

Then, as almost an *obiter dictum* of but two-and-a-half lines (759–761), he reminds the audience that his now-unransomable son is the *second* he has lost in his lifetime. For twenty years earlier, a slave had kidnapped his four-year-old boy. The fact that no one has made the slightest allusion to this traumatic event since the Prologue (lines 7–10) can hardly be called good dramaturgy — although there is no reason automatically to ascribe this weakness to Plautus.[32]

In any case, with the possible exception of two verses (to be discussed below), the so-called "serious" moments of the *Captivi* have been played out. At line 768, the parasite Ergasilus reappears to initiate the second farcical scene, which is also the second longest.

He rushes in, ecstatic at the prospect of a magnificent banquet:

> Iuppiter supreme, servas me measque auges opes,
>    maxumas opimitates opiparasque offers mihi,
> laudem, lucrum, ludum, iocum, festivitatem, ferias,
> pompam, penum, potationes, saturitatem, gaudium.
>
> (lines 768–771)

> Jupiter Supreme, you are my guardian and prosperer,
>    You have blessed me with superbly super sumptuosities,
> Praise and profit, jokes and fun — a festival of feasting full,
> Pastry on parade, potations — all the joys of partying.

The parasite is bringing news that will win him *aeternum cibum* (line 780). But to do so he has changed dramatic persona. Clearly having forgotten the Prologue's promise that this comedy would not be *ut ceterae*, Ergasilus proposes to behave *ut comici servi solent* (line 778), that is, play the stock running slave.[33] What ensues — at considerable length — is a gamut of comic badinage in which the self-aggrandized slave-parasite spouts *basilicas edictiones* (line 811), "kingly pronouncements," and tantalizes old Hegio by withholding the good news to ensure a feast of unprecedented lavishness.[34]

Not until the parasite demands the sacrifice of a fat lamb to his "godhead," to which Hegio agrees — and receives a homosexual insult for his compliance (line 867) — does Ergasilus deliver his message: that Philocrates has not only returned with his captive son, but also brought the evil slave who long ago kidnapped his other son as well. (Swift action for barely three minutes' stage time.)

But Hegio is understandably reluctant to credit this, fearing another trick. *Ludis me,* he retorts (line 877). The parasite then swears — in Greek — invoking a series of "deities" that are also puns for *barbaricae urbes* (lines 880–884). At the mention of these South Italian towns, Hegio finally begins to believe that Ergasilus speaks *bona fide* (line 890). But he still obliges the parasite to swear in solemn Roman contractural language: *spondeo.* "If this be true," he exclaims, "I am born again!" (line 891 *iterum gnatus videor*). This is the sort of remark that hints at the imminence of a traditional comic ending.[35]

As soon as Hegio scurries off to the harbor, Ergasilus colorfully reiterates his intention to gorge himself — all pork products in the city are especially at risk[36] — and dashes into the old man's house. Hegio returns almost immediately,[37] with a trio of new arrivals: his ransomed son, Philocrates, and the nasty slave Stalagmus (lines 922ff). There are now scarcely a hundred lines until the epilogue and many loose ends to tie up. It cannot be said that this is done with any theatrical finesse.

Hegio rejoices at the return of his captive son, an act which proves Philocrates' *fides firma* (line 927). But when Philocrates requests a reward for his *fides* — the return of the noble Tyndarus — Hegio embarrassedly confesses that *iratus ei feci male*, "I treated him badly" because *mihi data esse verba*, "I'd been bamboozled." (lines 943–945). To expiate his rashness, Hegio offers to free the slave: *sit liber* (lines 947–948). In one sense, this is the fulfillment of a *servus callidus'* dream. Indeed, were the play to end at this point, the brief epilogue of the *Epidicus* would be equally apposite here:

> Hic is homo est qui libertatem malitia invenit sua.
> Plaudite et valete.
>
> (lines 732–733)

> Here's a man who won his freedom, making good by
> acting bad.
> Now applaud and all go home.

But it will soon be discovered that Tyndarus is already freeborn — not to mention Hegio's long-lost other son.[38] We are racing — so it seems — down the main line of traditional comedy: towards the reunion of a family.

Still, there are difficulties — at least for some critics. Tyndarus has been condemned to the quarries, and when he returns he claims to have suffered the "pains of hell." There is no denying that the play's ending is problematical, but too much has been made of Tyndarus' entrance speech:

> Vidi ego multa saepe picta, quae Accherunti fierent
> cruciamenta, verum enim vero nulla adaeque est
> Accheruns
> atque ubi ego fui, in lapicidinis. Illic ibi demumst
> locus
> ubi labore lassitudost exigunda ex corpore.
>
> (lines 998–1001)

> Often have I seen depicted all the tortures found in
> Hell

Yet there's nothing that I saw can match the
quarrying for stones
That's where I've just been — a place where, when
you're tired
You can work off all your tiredness by working even
harder still!

How literally are we to take him? To begin with, there is some question as to how much time Plautus intends us to believe he spent there.[39] A lot may depend on how the actor speaks the first three lines, since by the fourth he is already cracking jokes. And from there on he makes an elaborate (Plautine) simile between his plight and various birds in the playful hands of *patriciis pueris* (lines 1002ff), concluding:

Itidem haec mihi advenienti upupa qui me delectem
datast.
(line 1004)

But playing with a crowbar's not a game to crow
about.

The actual reunion of father and son is, as many have observed, curiously unfestive — and dramatically lame.[40] Tyndarus suddenly recalls *quasi per nebulam* that as a boy he heard his father spoken of as Hegio. At this the old man replies, "That's me!" But neither father nor son addresses another word to each other for the remainder of the play. This has occasioned comment that the *Captivi* terminates not in reconciliation, but in lingering bitterness. To be sure, it is not the deftest of endings, though there is a possible hint of farce if we imagine both men trying to embrace, but being impeded by Tyndarus' grossly heavy chains.

Still, the play concludes two lines later without jubilation, or any sort of *komos*. All merely go into Hegio's house, without the slightest mention of the traditional concluding feast. One is tempted to speculate — on the basis of no textual evidence — that a few lines have somehow been lost: perhaps there was a musical finale (cf. *Stichus*, lines 758ff). That would have helped matters.

In any case, we are left to deal with what does remain in the text, namely the famous epilogue and its high-minded claims. Let us now examine their validity:

> Spectatores, ad pudicos mores facta haec fabula est,
> neque in hac subigitationes sunt neque ulla amatio
> nec pueri suppositio nec argenti circumductio,
> neque ubi amans adulescens scortum liberet clam
> suom patrem.
> Huius modi paucas poetae reperiunt comoedias,
> ubi boni meliores fiant.

> (lines 1029–1034)

> Folks, this play was played to foster chaste morality:
> You'll find in it no vulgar titillations or cheap love
> affairs;
> Absent too are children interchanged and cash
> bamboozlements,
> Nor have we seen lovers freeing sluts behind their
> fathers' backs.
> Playwrights find few comedies as lofty and as noble-
> toned
> Where the people who are good become yet better.

There are no literal *subigitationes*, but there is never overt bawdry on the Roman comic stage. Would it be excessive to argue that homosexual quips qualify as "titillations?" [41] They are not as crude as in the *Casina*, but they would nonetheless be piquant for the audience. Whatever their actual behavior, the early Romans publicly deplored — indeed, forbade —

homosexual relations. This was the attitude of "the philhellene Scipio Aemilianus as much as the antihellene Cato." [42] Significantly, there are very few references to homosexuality in extant New Comedy.[43] Perhaps Plautus' audience enjoyed these innuendos as a bit of exotic, "decadent Greek" spice.

*Amatio* seems only to refer to boy-girl romances and in that sense it is absent from the *Captivi*. But does the play really lack a *pueri suppositio*? To be literal-minded, we would have to call it an *adulescentis suppositio*, but the fact remains that one lad switches places with another for the sake of bamboozlement. As for the claims in line 1032, it is true that the only *scortum* in the play is Ergasilus (cf. lines 69ff). But Tyndarus does indeed free his beloved, lifelong friend *clam suom patrem*. Would not a Roman audience, so thoroughly familiar with the usual erotic intrigue, appreciate the new twist Plautus had given an old plot?

There is also an extra "metatheatrical" phenomenon that has been seldom noticed. It is not unlike the ironic delight enjoyed by Elizabethan audiences, where young boys played the female roles. Thus, in *Twelfth Night*, Viola, the heroine who disguises herself as a man, is enacted by a boy-playing-a-girl-playing-a-man, and Ben Jonson's *Epicoene* contains yet a further twist on this gender switching. The audience was well aware of all this — which added to their delectation.

Analogously, the Roman audience would have savored a comedy in which the hero is a slave-who-is-really-free masquerading as a free man — ultimately discovered to be truly free — being enacted onstage by an actual slave.[44]

There are other familiar conventions of which Plautus makes sport. At the end of the traditional New Comedy plot (whether Greek or Roman), the heroine is discovered to be of better birth than once supposed — and hence marriageable. Frequently she is thought to be a *meretrix* — often because she has been raised by one. But the happy ending reveals otherwise: she turns out to be *et pudica et libera* (*Casina*, line 81).

We are observing a parallel phenomenon in the *cognitio* of the *captivi*. In the *Curculio*, for example, Planesium is at first thought to be a slave girl belonging to the pimp Cappadox, who hints at the dénouement by remarking, *bene ego istam eduxi . . . et pudice* (line 518). Indeed, after some *fallacia* on the part of the clever slave, she is found to be freeborn, and since she was raised *bene et pudice* (repeated for emphasis at line 698 and slightly varied at line 699), she can marry the *adulescens* and live happily ever after. The prologue to the *Cistellaria* predicts a similar joyous fate for the supposed courtesan Selenium, informing us that the elder *meretrix educavit eam . . . bene ac pudice* (lines 172–173).

*Mutatis mutandis*, do we not have a similar situation in the *Captivi?* — a kidnapped child sold as a slave, perhaps intended for immoral sexual purposes,[45] ultimately discovered to be wealthy and freeborn, having had the good fortune to be able to retain his chastity, "bene pudiceque educatust" *usque ad adulescentiam* (line 992).[46] We need not go as far as some critics who argue that the Greek original might have contained a more serious homoerotic love plot,[47] for it is more likely that Plautus was here calling deliberate attention not to the familiar theme but to its unique variation.[48]

Yet the revelation of Tyndarus' purity surely endows the remarks of the epilogue (*ad pudicos mores . . . pudicitiae . . . praemium* [lines 1029, 1036]) with a new significance, since the *pudor* would relate directly to the play.

In any event, the Romans were not a romantic lot. Plautus' cynical treatment of love — as opposed to sensuality — is proof of this (as are the many *uxor dotata* gibes). In anachronistic but accurate terms, they were male chauvinists. Plautus' jokes are meant for the men. But though they laughed at *eros*, the Romans greatly respected *amicitia*. And this may provide a key to what especially appealed to them in the *Captivi*.

Cicero in *de Amicitia* describes the reaction to a scene from a play by Plautus' younger contemporary, Marcus Pacuvius:

I wept with exhaustion. It occurs to me now that some could have viewed these kinds of physical dealings with a four-year-old girl as inappropriate. He wrote an essay about me around then, which starts with a quote by D.H. Lawrence: "*She was a little bright wave of willfulness, so abandoned to her impulses, so white and smooth as she lay at rest, so startling as she flashed her naked limbs about. But she was growing too old for a young man to undress.*" He wrote beautifully, and always got me down perfectly—my voice and my vagaries, both when I was little and unself-conscious, and also later, when I was painfully so.

Finally, to my disappointment—and secret relief—my mother told him that he shouldn't be so rough with me, that even though I screamed in delight, I was also afraid. That was the end of our fun. Ken moved to San Francisco after college. This was in the early eighties, during the beginning of the AIDS epidemic in the Castro neighborhood. After a few years in San Francisco, when I was about eleven, he moved back to our town. He came over to the house one afternoon. I was shy to greet him at first, but his loud laugh and affectionate behavior soon put me at ease. Besides, he was someone I had loved and lived with growing up.

My mother served some food. We stood around on the patio and ate, while Ken told wild stories about all the boyfriends he'd had in the city. After a while, he became quiet.

"Pleasure has its price though, right?" he said. He was silent for several moments before continuing. "I got the virus."

My parents looked grim. I didn't understand.

"A disease for faggots," he explained. "Punishment for giving good blowjobs. I'll die of it, some day, but not for a long time."

I looked at him. He was smiling.

"A long time," he said again, "and definitely not until after you're all grown up, which is like, forever, right?"

I smiled back.

We spent a lot of time together after that. I was glad to have a grown up friend who took me seriously. He would often tease me, in a softly mocking tone, with his barely discernible Georgia accent, but he was big-hearted. Physically, he was slight and wiry, but everything else about him was big. The way he'd throw his head back and laugh

Qui clamores tota cavea nuper in . . . nova fabula, cum
ignorante rege uter Orestes esset, Pylades Oresten se esse
diceret, ut pro illo necaretur, Orestes autem, ita ut erat,
Oresten se esse perseveraret! Stantes plaudebant in re ficta.

(7.24)

What an uproar this new play caused recently in the
theater . . . when the king was uncertain as to which man
was the real Orestes, since Pylades was offering to be killed
instead of his friend. While he kept saying *he* was Orestes,
Orestes insisted that *he* was himself! This fictional scene
brought a standing ovation.

If anything sets the *Captivi* apart from the rest of the Plautine corpus, it is not, as we have seen, a lack of trickery, farce,
rich and abundant word play[49] and an essential — if innovative — comic structure. It is perhaps the scene where Tyndarus displays such loyalty to his childhood friend. This
would probably not bring tears to the Romans' eyes as it
does to old Hegio's but might, as in the case of Pacuvius, bring
them to their feet, applauding.

### Morality and Money: The Purpose of the *Trinummus*

The *Trinummus* is unique in the Plautine canon. For though
Plautus wrote plays both good and bad, this is his only boring
one — as Wilamowitz himself once remarked. A glance at
the dramatis personae explains much: the cast of eight features neither *fallax servus*, *durus pater*, *improba lena*, nor
*meretrix blanda*. In fact, excluding the abstract characters in
the prologue, there are no women at all. Moreover, no one
is either *libidinosus* or *gloriosus*, two quintessential comic ec-
centricities. Instead, the stage teems with senior citizens, no
fewer than four dull *senes*, all lacking humors either Theo-
phrastean or Jonsonian. What is more, these *patres familiae*

seem indistinguishable in their benign conservatism; none is as liberal as Micio or as harsh as Demea in Terence's geriatrically balanced *Adelphoe*. Even so, we discern the potential for comedy. Witness the many similarities between the *Trinummus* and the *Mostellaria*, not least of which is the prominent use of the house metaphor.[1]

But the differences! As the very slave names suggest, the ghost play scintillates through τρανής (piercing, sharp) Tranio, whereas the *Trinummus* muddles with στάσιμος (static) Stasimus. Indeed, the *Trinummus* stands as Plautus' *fabula stataria*.[2] While the *Mostellaria* has an onstage *komos*, the *Trinummus* merely mentions yesterday's cakes and ale while praising tomorrow's virtue. The two *adulescentes* of the happier play enjoy comely companions like Philematium and Delphium, while the boys in the bland *Trinummus* abjure such pleasures completely.[3]

But the contrast is most striking when one considers the cardinal feature shared by the *Trinummus* and *Mostellaria*: they both derive from comedies by Philemon. Our acquaintance with the Greek author is fragmentary, and the differences between the two comedies shed little light on his Muse.[4] But our knowledge of Plautus is considerable and we may well ask why his adaptation of the *Thesauros* is so atypical of his work. Why, despite the many Plautine verbal coinages, does the *Trinummus* seem plodding and verbose? There is, in fact, but one moment worthy of the Latin master, the "title scene," in which a threepenney operator, a trickster hired for *tres nummi*, tries to bamboozle old Charmides.[5] This provides the only comic relief in what is otherwise a work less typical of Plautus than of Aeolus, god of the winds, replete with what he elsewhere mocks as *longos logos*.[6]

Yet the playwright wanted it so. The prologue emphasizes Plautus' creative responsibility, the same artistic "volition" that characterizes his rendition of Diphilus' *Kleroumenoi denuo latine* into the farcical *Casina*. Diphilus had presented a pretty young thing and an ardent suitor, but in Plautus we never see the lovers. Of the youth, the prologue states:

> Is, ne exspectetis, hodie in hac comoedia
> in urbem non redibit: Plautus noluit.
>
> > (lines 64–65)

> But don't expect to see *him* on the stage today.
> He won't come back to town, Plautus won't let him.

The *noluit* reveals the *ars poetica*: Plautus chose what *he* wanted to show, and cut what *he* wanted to cut. The same holds true for the *Trinummus*, although one might well question his choice of material.

The brief prologue is spoken by Luxuria personified, assisted by her daughter Inopia, who has but one line.[7] Alas, this style prefigures the dramaturgy to come, namely monostich evoking monologue. But here, no less than in the *Casina*, Plautus declares his independence:

> Primum mihi Plautus nomen Luxuriae indidit;
> tum hanc mihi gnatam esse voluit Inopiam.
>
> . . . . . . . . . . . . . . . . . . .
>
> Huic Graece nomen est Thensauro fabulae:
> Philemo scripsit, Plautus vortit barbare,
> nomen Trinummo fecit, nunc hoc uos rogat
> ut liceat possidere hanc nomen fabulam.
>
> > (lines 8–9, 18–21)

> First Plautus chose to name me Luxury,
> And wished my daughter to appear as Poverty
>
> . . . . . . . . . . . . . . . . . . .
>
> In Greek this play is called the *Treasure Trove*
> But Plautus barbarized the text of Philemon
> And give to it the name, *Threepenny Day*. He begs
> That you permit the play to keep its Roman title.

In a dozen lines, the Latin author drops his own name twice; Terence never does so even once. We respect Plautus' *voluit* and understand his change of title, since he characteristically names his plays after their liveliest moments (e.g., *Rudens*). But why did he accentuate the sermons on morality? Perhaps we may regard the *Trinummus* (and to some extent the *Captivi*) as a glorification of contemporary ideals, a Plautine venture in Roman propagandistic mythopoesis.[8] Let us follow the points that Plautus drives home.

As in many more successful comedies (e.g. the *Mostellaria*, Menander's *Samia*), the action begins with the hero's father off on a voyage. Before leaving, old Charmides appointed his friend, old Callicles, to take care of his household: a son, Lesbonicus, a daughter with no name, and a buried treasure. True to type, Lesbonicus took to prodigal roistering, and as the play begins, he has already run *res paterna* (line 13) into a sandal string. In fact, he became so desperate that he was obliged to offer the family house for sale. To prevent the hidden hoard from falling into alien hands, Callicles purchased the house himself.

In the opening scene old Callicles is confronted by yet another *senex*. Megaronides, essentially a protatic persona, has the impression that Callicles has abused his friend's trust. Ah, but it is part of the general moral decline, he philosophizes. Nowadays, *mores boni* have been weakened (line 28) and *mores mali* (lines 30, 32) flourish everywhere. Megaronides feels bound by *fides* (line 27) to reprimand Callicles for betraying *fides et fiducia* (line 117). But Callicles then reveals that it was this very *fides et fiducia* (line 142) and *fidelitas* (line 164) that inspired both his financial rescue and his discreet silence. He recounts how the boy's father tearfully implored him *per amicitiam et per fidem* (line 153) never to disclose the presence of the aureate *aulula*. Thus, each of the first three characters has displayed a conspicuous concern with *fides*.

Now the subplot. Enter young Lysiteles, an upstanding friend of declining young Lesbonicus. Lysiteles sings of his quandary — which life-style to choose, business or pleasure.

> Amorin med an rei opsequi potiu' par sit,
> utra in parte plus sit voluptati' vitae
>        ad aetatem agundam.
>                         (lines 230–232)

> Amorous feelings or practical dealings,
> Which course will offer most pleasure for me
>        My whole life long?

*Amor* is enticing, he reasons, but it brings ruin. The young man's words anticipate Lucretius:

> Nam qui amat quod amat quom extemplo saviis
>                         saggittatis perculsust,
> ilico res foras labitur, liquitur.
>                         (lines 242–243)[9]

> But a lover in love commonsense soon dismisses:
> Once struck by the arrows of kisses
> He lets business just slip from his grip and
>                         dissolve.

Rather than flee duty, he will flee love: *apage te, Amor, tuas res tibi habeto* (line 266), the precise language of divorce.[10] He thus resolves to seek the polar opposite of love, namely, marriage. He intends to wed the (nameless) sister of his impoverished friend.

The young man tries to convey his desire to his father Philto (the fourth *senex*), who must first lecture his son on *pietas* (line 281) and bemoan the general current decline in *mores* (lines 283ff). He urges the youth to follow *mores maio-*

*rum* (line 292) and lead his life *moribus antiquis* (lines 295–296). Small wonder that some — including Fraenkel — have detected Ennian influences in this play.[11] The father's metaphor, *benefacta benefactis aliis pertegito, ne perpluant* (line 232), "roof your deeds of good with more good deeds lest they be rained upon," reminds us of Philolaches' "unroofing" in *Mostellaria* (lines 108ff) as well as the words of a craven slave in that same play:

> Si huic imperabo, probe tectum habebo,
> malum quom impluit ceteris, ne impluat mi.
> (lines 870–871)

> If my hand is commanded, my roof will stay strong.
> Let it rain upon others, let others do wrong.

But the glass house of the *Trinummus* is so well polished that not even verbal stones are thrown.

After some persuasion, Philto grants his virtuous son permission to wed *sine dote*. In the long run, such magnanimity will bring *fama*, *amicitia*, and *gratia* to the family name (line 379). It is more difficult to persuade Lesbonicus: he too has family pride. He stubbornly insists upon selling his last remaining asset in the world — a little farm — to provide his sister with a dowry.

It remains for his comrade Lysiteles to convince him by insisting that such obduracy yields neither *gloria* nor *fama* (line 629). Lysiteles argues that the prodigal is now going to the opposite extreme, to avoid betraying the *fama* and *virtus* of his *maiores* (lines 641ff). But if you would truly repent, he says, *in foro operam amicis da, ne in lecto amicae, ut solitus es* (line 651), "help your friends in court instead of courting in your bed." After all, the only Roman way leads straight to the forum.[12] And miraculously, the prodigal repents, recants, reforms, now painfully aware of how he has ruined *rem patriam et gloriam maiorum* (line 656).

With the young man's sudden reformation, the *Trinummus* achieves an odd consistency: everyone in the play has now pronounced upon *mores* except the slave Stasimus. The omission will soon be rectified, however, for as Aristophanes' Euripides quips in *The Frogs*, "everyone should speak — it's the democratic way." Meanwhile, moralizing briefly diminishes and dramaturgy perks up. Old Charmides, the absent father, unexpectedly appears. Brimming with *pietas*, he blesses Neptune for returning him — and his riches — intact (lines 820ff). Father Theopropides in the *Mostellaria* thanks Neptune in similar fashion when he returns.[13] But Theopropides then suffers a *frustratio* "worthy of Philemon or Diphilus" (lines 1149–1151). By contrast, what little deception is performed in the *Trinummus* is done *by* the oldster *to* the trickster. Plautus presents this incident as a kind of little play-within-a-play. For the *sycophanta*, who spouts much theatrical lingo in describing his assignment,[14] introduces himself with a kind of prologue:

Huic ego die nomen Trinummo facio: nam ego operam
meam
tribu' nummis hodie locavi ad artis nugatorias.
(lines 843–844)

Threepenney is the name I give this day, because I will
receive
Threepence for the job of acting out a silly comic
sketch.

The trickster has named the day, precisely as Plautus has named the play (cf. lines 9, 19–20). The problem is that the *sycophanta* has been hired to play an emissary of old Charmides (bearing dowry money), a difficult role since his first audience turns out to be Charmides *ipsissumus* (line 989). Unmasked, the con man retreats, wishing the old man a good beating at the hands of the *novi aediles* (lines 990–997).[15] Old Charmides astutely concludes that something is up; *numquam edepol temere tinnit tintinnabulum* (line 1004), "a bell that's ringing's always bringing something winging." But what is truly up is another *mos maiorum* monologue, this time by the slave Stasimus.[16]

This jeremiad certainly comes unexpected and seems un-called for. Nonetheless it comes, and at lines 1028ff Stasimus begins a long lament:

> Utinam veteres homin<um mor>es, veteres parsimoniae
> potius <in> maiore honore hic essent quam mores mali!

> Would the moral ways of yore, the good old thriftiness,
> Were in greater favor than the current moral shiftiness!

Stasimus' repetition of *mores* outdoes even old Philto (cf. lines 280ff), and old Charmides, who is eavesdropping, quips that Stasimus himself is acting *more maiorum* (line 1031), a famil-iar and feeble gag, since slaves were legally *nullo patre*.[17]

When the master hears the apparent bad news, he is terribly angered, and he confronts the man he trusted:

> CHARMIDES: O Callicles, o Callicles, o Callicles!
> Qualine amico mea commendavi bona?
> CALLICLES: Probo et fideli et fido et cum magna fide.
> (lines 1094–1096)

> CHARMIDES: O Callicles, O Callicles, O Callicles!
> What kind of friend have I left with my
> property?
> CALLICLES: A good and faithful friend of fidelity.

The central question of the play is here asked and answered, the question of friendship, of *fides*. The answer is positive, as Stasimus concludes:

Hic meo ero amicus solus firmus restitit
neque demutavit animum de firma fide,
sed hic unus, ut ego suspicor, servat fidem.

(lines 1110–1112)

Now here's a man who stayed a faithful friend to master
And he never wavered in fidelity
Yet I think that he alone has kept his faith.

This sentiment is repeated with even greater emphasis by father Charmides himself:

Neque fuit neque erit neque esse quemquam hominem in
terra arbitror
quoi fides fidelitasque amicum erga aequiperet tuam;
nam exaedificavisset me ex his aedibus, apsque te foret.

(lines 1125–1127)

Never was there, never will there be, a man in all the
world
Whose faith and fond fidelity to friends has been as firm
as yours.
But for you, he would have dislodged me from his own
lodging here.

The pun on *exaedificare* recalls its earlier usage in reference to the son's *ignavia* (line 132). Once more, the *Mostellaria* comes to mind. But unlike the haunted house–party play, the *Trinummus* has had a "utilitarian" purpose: to present the triumph of friendship and its nuclear quality, *fides;* and *fidelitas*, which appears but twice in the entire Plautine corpus — both times in the *Trinummus*.[18]

The words emphasized in this essay are the words Plautus emphasized in his play. One key term is *fides*. We know from Eduard Fraenkel's famous essay that with a single exception the word did not have its moral and religious connotations in

early Latin (and until Cicero's time). The exception is not
Ennius, but Titus Maccius Plautus. Here, according to Fraenkel, the term may indeed mean *Glauben*, *Vertrauen*.[19] But
why this unlikely likelihood?

D. C. Earl's study of Plautus' political vocabulary is most
helpful. He calls attention to the Roman reverberations of
such terms as *virtus*, *gloria* and that oft-bandied term in the
*Trinummus*, *mores*. Using Tenney Frank's 1932 article as
point of departure, Earl concludes that the language of the
*Trinummus* is very much "in the tradition not only of Polybius, but also of Ennius and the Scipionic Elogia."[20] He argues that *mores* in Plautus could never have anything *but* a
Roman connotation. And yet he does not mention that the
word appears no fewer than twenty-one times in the *Trinummus*. This is almost triple the incidence in any other Plautine
play, including the *Captivi*. There must be a specific reason.

Was Plautus politically engagé? This has been a frequent if
unfruitful hypothesis. Tenney Frank read the *Trinummus* as
a comment on the rivalry between Cato and Scipio, a possibility also admitted by Gagliardi.[21] C. H. Buck's entire chronology presumes that the plays "provide a mirror of Roman public opinion in the politics of the day," and they are datable
according to the waxing and waning of Scipio's career.[22] Many
view Plautus as an advocate, arguing for Cato. And yet Plautus seems to have lived more as *cliens* than *patronus*. That is to
say, he wrote to *be* supported. After all, the primary concern
of the professional playwright is to be financially engagé.
Horace's criticism of Plautus actually confirms this (*Epist.*
2.1.175–176):

Gestit enim nummum in loculos demittere, post hoc
securus cadat an recto stet fabula talo.

The man is just anxious to put a penny in his pocket.
After that he doesn't care a whit whether the play stands
                                         or falls flat.

a huge, loud laugh. He was quick and bright and loved to talk. And when I talked, he'd lean in and listen, giving me his full attention. He was affectionate, persuasive, and flirted with everyone. Sometimes, as a kind of game, he'd try to convince his straight male friends to fool around with him. Sometimes he'd succeed, too.

My parents would host dinner parties for the professors and students at the college, where Ken's genius was widely acknowledged. Everyone would come over. My mother would cook. The adults ate, drank wine, and talked about music and movies and books and art while I sat and listened. Everyone was mostly staid and well-behaved, but then there was Ken. He was never drunk, but was invariably loud, almost wild. He laughed, and he made everyone else laugh while I watched and admired. One night, Ken came over for dinner with some other students, a couple. They had given him a ride in their truck.

"I got to sit in the middle," Ken said, as they came into the house. "I gave them both handjobs on the drive here." He threw back his head and laughed. The couple looked startled, and a little embarrassed. I stared, also a little embarrassed. I wasn't sure if he was joking, but I hoped not.

Ken was something like a big brother, one who doted on me. He sent me cards when I went away to violin camp for the summer; one card a week for the eight weeks that I was gone. Inside the cards, he would write about what he'd been doing that week, often with little cartoon–like drawings to illustrate. His words and drawings were often obscene, but the tone was always lively and affectionate. I was touched by these efforts to amuse me, and felt lucky. Ken was also generous. Later, when I'd gone off to college, he had insisted on sending me fifty dollars a month, no questions asked.

"Do whatever you want with it," he said. "Throw it away, burn it, I don't care. I'm just sorry I can't send more."

As I grew older, our relationship changed a little—I thought he was cute and he knew it. He started holding my hand when we walked, and putting his arm around me.

"Can I be your *boyfriend?*" he'd say mercilessly, as I blushed to my ears and stared at the ground. I hated him then, because I knew, as a girl, how safe I was. For a few years I wanted nothing more than to be a boy, a cute boy who Ken would actually be interested in.

Rather uncharitably, Horace neglects to mention that Plautus had no Maecenas; he *had* to work for a day's *nummi*.

And who paid the playwrights? The spectators gave their applause, but the cash came ultimately from the aediles. These men held the purse strings and usually supplemented the senatorial appropriation. In fact, the practice whereby the aediles personally added to the largesse of the *ludi* was begun only in Plautus' day — according to Pliny (*NH* 21.4) — by an official almost theatrically named Crassus Dives. Is it not then logical that Plautus would be working to earn the favor of the very *novi aediles* to whom his favorite character refers?[23] This would do much to explain the odd disproportion of *utile* to *dulce* in the *Trinummus*.

How would the officals find this play "useful?" We are, of course, seeking intent, not result. For one thing, old men hold the stage, and they are *not* the butt of jokes (as they are in most Plautine comedies, like the *Mostellaria*).[24] Moreover, the sons are atypically respectful, dutiful, and virtuous — if dull. *Fides*, queen of virtues, reigns in word and deed. For once on a Plautine stage, *mos maiorum* is praised, not damned.[25] We see *amicitia* in its best Roman sense, honorable dealing with friends, in praiseworthy paradigm. (It is yet another feature in common with the *Captivi*.[26])

And these are Roman virtues which transcend Catonian or Scipionic factions, though they do reflect a current mood. For at the time the *Trinummus* was presented — roughly in the mid-190s — conservative feeling, or at least propagandizing, was on the rise.[27] The decade between Cato's consulship and censorship was a moralizing crescendo, culminating in what Livy calls *tristis et aspera in omnis ordines censura* (39.44.1). This year (184 B.C.) was, as Scullard observes, "the last real attempt of old-fashioned Romans to re-establish a more austere manner of life in the face of the social and moral decline"[28] To Grimal, Cato and Valerius Flaccus represent no less than "le triomphe du *mos maiorum* et du conservatisme le plus étroitement réactionnaire." [29] And for more than a decade preceding 184, Roman voices decried the increasing *luxuria* pouring in from the East.[30]

But the mythical moments of the *Trinummus* briefly turn the tide. In art, if not in life, *mos maiorum* prevails, stronger than ever. In fact, here it is both past precedent and future perfect. But myth it was, as much a legend to the Roman mind as the *Saturnia regna*, an aureate past by which they could measure the present and find it wanting — except in the *Trinummus*, which is quite simply a morality play. Consider the young men's *redende Namen*: Lesbonicus, "passion triumphant," [31] Lysiteles, Λυσιτελής, *utilis*, perhaps. It is Plautus who chose these names, as is his wont.[32] And regardless of whether the prologue was in Philemon's original, it nonetheless confronts the Romans with their national nemesis. As Cicero remarks (*Pro Murena* 76), *odit populus Romanus privatam luxuriam*. And we recall who named the Latin prologue, *mihi Plautus nomen Luxuriae indidit* (line 8). How far are we from the spirit of such doctrinal dramas as *Everyman*?

> I pray you all give your audience,
> And hear this matter with reverence,
> By figure, a morality play.

Is the *Trinummus* any less "by figure"? Indeed, if the church could promote such entertainment, why not the state?[33] And if the *Trinummus* is indeed propaganda, it would hardly be the last time Rome would manipulate its myths. Who, after all, publicized Ascanius' transformation to Iulus, thus making him founder of the *gens Iulia?* But of course men like Virgil worked for more than *trium nummum caussa* (line 848). In fact, Servius relates how a short laudatory passage in *Aeneid* 6 reaped the poet a huge fee.[34] For Roman artists, myth was not only rich, it was lucrative.

But in this sense the Roman attitude was quite advanced.

Only in our own day has the propaganda value of myths been acknowledged. As Georges Sorel wrote, "il faut juger les mythes comme des moyens d'agir sur le présent." [35] And this may well be the way to judge the *Trinummus*, for *fides* and *mos maiorum* are great mythical attempts at moral rearmament. Consider the wise, if not too wise, definition of *le mythe* in the great Littré dictionary: "ce qui n'a pas d'existence réelle. On dit qu'en politique la justice et la bonne foi sont des mythes." [36]

And consider the climactic moment of the play we have just examined:

> Neque fuit neque erit neque esse quemquam hominem in
> terra arbitror
> quoi fides fidelitasque amicum erga aequiperet tuam.
>
> (lines 1125–1126)

> Never was there, never will there be, a man in all the
> world
> Whose faith and fond fidelity to friends has been as firm
> as yours.

No further mention is ever made of the hidden treasure; [37] *mores* supersede materialism.[38] Yet what is perhaps more important — for Plautus — is that the playwright may have put more than three pennies in his own pocket.

# ABBREVIATED TITLES

| | |
|---|---|
| *AJP* | *American Journal of Philology* |
| Barber | C. L. Barber, *Shakespeare's Festive Comedy* (Cleveland and New York 1963) |
| Bergson | Henri Bergson, "Laughter," trans. Cloudesley Brereton and Fred Rothwell, in *Comedy*, ed. Wylie Sypher (New York 1956) |
| Duckworth | George E. Duckworth, *The Nature of Roman Comedy* (Princeton 1952) |
| Ernout | Alfred Ernout, *Plaute. Comédies. Texte et Traduction*, 7 vols. (Paris 1932–1940) |
| Fraenkel | Eduard Fraenkel, *Elementi Plautini in Plauto*, rev. ed. of *Plautinisches im Plautus* (Berlin 1922) translated into Italian by Franco Munari (Florence 1960) |
| Freud | *The Complete Psychological Works of Sigmund Freud*, ed. James Strachey, Anna Freud, Alix Strachey, and Alan Tyson, 24 vols. (London 1953 ——) |
| "The Glorious Military" | John A. Hanson, "The Glorious Military," in *Roman Drama*, ed. T. A. Dorey and Donald R. Dudley (New York 1965) |
| Grotjahn | Martin Grotjahn, *Beyond Laughter* (New York 1957) |
| Handley | Eric W. Handley, *Menander and Plautus: A Study in Comparison* (London 1968) |
| *HSCP* | *Harvard Studies in Classical Philology* |
| Kock | T. Kock, *Comicorum Atticorum Fragmenta*, 3 vols. (Leipzig, Teubner, 1880–1888) |
| Legrand | Philippe Legrand, *The New Greek Comedy*, trans. James Loeb (London and New York 1917) |
| Leo, *P.F.*[2] | Friedrich Leo, *Plautinische Forschungen* (2nd ed., Berlin 1912) |

| Meredith | George Meredith, "An Essay on Comedy," in *Comedy*, ed. Wylie Sypher (New York 1956) |
|---|---|
| Paratore | Ettore Paratore, *La Storia del Teatro Latino* (Milano 1957) |
| Pauly-Wissowa | Wissowa et al., *Paulys Realencyclopädie der classischen Altertumswissenschaft* (Stuttgart 1894 ——) |
| Perna | Raffaele Perna, *L'originalità di Plauto* (Bari 1955) |
| "Religion in Plautus" | John A. Hanson, "Plautus as a Source-Book for Roman Religion," *TAPA* 90 (1959) 48–60 |
| Spranger | Peter P. Spranger, "Historische Untersuchungen zu den Sklavenfiguren des Plautus und Terenz," *Akademie Mainz. Geistes und Sozialwissenschaftlichen Klasse* 1960 no. 8 |
| *TAPA* | *Transactions and Proceedings of the American Philological Association* |

The text of Plautus quoted is that of Friedrich Leo as followed by Paul Nixon in his *Plautus*, Loeb Classical Library, 1916–1938, 5 vols. All line numbers, speech divisions, and spellings conform to this edition, except where noted.

For the Appendix in the second edition of this book, the text of W. M. Lindsay, *T. Macci Plauti Comoediae* (Oxford 1904) has been used.

# NOTES

1. For an annotated bibliography, the reader is referred to my "Scholarship on Plautus 1965-1976," *Classical World* 74 (April/May 1981). A survey on the subsequent decade will appear in 1987. There have also been two imaginative books on Plautus in English: N. W. Slater, *Plautus in Performance: The Theatre of the Mind* (Princeton 1985) and one that focuses on six Plautine and two Terentian plays, David Konstan, *Roman Comedy* (Ithaca 1983). For an excellent overview of the entire New Comedy–Roman Comedy scene, see W. G. Arnott, *Menander, Plautus, Terence*, Greece & Rome, New Surveys in the Classics No. 9 (Oxford 1975). For a general introduction to Menander, see Carroll Moulton's chapter on the playwright in *Ancient Writers: Greece and Rome*, ed. T. James Luce (New York 1982) 1:435-447.

2. *Menandri reliquiae selectae*, ed. F. H. Sandbach (Oxford 1972). This volume was followed a year later by the 760-page *Menander: A Commentary*, ed. A. W. Gomme and F. H. Sandbach (Oxford 1973).

3. And we now understand the sly humor lying behind that seemingly vague boast of the clever slave in the *Bacchides* (lines 649-650):

> Non mihi isti placent Parmenones, Syri,
> qui duas aut tris minas auferunt eris.

> I couldn't give a damn about those Parmenos and Syruses,
> That merely trick their masters for a paltry coin or two!

For Handley's papyrus has shown us that the name of the slave in Menander's play was in fact Syrus. Plautus not only changed it to a more colorful and pun-worthy Chrysalus, but alludes to his alteration with a typically Plautine in-joke (cf. Handley p. 19 n. 5).

4. Notwithstanding the many valid observations in examining "the fallibility of Fraenkel's theory" made by N. Zagagi, *Tradition and Originality in Plautus* (Göttingen, 1980). See my review in *AJP* 103 (1982).

5. For example, W. S. Anderson, "A New Menandrian Prototype for the *Servus Currens* of Roman Comedy," *Phoenix* 24 (1970) 229ff.

6. Sander M. Goldberg, *The Making of Menander's Comedy* (London, 1980) 39. See also W. Thomas MacCary, "Menander's Slaves: Their Names, Roles and Masks," *TAPA* 100 (1969) 277ff, who observes, "there is no indication in the published fragments of any Menandrean play of a slave's part of the scope characterizing Plautus' masterpieces, the *Pseudolus* and the *Bacchides*" (pp. 292-293).

7. An important book by John Wright examining the fragments of

other *palliata* authors suggests that they too may have written "Plautine" comedy: *Dancing in Chains: The Stylistic Unity of the Comoedia Palliata*, American Academy in Rome Papers and Monographs 25 (Rome 1974).

8. A. S. Gratwick, *CR* 20 (1970) 334. Gratwick is a formidable Plautine scholar as may be seen in his excellent chapters on early Roman drama in *The Cambridge History of Classical Literature*, ed. E. J. Kenney and W. V. Clausen (Cambridge 1982) 2:77ff. Since this is mainly for classicists, the general reader would be best served by John Wright's excellent chapter on Plautus in *Ancient Writers: Greece and Rome* (above, n. 1) 1:501–523.

## INTRODUCTION

1. Cf. Horace *Epistles* 2.1.175–176:

> Gestit enim nummum in loculos demittere, post hoc
> securus cadat an recto stet fabula talo.

The man only gets excited about adding a coin to his money box. After he does, he couldn't care less whether the structure of his play stands straight or falls flat.

Being a true man of the theater — as well as a classicist — the Spaniard Lope de Vega understood, as Horace could not, that good rules do not necessarily make good (i.e., successful) plays. Quite the contrary, says Lope in his *Arte nuevo de hacer comedias*, if one wishes to enjoy public favor, one must completely ignore the classical precepts. The Spaniard began his own playwrighting process as follows: "encierro los preceptos con seis llaves" ("I lock up the rules with six keys"). And, after all, Horace's *Ars Poetica* virtually ignores the greatest theatrical skill, for, according to Molière, "le grand art est de plaire."

2. *In pauca confer: sitiunt qui sedent* (*Poenulus* 1224). Among many similar examples, we might cite *Casina* 1006 and *Pseudolus* 720–721, wherein Plautus' characters express concern about keeping the audience attentive and content. Of course this attitude is not a Plautine innovation, as witness Aristophanes *Ecclesiazusae* 581ff.

3. Gellius *Noctes Atticae* 3.3.14. Perhaps there is all fancy and no fact in this *vita*; it may describe the plays and not the playwright. Leo (*P.F.*², pp. 63–86) demonstrates how the famous story of Naevius' imprisonment could have been based on the poet's *Hariolus*. And there is a suspicious similarity between both Plautus' and Naevius' writing plays while incarcerated. Many scholars regard the tale of Plautus' being sent *in pistrinum* to be a reflection of the countless references to such punishment in his comedies. Still, Gellius insists that his authority is the great Varro *et plerique alii*.

The strongest evidence for Plautus' unique success is statements like those added to the prologue of the *Casina* for a revival performance (lines 11-13, 17-18):

> Nos postquam populi rumore intelleximus
> *studiose* expetere vos Plautinas fabulas,
> antiquam eius edimus comoediam.
>
> .   .   .   .   .   .   .   .   .   .
>
> haec cum primum acta est, vicit omnis fabulas.
> ea tempestate flos poetarum fuit . . .

> After the uproar of the people let us know
> You're all *so very anxious* to see Plautine plays,
> We've re-produced this ancient comedy of his.
>
> .   .   .   .   .   .   .   .   .   .
>
> When first presented, this play beat all other plays.
> Those were the days when greatness flourished on the stage.

4. *Apporto vobis Plautum — lingua non manu*, "I bring you Plautus — not in person, just his play," *Menaechmi* 3. On the rowdy, intoxicated audience, cf. Horace *Ars Poetica* 225.

5. The playwright Accius (c. 170–c. 86) is the first known scholar of Plautinity; it seems reasonable to assume that the "authenticity question" became a live issue right after the poet's death. See Paratore, p. 80.

6. Karl von Reinhardtstoettner, *Plautus: Spätere Bearbeitungen plautinischer Lustspiele* (Leipzig 1886).

7. Friedrich W. Ritschl, *Parerga zu Plautus und Terenz* (Leipzig 1845) (rep. Amsterdam 1965); T. B. L. Webster, *Studies in Later Greek Comedy* (Manchester 1953). Other major works which stress Plautus as a "spoiler" of his models include Legrand, *The New Greek Comedy*, and Gunther Jachmann, *Plautinisches und Attisches* (Berlin 1931) [= *Problemata*, Heft 3].

8. Webster (above, n. 7) 2–3. With these principles set forth, Webster can then discuss such Greek plays as "Diphilos' *Rudens*" (p. 7).

9. Gilbert Norwood, *Plautus and Terence* (New York 1932) 27–28.

10. Studying a complete comedy by Menander enables L. A. Post to dissociate the Greek playwright "from the frivolous inconsequence of Plautus and Terence" ("Some Subtleties in Menander's *Dyscolus*," *AJP* 84 [1963] 37). Plautus is defended in the next issue by Robert B. Lloyd, "Two Prologues: Menander and Plautus," *AJP* 84 (1963) 146–161.

11. Fraenkel, *Elementi Plautini in Plauto*. The discovery of *Dyskolos* has called some of Fraenkel's conclusions into question. For example, Walter R. Chalmers observes that Menander's mythological passage in lines 153ff is, by Fraenkel's criteria, "Plautine" ("Plautus

and His Audience," *Roman Drama*, p. 48 n. 22). Several scholars have pointed out the similarity between the boisterous finales of the *Dyskolos* and the *Pseudolus*.

12. Webster (above, n. 7) 98.

13. D. C. Earl, "Political Terminology in Plautus," *Historia* 9 (1960) 234–243. (Earl studied these same elements in a subsequent article on Terence, with less rewarding results: *Historia* 11 [1962] 469–485.)

John A. Hanson, "Plautus as a Source-Book for Roman Religion," *TAPA* 90 (1959) 48–60, hereafter cited as "Religion in Plautus."

———— "The Glorious Military," *Roman Drama*, pp. 51–85.

Gordon Williams, "Some Problems in the Construction of Plautus' *Pseudolus*," *Hermes* 84 (1956) 424–455.

———— "Evidence for Plautus' Workmanship in the *Miles Gloriosus*," *Hermes* 86 (1958) 79–105.

———— "Some Aspects of Roman Marriage Ceremonies and Ideals," *Journal of Roman Studies* 48 (1958) 16–29.

14. See, for example, Perna's discussion of the *Amphitruo*, *L'originalità*, p. 91. For a recent survey of the "Plautinisches-Attisches" debate, see Perna, pp. 10–37 (although the author's critical bias must be borne in mind).

A fine general introduction to the contemporary view of Plautus may be found in Chalmers (above, n. 11) 21–50. Chalmers' essay appeared just after the first draft of this book was completed; certain similarities in our observations are coincidental and would seem to indicate the present trend in Plautine scholarship. Invaluable to the specialist is John A. Hanson's "Scholarship on Plautus since 1950," Parts I and II, *Classical World* 59 (1965–1966) 101ff, 141ff.

15. These critics of Roman Comedy say precisely what Terence's literary enemies said of him: he made good Greek plays into bad Latin ones, *ex Graecis bonis Latinas fecit non bonas* (*Eunuchus* 8).

16. Fraenkel, p. 6.

17. *Antony and Cleopatra* II ii 191ff.

18. Cf., for example, Gordon Williams, "Pseudolus" (see above, n. 11) 448ff.

19. Gellius *N.A.* 2.23. This early exercise in comparative literature concludes with the scholar's unhappy observation that the Latin poet *nescio quae mimica inculcavit*, "he stuck in some farcical stuff," a criticism echoed by Boileau when he complained that Molière in *Les Fourberies de Scapin* "à Térence a allié Tabarin."

20. Fraenkel makes this same point, p. 324. Many scholars believe that Naevius influenced Plautus (e.g., Duckworth, p. 394), and some of the fragments suggest as much. I have tried to incorporate these fragments into my discussion.

21. On the two traditions of dramatic literature evident even from the earliest times, see Paratore, p. 64.

22. *Ibid.*, p. 18.

23. See J. H. Waszink, "Varro, Livy and Tertullian on the History of Roman Dramatic Art," *Vigiliae Christianae* 2 (1948) 229.

24. Cf. Virgil *Georgics* 2.38off. Horace's account describes how the *libertas* of fescennine jesting grew bolder and bolder, hence the strict Roman law against libel on the Twelve Tables. See my discussion on pp. 9–10.

25. The "saturnalian" tradition in Italy has been studied in depth by Paolo Toschi of the University of Rome (*Le Origini del Teatro Italiano* [Torino 1955]). It is Toschi's thesis that Italian popular comedy from the very first (and who is to say where Roman ends and Italian begins?) reflects the atmosphere of Carnevale, the Italian festival celebrated at the same time as the Saturnalia and without question a descendant of the Roman event (p. 112). Carnevale, says Toschi, is a "frenesia gioiosa . . . un momentaneo allentamento nei vincoli di una rigida morale" (p. 9), which could be an equally apt description of the holiday being enjoyed by Horace's *agricolae prisci*.

26. Sir James Frazer, *The Golden Bough* (one vol. abr. ed., New York 1951) 675.

27. There was never any drama associated with the Saturnalia in classical times (perhaps because of the weather), although it was the occasion for the revival of Roman comedies during the Renaissance.

28. G. Wissowa connects Saturnus with *sero-satus*, assuming him to have originally been a god of sowing; *Religion und Kultus der Römer* (2d ed., Munich 1912) 204. This etymology is questionable because of the difference in vowel quantity: *Sāturnus-sătus*. Its origin may be Etruscan. See H. J. Rose, *Religion in Greece and Rome* (New York 1959) 225.

29. W. Warde Fowler, *The Roman Festivals* (London 1925) 177.

30. Barber, p. 78. I have already acknowledged how deeply this entire study is indebted to Barber's work.

31. Cf. Juvenal *Sat.* 6.67–69:

> . . . aulaea recondita cessant
> et vacuo clusoque sonant fora sola theatro
> atque a Plebeis longe Megalesia . . .

[female theater fans have nothing to watch] when the stage curtains lie quietly stored away, when the theater is empty and closed — only the forum's now alive with noise — and it will be a long time between the Megalensian Games and the Plebeian.

In Plautus' day, in addition to the *ludi Romani*, the *ludi Plebeii* (November), *ludi Apollinares* (July), and *ludi Megalenses* (April) were

"Grief turns out to be a place that none of us knows until we reach it."
—Joan Didion, *The Year of Magical Thinking*

At school, I was learning that to be anything other than homophobic was unacceptable. I found that I couldn't relate to the other kids. I started cutting classes. Some stoners had shown me a hole in the fence that they'd discovered behind the track field. At lunchtime, I'd make sure no one was watching, then squeeze through the hole and walk downtown to the library where Ken had a part-time job doing something that didn't seem to require much attention. I'd hang out in his cubicle and talk to him about boys, or read if he had work to do. On weekends we'd go hiking. Later, when I had boyfriends in high school, I'd bring them over to Ken's apartment. I wanted to show him off, but it was also a test: "This is my cool, cute, brilliant *gay* friend. If *he* doesn't love you, then I certainly can't." I was proud and defensive of him at a time when it seemed like everyone else in the world was a bigot. Alone with Ken I'd ask, "Well? Isn't he cute? Will he do?"

Ken despised officiousness and artificiality. He taught me to laugh at prudery. We would act deliberately obscene if we sensed a prude or phony in our midst. He might say something like: "So, I was making out with my boyfriend last night—" and then wink at me. In the mid-eighties, this was provocative enough to get him beaten up.

"Did you blow him?" I'd ask, thrilled at my own audacity.

We'd stop talking and watch for a reaction. And sure enough, expressions would harden—eyes would narrow, lips purse in disapproval. It was confirmation that they deserved it. It was fun and kind of pathetic all at once, but most importantly, it was defiant. It was an attempt to "own it," when owning it meant being attacked, ostracized, and despised.

That kind of goofing around was just innocent fun, more or less, but as Ken got sicker he started to become unpleasant. His personality, the part of his personality that depended on being in good health, had changed. He grew thinner, more irritable. But his laugh was still loud, and he still showed me flashes of his old affection.

He was very thoughtful and deliberate about the process of waiting to die. And although we never talked about it, he was thoughtful and deliberate in the way that he tried to prepare me for his death.

I remember one time when we were hiking up in the mountains, a couple of years before he died. We were halfway up a switchback on occasions for theatrical entertainment. See Lily Ross Taylor, "The Opportunities for Dramatic Performances in the Time of Plautus and Terence," *TAPA* 68 (1937) 284ff. Or, more briefly, Duckworth, pp. 76ff.

32. Freud, XIII, p. 140, in "Totem and Taboo."

33. Plato *Republic* 10.605a–b. It is interesting to note that both Plato and Freud see comedy as affecting man's inner desire to "break rules." But while the Greek philosopher objects to comedy because it may lead its spectators to *enact* the disgraceful things they see on stage, the psychoanalytic view is the exact opposite! Drama to Freud affords man the opportunity to "act out" (inwardly) the potential aberration, thereby serving a useful social function.

34. Max Beerbohm, "Laughter," in *And Even Now* (New York 1921) 308: "[for great laughter] nothing is more propitious than gravity. To have good reason for not laughing is one of the surest aids. Laughter rejoices in bonds."

35. *Inst. Orat.* 10.1.65.

36. *Epist.* 2.1.23.

37. On the very strict laws against libel, see Harold B. Mattingly, "Naevius and the Metelli," *Historia* 9 (1960) 416. Some scholars have discerned covert allusions to proper names in Plautus (e.g., R. W. Reynolds, "Criticism of Individuals in Roman Popular Comedy," *Classical Quarterly* 37 [1943] 37–45), but this is unlikely. Mattingly argues that even the famous story of Naevius' imprisonment for slandering the Metelli is fictitious (p. 423); in fact *metelli* may not have been a family name at this early time.

38. Crane Brinton, *A History of Western Morals* (New York 1959) 111.

39. Plutarch *Cato Maior* 17.7. Here as elsewhere the Roman moral outlook is like that of the Middle Ages. One may compare Cato's attitude toward the "kissing senator" to Peter Lombard's argument that to have great love for one's wife was, in effect, a grave sin: *omnis ardentior amator propriae uxoris adulter est*. This morbid severity contrasts sharply with Oscar Wilde's ironic description of the very same situation: "The amount of women in London who flirt with their husbands is scandalous. It looks so bad. It is simply washing one's clean linen in public" (*The Importance of Being Earnest*, Act I).

40. In fact Pliny (*N.H.* 8.78.209), in discussing the Sumptuary Laws, mentions that Publilius Syrus, composer of mimes, was notorious for his flagrant infringement of the dietary prohibitions. Yet Publilius does not appear ever to have suffered for his "crimes."

41. For example, Cato's famous speech on the status of women (195 B.C.), as quoted by Livy 34.2.11.

42. The verses quoted follow an evocation by Horace of "the good

old days," which, from the poet's standpoint, are the days of Cato and the Punic Wars.

43. Cf. also *Epode* 7.

44. In *Eclogue* 4, Virgil predicts that Pollio's consulship will restore the Golden Age, purging mankind of its old "traces of sin" (lines 13–14):

> Te duce si qua manent sceleris vestigia nostri,
> inrita perpetua solvent formidine terras.

John Dryden's rendering of these lines is interesting:

> The father banished virtue shall restore;
> And crimes shall threat the guilty world no more.

45. A. A. Brill (ed.), Introduction to *The Basic Writings of Sigmund Freud* (New York 1938) 12.

46. Of course it is impossible to state with certainty that the average Roman was *gravis*. But the fact that the Romans constantly praised and preached *gravitas* is clear beyond doubt, and it is this fact which is important for our discussion. After all, the precondition for French Boulevard Comedy (or any bedroom farce, for that matter) is merely an awareness among the audience that the Seventh Commandment *exists*.

47. Ernst Kris, *Psychoanalytic Explorations in Art* (New York 1952) 182.

48. If the Roman obsession with order and precision needs any documentation at all, one might cite Fabius Pictor's mission to Delphi in 216 B.C., when he carried an itemized list of the gods and goddesses, the exact manner in which each was to be addressed, etc. (Livy 23.1–6).

49. Allardyce Nicoll, *Masks, Mimes, and Miracles* (London 1931) 19.

50. It is distortion enough when Gilbert Norwood prefaces a discussion of Plautus by calling him "the worst of all writers who have ever won permanent repute" (*Plautus and Terence*, p. 4), but Albert Cook goes still further, entirely omitting any consideration of Plautus (or Terence) from his study of the comic tradition because "only the accident that Western Europe had nothing in the genre for a long time could have imparted such an undeserved reputation to works so devoid of ideas" (*The Dark Voyage and the Golden Mean* [Cambridge, Mass. 1949] p. i).

51. *De Officiis* 1.29.104: *Duplex omnino est iocandi genus, unum illiberale, petulans, flagitiosum, obscenum, alterum elegans, urbanum, ingeniosum, facetum. Quo genere non modo Plautus noster et Atticorum antiqua comoedia, sed etiam philosophorum Socraticorum libri*

*referti sunt*, "There are two completely different categories of wit: the first coarse, wanton, shameful, and foul, the other graceful, civilized, inventive, and charming. This second category includes not only our own Plautus and Attic Old Comedy, but it abounds as well in the books of the Socratic philosophers."

## I. "O Tempora, O Mos Maiorum"

1. In supporting Jachmann's claim that these lines are Plautine additions, Gordon Williams remarks that the young man's "tasteless joke about his mother is out of place" ("Some Problems . . . ," p. 426; see above, Introduction n. 13).

2. Calidorus repeats this sentiment, ironically, in a later exchange with Ballio the pimp. To the *leno*'s suggestion that he go "filch from father," *surrupere patri* (line 288), a suggestion, by the way, which parallels Mnesilochus' plan (*aliquid surrupiam patri, Bacchides* 507), Calidorus indignantly retorts, *atque adeo, si facere possim, pietas prohibet* (line 291), "Even if I could, my *pietas* prevents me." This very plan has, of course, already been set in motion by the pious son and his man Pseudolus.

3. Later in the play, Chrysalus, the clever slave, echoes his young master's words in the rhetorical style which Fraenkel (p. 57) described as uniquely Plautine (line 947):

> Mnesilochust Alexander, qui erit exitio rei patriae suae.
> He will, like Paris, ruin his father's real estate.

For the very Roman association of father and fatherland, see my argument below, p. 19.

4. Freud, XIII, p. 159, in "Totem and Taboo"; XXI, p. 183, in "Dostoyevsky and Parricide."

5. Georgia Williams Leffingwell, *Social and Private Life at Rome in the Time of Plautus and Terence* (New York 1918) [= Columbia University Studies in Politics, Economics and Public Law 81, 1] 58–59.

6. Livy 8.7. See also Valerius Maximus 2.7.5 (*de disciplina militari*). Quite understandably he also cites this incident under *de severitate patrum in liberos*, 5.8.

7. Livy 2.3–5 (509 B.C.).

8. Cf. Freud, XXI, pp. 124 and 132, in "Civilization and Its Discontents."

9. In Plutarch *Cato Maior* 20.5 there is a statement which evokes thoughts of the impious deed of the sons of Noah. The historian says that in Cato's day, relations between the generations were so strict that elders would not undress in the company of younger men. On the psychological significance, see Grotjahn, p. 28.

10. The main features of "matrist" and "patrist" systems are outlined and discussed by G. Ratray Taylor, *Sex in History* (London 1954) 83ff. Taylor's concise tabulation of the attitudes prevalent in "patristic" societies (p. 83) bears quoting in full, since so many of these attitudes are prominent in the Rome we are discussing:

"1. Restrictive attitude towards sex
2. Limitation of freedom for women
3. Women seen as inferior, sinful
4. Chastity more valued than welfare
5. Politically authoritarian
6. Conservative: against innovation
7. Distrust of research, enquiry
8. Inhibition, fear of spontaneity
9. Deep fear of homosexuality
10. Sex differences maximized (dress)
11. Asceticism, fear of pleasure
12. Father-religion"

11. Scipio Africanus won renown at age 18 for saving his father's life at the battle of Ticinus; Livy *Periocha* 21, Polybius 10.3. Cf. also Aurelius Victor *De Viris Illustribus* 3.49.

12. Grotjahn, p. 115.

13. Freud, VIII, pp. 108–109, in "Jokes and Their Relation to the Unconscious": "the object of a joke's attack may equally well be institutions, people in their capacity as vehicles of institutions, dogmas of morality or religion, views of life which enjoy so much respect that objections to them can only be made under the mask of a joke and indeed of a joke concealed by its facade."

14. We may compare, for example, the instances cited at the beginning of this chapter, in which Plautus' young men set out to swindle and bankrupt their fathers, with Terence *Eunuchus* 380ff, where young Chaerea explains to his slave Parmeno that he will disguise himself as a eunuch so that he will *not* have to deceive his parent (lines 386–387):

An potius haec patri aequomst fieri, ut a me ludatur dolis
quod qui rescierint, culpent.

Would it be better if I went and tricked my father?
Whoever learned of *that* would criticize me . . .

It is even more revealing to contrast the sentiments of the Plautine lovers who wish their parents dead because they adore their mistresses so much with Terence *Adelphoe* 696ff, when young Aeschinus speaks to his father of his beloved Pamphila (lines 701–703):

AESCHINUS: Di me pater
omnes oderint ni magis te quam oculos nunc amo meos.

MICIO:  Quid? Quam illam?
AESCHINUS:  *Aeque.*

AESCHINUS:  O father!
May the gods all hate me if I don't love you above all else.
MICIO (*pointing to the girl*):  Even more than *her?*
AESCHINUS (*a pause for reflection*):  As much.

15.  Donatus *ad Ter. Adelph.* 4.1.5.
16.  The tutor replies with an equally clever (and equally hostile) allusion (*Bacchides* 156–157):

Pol metuo magis, ne Phoenix tuis factis fuam
teque ad patrem esse mortuom renuntiem.

By Pollux, I'm afraid you'll turn me into Phoenix,
That is, the man who tells your father that you're dead.

17.  See above, n. 6.
18.  Cf. "Religion in Plautus," p. 91.
19.  *Aeneid* 2.777–789.
20.  Propertius 4.11. Cf. especially lines 73–74, which echo Creusa's *nati serva communis amorem* in *Aeneid* 2.789.
21.  Cf. Cato on the proper role of women (195 B.C.): *Maiores nostri nullam, ne privatam quidem rem agere feminas sine tutore, auctore voluerunt, in manu esse parentium, fratrum, virorum* (Livy 34.2.11), "Our forefathers would not allow women to undertake even a private business matter without the supervision of a *tutor*; they wished women to remain in the custody of fathers, brothers, or husbands."
22.  *Iliad* 6.429–430.
23.  Gilbert Murray, *Aristophanes* (Oxford 1933) 251.
24.  Williams, "Some Aspects . . . ," p. 28 (see above, Introduction n. 13). On p. 25, Williams quotes several Latin epigraphs which laud wifely *obsequentia.*
25.  Susarion's primeval witticism (as told in Tzetzes, Kaibel p. 77) was of the *nec tecum nec sine te* variety. Cf. Menander frag. 651 Kock ("marriage . . . is a necessary evil [ἀναγκαῖον κακόν]"). Freud offers psychological explanations for the fact that from the earliest times marriage has been a popular object of comic attack. See Freud, VIII, p. 110, in "Jokes and Their Relation to the Unconscious." Petronius (*P.L.M.* 78, ed. Baehrens) would seem to have anticipated Freud's argument when he defined a wife as a *legis onus,* "a legalized hardship."
26.  Quoted by Gellius *N.A.* 2.23.10, who comments in dismay, *quantumque mutare a Menandro Caecilius visus est,* "how much Caecilius has distorted Menander."

27. Harry Levin, "Two Comedies of Errors," in *Stratford Papers on Shakespeare* (Toronto 1963) 44.

28. Menaechmus II threatens his brother's wife still more violently (lines 846ff).

29. For line 404 I have followed Ernout's reading, vol. II, p. 183. Giving the second half of the line to Cleostrata seems to make the best dramatic sense.

30. Cf. Moses I. Finley, "The Silent Women of Rome," *Horizon* 7 (winter 1965) 56–64.

31. On the significance of being *morigera*, see Williams, "Some Aspects . . . ," pp. 28–29 (see above, Introduction n. 13). This term is used with its normal noble connotation by Alcumena in *Amphitruo* 842.

32. *Aeneid* 2.792–795 and 6.701–703.

33. The exact reading of *Menaechmi* 152 is a matter of much critical dispute. Both Lindsay and Ernout print *ubi sepulcrum habeamus* for *ubi pulchre habeamus*. But the *clam uxorem* with which I am supporting my present argument is not in dispute. My own analysis of this comedy as presenting a typically Plautine conflict between *bene habere* and *male habere* ("The *Menaechmi*: Roman Comedy of Errors," *Yale Classical Studies* 21 [1968]) helps to explain my preference. Some aspects of this article are presented in slightly altered form in Chap. II, pp. 43ff.

34. This same description applies to part of the conflict in Molière's *L'Avare* in which father and son are fighting for the same girl. In II i, young Cléante also expresses an outlook similar to that of the Plautine sons: "Voilà où les jeunes gens sont réduits par la maudite avarice des pères; et on s'étonne, après cela, que les fils souhaitent qu'ils meurent." ("Look at the point to which young men are reduced by the miserliness of their fathers; is it any wonder that sons wish their fathers to drop dead?")

35. Cf. *Casina* 50–51:

> Nunc sibi uterque contra legiones parat
> paterque filiusque, clam alter alterum.

> Now each prepares his legions 'gainst the enemy:
> Father versus son — each unbeknown to each.

36. "Their every breath" is not a metaphor chosen at random. Caecilius adds the unattractive feature of bad breath to Menander's wife in his reworking of the *Plokion*. Cf. also Plautus *Asinaria* 893ff.

37. Cicero *Part. Or.* 22.78: *Iustitia . . . erga deos religio, erga parentes pietas . . . nominatur.*

38. Frag. 715 Kock:

> ὁ λοιδορῶν τὸν πατέρα δυσφήμῳ λόγῳ
> τὴν εἰς τὸ θεῖον ἐκμελετᾷ βλασφημίαν.

He who lashes out at his father with evil speech
Is rehearsing blasphemy against the divine.

Of further interest here is Menander's use of what may be a theatrical metaphor: he who abuses his father is "rehearsing" for blasphemy of the gods. The Latin equivalent of ἐκμελετᾶν is *meditari*, a verb used often by Plautus to describe the preparation of actors for their performance. Still more significant and thought-provoking is F. M. Cornford's discussion of the possible etymological relation of λοίδορος to *ludus* (*The Origin of Attic Comedy*, ed. Theodore Gaster [Garden City 1961] 113).

39. Duckworth, pp. 296–300.

40. "Religion in Plautus," p. 50. On p. 97, Hanson cites seventy-seven passages which contain technical references to sacrifice and ritual. This, of course, is strong support for Lily Ross Taylor's thesis that a sacrifice immediately preceded the dramatic performance ("Lucretius and the Roman Theater," *Studies in Honor of Gilbert Norwood*, ed. Mary E. White [Toronto 1952] 151).

41. "Religion in Plautus," pp. 54–60.

42. *Bellum Punicum*, frag. 13.

43. M. Cary, *A History of Rome* (2nd ed., London 1957) 54.

44. Livy 22.57.2.

45. As for everything in literature, there is a Homeric precedent: cf. *Iliad* 1.565–567 and 15.14ff, scenes in which Zeus threatens Hera with bodily injury.

46. Cf. the rough behavior of the bully Pyrgopolynices, anxious to rid himself of his present mistress: *si voluntate nolet, vi extrudam foras* (*Miles* 1124), "If she's unwilling, then I'll kick her out by force!"

47. Nor was Mary ever mocked in the medieval revels. On the psychology of ridiculing a mother-figure, see Grotjahn, p. 98.

48. Cf. Williams on *Casina* 815–824, "Some Aspects . . . ," p. 18 (see above, Introduction n. 13): "the solemn ritual language of Roman religious institutions is parodied with its pleonasm and parallelism, archaism and alliteration . . . The advice here given . . . is also the reverse of normal and ordinary life . . . The humour, in fact, is that here convention is stood on its head."

49. See *Epidicus* 349ff. The "parricidal puns" in this passage are thoroughly explained by Ernout, vol. III, p. 141 n. 1. This is one of the passages cited by Fraenkel (pp. 22ff) as a typical Plautine elaboration. In *Pseudolus* 213, the pimp Ballio, arch-perverter of *pietas*, threatens one of his *filles de joie* with the horrible punishment for

parricides, should the girl not heed his fatherly advice — to be rapacious.

50. This irreverence is not quite universal. Plautus' freeborn women are the unique exception. Alcumena in the *Amphitruo*, for example, and Palaestra in the *Rudens* are each the quintessence of *pietas*; cf. "Religion in Plautus," p. 90.

51. Legrand, p. 106.

52. Gilbert Norwood, *Plautus and Terence* (New York 1932) 26.

53. Aristotle *Rhetoric* 1406b cites as a "ridiculous and inappropriate" statement Alcidamas' description of the *Odyssey* as καλὸν ἀνθρωπίνου βίου κάτοπτρον, "lovely *mirror* of human life."

54. Legrand, p. 43; Duckworth, p. 272; Paratore, p. 92. Even Perna (p. 225) believes Plautus is reproducing the Hellenic world, "fuori d'ogni dubbio." Another group of scholars takes the *speculum vitae* theory of comedy less literally and sees the setting of Plautine comedy as somewhere "between life and reality" (Leo, *Geschichte der römischen Literatur* [Berlin 1913] 144). Also Fraenkel, pp. 378–379, and Pierre Grimal, *Le Siècle des Scipions* (Paris 1953) 49.

55. Cicero quotes Ennius' famous phrase from the *Annales* (frag. 467 Warmington) at the beginning of *De Republica* 5.

56. After D. C. Earl's pioneering study, it is impossible to read references in Plautus to *mores* without taking into consideration the fact that this term had extremely Roman reverberations for the audience. See "Political Terminology . . . ," p. 237 (see above, Introduction n. 13). A more moderate view, but one which still acknowledges that this line would have some Roman (if not specifically political) connotations is taken by Donato Gagliardi, "Aspetti del Teatro Comico Latino. La 'Politica' di Plauto," *Le Parole e Le Idee* 5 (1963) 163.

57. Another example is *Casina* 67ff. The prologue tells the audience not to doubt its eyes, slave weddings did indeed take place in Greece, Carthage, and Apulia.

58. Legrand, p. 216. Similarly, Duckworth, p. 291, and Perna, p. 228. Perna also sees *pergraecari* as a sort of apology (p. 229).

59. Accius' account is quoted by Macrobius *Sat.* 1.7.37. Macrobius describes the Greek Kronia as ancestor to the Roman Saturnalia.

60. Cf. also *Mostellaria* 959–960. In the *Bacchides*, the reveling is referred to both as *congraecare* (743), and *pergraecari* (line 813). In *Poenulus* 603 and *Truculentus* 88, *pergraecari* is employed with similar connotations. Cf. *graecari* as used by Horace in *Sat.* 2.2.11.

61. I. Lana holds that Terence was motivated to "rehabilitate" the Greek world which Plautus had so disparaged; see "Terenzio e il movimento filellenico in Roma," *Revista di Filologia Classica* 25 (1947) 44–80, 155–175. This extreme view has never gained much

acceptance. See, for example, the refutation by Gagliardi (above, n. 56).

62. According to the *didascalia*, the *Stichus* was adapted *Graeca Adelphoe Menandru*. The source for Terence's *Adelphi* is a different Menandrian play of the same title.

63. See Leo, *P.F.*², p. 386; Fraenkel, p. 268. Also P. J. Enk, "Quelques observations sur la manière dont Plaute s'est comporté envers ses originaux," *Revue de Philologie, de Littérature, et d'Histoire Anciennes* 64 (1938) 290ff. Perna (pp. 57ff) reviews the history of theories concerning the structure of the *Stichus*, all of which began with Ritschl's *De Stichi Plauti vetere retractatione* (Bonn 1850).

64. Pliny (*N.H.* 29.14) quotes Cato's indignant *nos quoque dictitant barbaros!* On Cato's anti-Greek attitude, see also Plutarch *Cato Maior* 23.

65. Paul Nixon, *Plautus* (Loeb Classical Library) II, 81.

66. *Poenulus* 53–54:

> Carchedonius vocatur haec comoedia,
> latine Plautus "Patruus" Pultiphagonides.

> This comedy, called *Carchedonius* before,
> Is "Uncle," Latinized by Plautus-son-of-Porridge.

Ernout, V, 173 n. 1, refers to *puls* as "l'aliment national du peuple italien." Cf. Juvenal 14.171, Varro *L.L.* 5.105, Pliny *N.H.* 18.19. Most translators prefer to render *pultiphagonides* with *Patruus*, assuming that the *Poenulus* himself is the porridge-eater. I would hope that my argument justifies giving the epithet to Plautus who is, after all, boasting that he prepared his play for Roman consumption.

67. This interpretation may be supported by citing *Bacchides* 115ff, where a man who does not believe in the divinity of *Suavisaviatio* ("Kissy-kissy-kissy") is twice called *barbarus* (lines 121 and 123). See Chap. III, p. 98.

68. Polybius 3.2.

69. Cf. Cato's famous advice to his son, to read a bit of Greek literature (*inspicere non perdiscere*) but to beware the men of this perverse and corrupting race, *nequissimum et indocile genus* (quoted by Pliny *N.H.* 29.7.14). Of course the celebrated Roman chauvinism also fed the fires of distrust for foreigners. To be able to say *civis Romanus sum* was always a glorious privilege. This pride is perhaps best expressed by Annius Florus, a poet of the second century A.D. (*Anthologia Latina* #250, ed. 2 Riese):

> Sperne mores transmarinos, mille habent offucias.
> cive Romano per orbem nemo vivit rectius:
> quippe malim unum Catonem quam trecentos Socratas.

Shun the ways of foreign peoples, they've a thousand treacheries.
No man in this world's more upright than a Roman citizen:
I'd prefer one single Cato to three hundred Socrates.

70. Cf. *Aeneid* 2.65–66:

Accipe nunc Danaum insidias et crimine ab uno
disce omnis.

Now listen to the tricks of the Greeks:
From this one crime you'll know them all.

The credulous Trojans (= Romans) are pictured by Virgil as "unaware of sins of such magnitude and of Greek guile": *ignari scelerum tantorum artisque Pelasgae* (2.106). As Hanson points out ("Religion in Plautus," p. 91), *scelus* is the term which denotes the precise opposite of *pietas*.

71. Paul Lejay, *Plaute* (Paris 1925) 237.

72. Cf. Eduard Fraenkel, "Zur Geschichte des Wortes *fides*," *Rheinisches Museum* 71 (1916) 187ff.

73. *Volpone* III iii 296–297. Cf. also *Twelfth Night* IV i 17, when Sebastian says to the Clown, "I prithee foolish Greek, depart from me." Hence there is an extra touch of irony when Shakespeare's Cressida describes the lascivious Helen as "a merry Greek indeed" (*Troilus and Cressida* I ii 104). The origin of this Elizabethan stereotype may perhaps be seen in a remark by one of the characters in Thomas Dekker's *Shoemaker's Holiday* (iv 157): "drink you mad Greeks, and work like true Trojans!" Clearly, Virgil's *Aeneid* had captured the Elizabethan imagination (see above, n. 70).

74. It is interesting to note that the stereotype which attributes all perfidies to foreigners (and especially to enemies) is nowhere more factitious than in Plautus' initial description of Hanno the Carthaginian. While the prologue of the *Poenulus* emphasizes his dissimulation, his shrewdness, *docte atque astu* (line 111), and what might be termed a general *Graeculus* character, his actual behavior during the play bears out Hanson's observation that he is the male character in Plautus "most strongly characterized by *pietas*" ("Religion in Plautus," p. 92). Plautus was never a man to deny his audience what they wanted to hear, even if it was at odds with the characterization he was about to present. Since the prologue is a *captatio benevolentiae*, it may be concluded that Plautus' audience *wanted* to see foreigners of the *Graeculus* type. There is, of course, no way of knowing whether Hanno's subsequent "good behavior" disappointed them.

75. *De Officiis* 1.38. For Cicero on the Greeks, see above, p. 37.

76. Juvenal *Sat.* 3.73–78.

77. Duckworth, p. 323.

Rattlesnake Trail and had stopped to catch our breath. We sat down close together on a large rock that looked out over the canyon. I leaned my head on his shoulder. He was quiet for a moment, then pulled out his wallet and started looking through it.

"Look, I'm a member," he said, handing me what looked like a business card. It had a drawing of a tree on it, and said "Hemlock Society."

"I don't understand," I said.

"It's a pill to help me die," Ken said.

"Oh."

"It's the only club that would have me," he added, and laughed.

Eventually, Ken began to get really sick. The disease was attacking his nervous system. He continued to work at the library, while living very thriftily in a room that he rented from a friend. He had plenty of friends who would have helped him, but he was adamant about being self–sufficient. He had been saving up to buy a motorcycle, something he'd always wanted. He brought it over one day and gave me a ride around the block. It was a big, red, ugly thing, and expensive. He looked like hell sitting on it, weak and emaciated, and I was afraid we'd fall off. After a couple of months, he became too sick to ride, but continued to work at the library. He wanted to keep working as long as he could, he said, so that he could "pay off the bike in time."

Ken went downhill pretty fast after he paid off the bike. He was dizzy, in pain, and could barely stand. He was thirty-six. I was nineteen, and had just gone back to Ohio for my second year of music school. I had been unsure about leaving him again.

"No," he had said. "You go. Maybe I'll come visit. We can molest all of the cute boys."

Back home, my mother had started to make the rounds of her doctor friends. One of them was an oncologist who agreed to give her some morphine, which she delivered regularly to Ken, sometimes along with soup. It wasn't long before he was beyond the soup. He called me at school one day to say goodbye, although he didn't say it in so many words. I pretended not to know why he was calling. I asked if I could come home to see him.

78. As Grimal (p. 98) says of Plautus' multi-metrical, colorful *cantica* (see above, n. 54), "quoi de plus contraire à l'austerité romaine?"

79. Freud, XIII, p. 140, in "Totem and Taboo": "Excess is the essence of a festival; the festive feeling is produced by the liberty to do what is as a rule prohibited."

80. Juvenal *Sat.* 3.100. This recalls Messenio's description of the citizens of Epidamnus (*Menaechmi* 258ff: *ita est haec hominum natio . . .*). They are a nation of revelers. See Chap. II, p. 49.

81. Leo, *P.F.*², p. 95.

82. Donatus *ad Eunuchum* 57: *concessum est in palliata poetis comicis servos dominis sapientiores fingere, quod idem in togata non fere licet.*

83. Livy 34.4.3.

84. Freud, VIII, p. 165 and *passim*, in "Jokes and Their Relation to the Unconscious." Grotjahn (p. 13) summarizes the Freudian view: "Wit is an aggressive wish 'disguised.' If the disguise is successful, the aggression passes the censor, escapes further repression, and may be consciously enjoyed."

85. Kris (above, Introduction n. 47) 185.

86. Juvenal *Sat.* 11.204. Cf. Martial's lines to Juvenal (12.18) which more literally equate freedom from cares with the "untoga-ed life." Seneca in *Epist.* 18.2 describes the festivities at the Saturnalia as "a time for merrier dining and throwing off the toga," *hilarius cenandum et exuendam togam.* In *Amphitruo* 68, Plautus calls attention to the togas his own audience is wearing.

## II. From Forum to Festival

1. Catullus provides a ready example. He depreciates his own poetry as *nugae* (1.4) and refers to the writing of verse as trifling *ludere.* E.g., *multum lusimus in meis tabellis* (50.2) and his famous renunciation of poetry, *multa satis lusi* (68.17).

2. Johann Huizinga comments on the appropriateness of the term *ludi* to describe Roman holidays in his fascinating study of "play" as a cultural phenomenon, *Homo Ludens: A Study of the Play Element in Culture* (English trans., Boston 1950) 174.

3. Menaechmus' use of hostile military language has already been discussed in Chap. I, p. 24.

4. As stated earlier (Chap. I n. 33), I am aware that *pulchre habeamus* is not the favored reading for *Menaechmi* 152.

5. Williams comments on the significance of *morem gerere* as an important virtue for Roman wives, "Some Aspects . . . ," pp. 28–29

(see above, Introduction n. 13). As usual in Plautus, the wives behave in a manner which is precisely the opposite of the ideal. Ironically, Menaechmus refers to Erotium as *morigera* (line 202).

6. Fraenkel (p. 394) sees "das Properare" as a quality extremely Plautine. Elsewhere (p. 296), he interprets the *Casina* as a conflict between speed (Lysidamus and Olympio) and delays (the wives). This serves equally well as a description of the fate of Menaechmus I, whose experience in the forum is like those of Molière's protagonist in *Les Fâcheux*, who is constantly stopped on his way to an amorous rendezvous. It is perhaps significant that one critic sees this as a theme of Molière's comedy in general (Alfred Simon, *Molière par lui-même* [Paris 1957]).

7. Pliny *N.H.* 8.78.209. Pliny admits, however, that the censors' strictures had little real effect on the eating habits of the populace. But here again the mere fact that there were such prohibitions provides the basis for comedy (see Introduction, p. 11).

8. Pliny *N.H.* 8.78.210. Cf. such portions of proscribed cuts of pork in Plautus as *Pseudolus* 165–167 and *Curculio* 323.

9. Naevius, frags. 22–24, mentions *volvula madida*, which recalls Menaechmus' menu not only because of the forbidden meat but because it seems to be another "drunken dinner" (cf. *Menaechmi* 212). Naevius presents another such bill of fare in frag. 104.

10. Long catalogues of food were already a familiar comic motif in the days of Aristophanes. Cf. the antiphonal offers of delicacies made by the Paphlagonian and the Sausageseller to Demos in *Knights* 1162ff, not to mention *Ecclesiazusae* 1167ff, a menu for which Aristophanes concocted a seventy-nine-syllable dainty (lines 1169–1175), a bit of verbal audacity which makes a Plautine coinage like *glandionida* seem tame indeed. And yet, in content if not in expression, Menaechmus' menu is a more daring comic utterance, containing, as it does, a list of *forbidden* delights. Also of significance is Fraenkel's argument (pp. 238ff and 408ff) that the references to pork are peculiarly Roman and most probably Plautine additions.

11. The special "Roman-ness" of *Menaechmi* 571–601 has often been remarked upon. Fraenkel (pp. 152ff) believes that when Menaechmus says *hoc utimur maxime more* (line 571) he is saying "we Romans." This is supported by Earl's conclusions on the significance of *mos* and *mores* to the ears of Plautus' public ("Political Terminology . . . ," p. 237; see above, Introduction n. 13). But we need not go so far as some scholars who believe that Plautus is alluding in this passage to the Lex Cintia regarding the relationship between *clientes* and *patroni* (see Perna, p. 291 n. 1). In fact, even if we conceive of Menaechmus as heading off to the *agora*, the polarity between *industria* and *voluptas* remains the same.

12. Plautus stresses the "tenacity" of the many ties which bind Menaechmus by using three variations of *tenere*. First *retinere* (line 114) in reference to Menaechmus' wife, then *attinere* and *detinere* (line 589) to describe his clinging client.

13. Cf. *Menaechmi* 591-595. To his credit, Menaechmus has performed well; the suit has been lost because of his client.

14. This view may be further substantiated by examining an instance of the same phenomenon in the opposite direction. Simo, the next-door neighbor in the *Mostellaria*, has been dining at home. His wife has been especially lavish in her preparations, providing him a *prandium perbonum* (line 692). But Simo realizes that this festive meal is "to get him in the festive mood," as it were. He slips out of the house, however, explaining to the audience that he wishes to avoid the sensual experience and will head in the opposite direction (lines 696, 698, 707):

> Voluit in cubiculum abducere me anus
>
> . . . . . . . . . .
>
> clanculum ex aedibus me edidi foras
>
> . . . . . . . . . .
>
> potius hinc *ad forum* quam domi cubem.

> My ancient wife tried to entice me to the bedroom
>
> . . . . . . . . . .
>
> But secretly I sneaked outside the house unseen
>
> I'd rather go to business in the forum than to bed at home.

Simo would gladly have traded clients with Menaechmus. Earl ("Political Terminology . . . ," p. 236; see above, Introduction n. 13) sees what I have described as the forum-festivity polarity in *Trinummus* 259ff and especially *Trinummus* 651: *in foro operam amicis da, ne in lecto amicae*, "Go serve your friends in court, not court your friend in bed." He considers the references to be Plautus' articulation of a Roman aristocratic ideal, concern with one's *clientela*.

15. Some of the prologue to the *Casina* is obviously post-Plautine, but the later interpolations are obvious enough and bear no relation to our argument. Friedrich Leo, who was, if anything, overzealous in distinguishing non-Plautine lines, considers the passage under discussion to be authentic: "in fact, if we disregard the specific revisions, that is, remove verses 5-20, we can consider the entire prologue as Plautine" (*P.F.*², p. 207 n. 2). Leo's view has found almost universal support. For a list of recent scholarship on this question, see Perna, p. 250 n. 3.

16. Even though *ludum dare* is the conventional way of saying "to give a holiday to someone," there may well be, as Mason Hammond suggested to me, a subtle insinuation of *ludificatio* in the Prologue's speech, inasmuch as so many Plautine comedies involve the bamboozlement of "banking" types.

17. In his first oration against Verres, Cicero complains that the opposition is stalling until the *ludi* begin, during which there can be no business. Hence the trial will be suspended and the force of Cicero's argument will, by the passage of time, be *defessa ac refrigerata* (*In Verrem* 1.10.31).

18. Pliny *N.H.* 7.139ff.

19. Leffingwell, p. 132 (see above, Chap. I n. 5).

20. Plutarch *Cato Maior* 21.8.

21. Max Eastman, *The Enjoyment of Laughter* (New York 1936) 150.

22. Freud, VIII, p. 187, in "Jokes and Their Relation to the Unconscious." Barber, p. 99, writes, "festivity in wit is language which gives you *something for nothing*" (italics mine).

23. See especially pp. 82ff.

24. See above, p. 40.

25. In evaluating these remarks, we must once again refer to Earl's observations on the term *mores* in Plautus (see above, n. 11).

26. Cf. Horace's disappointment that Roman education spends too much time on bookkeeping instead of books (*Ars Poetica* 325–326):

> Romani pueri longis rationibus assem
> discunt in partis centum diducere . . .

Roman schoolboys, by long calculation, learn how to divide a single penny into a hundred parts.

Horace criticizes this curriculum aimed to teach a youngster *rem [posse] servare tuam* (line 329); he decries the Roman *cura peculi* (line 330). Yet in the "Roman day," he had nothing but praise for those elders who taught their sons not merely to guard their assets, but how to have them increase, *per quae / crescere res posset . . .* (*Epist.* 2.1.106–107).

27. "This businesslike disposition, this primeval inheritance, survived through the ages," J. Wight Duff, *A Literary History of Rome* (3rd ed. rev., London 1960) 33.

28. *Epist.* 1.1.53–56:

> "O cives, cives, quaerenda pecunia primum est;
> virtus post nummos." haec Ianus summus ab imo
> prodocet, haec recinunt iuvenes dictata senesque.

"O citizens, citizens, get money, first of all, get money. Be worth a lot — then afterwards be worthy." These words great Janus, banking deity, proclaims across the forum, and these same dictates are echoed by the young and by the old.

29. Plutarch *Cato Maior* 21.5–8. In view of this statement that even the good Cato was profit-mad, it is interesting to note that Brutus, Shakespeare's "noblest Roman of them all," was, at least to Cicero, more Shylock than saint. The orator accuses him of the most exorbitant usury in *ad Att.* 6.2.

30. Evander's famous remarks to Aeneas (8.364) became proverbial in Rome. Juvenal mocks them ironically in *Sat.* 11.60, and Seneca quotes them with what he would have his reader believe is moral fervor (*Epist.* 18.12). But it is hard to imagine that this millionaire-philosopher was really a *contemptor divitiarum* except in the sense Livy used the term to praise Cato.

31. Tibullus 1.1 is a locus classicus: *divitias alius fulvo sibi congerat auro*, "Let someone else pile up a wealth of shining gold." On a grander scale we have the most un-Roman remarks of Shakespeare's Antony, who forsakes duty for Cleopatra's arms (I i 33–37):

> Let Rome in Tiber melt and the wide arch
> Of the rang'd empire fall! Here is my space.
> Kingdoms are clay; our dungy earth alike
> Feeds beast as man. The nobleness of life
> Is to do thus (*embraces Cleopatra*) . . .

32. Legrand, p. 48, calls attention to this phenomenon.

33. Claudio in *Much Ado About Nothing* is another "money-minded" Shakespearean lover. Cf. Act I i, esp. 262ff.

34. Polybius 32.13. Cf. also Leffingwell (above, Chap. I n. 5) 46.

35. The countess' remark is from *Le Marriage de Figaro* IV iii, the song from the *premier couplet* in V xix.

36. Cf. Molière, *L'Avare* I v. To keep the record straight, Megadorus in the *Aulularia* is neither an *adulescens* nor impoverished like the young Plautine lovers in the rest of this discussion.

37. Strangely enough, Ernout (vol. VII, p. 14) believes it was *this* dialogue which inspired the "sans dot" of Molière's miser.

38. In Menander's *Dyskolos* young Sostratus protests that he wants Knemon's daughter "sans dot," but he gets one all the same; the *dyskolos* is not really a pauper. And even the soldier Polemon in Menander's *Shearing of Glykera* receives a dowry of three talents (cf. frag. 720 Kock).

39. True enough, Selenium is finally "recognized," in typical New Comedy fashion, and Alcesimarchus ends up with love and money. It is equally true, however, that the young man's actions are never motivated by gain. As Lejay rightly observes (above, Chap. I n. 71), p. 129, "nulle part il n'y est question d'argent." Of interest may be

Paratore's opinion (p. 123) that the *Cistellaria* is the most Menandrian of Plautus' comedies. See also the preceding note.

40. But the Plautine hero, unlike both the Terentian and the Balzacian protagonist, does not look to get *married* under any circumstances. He longs for a *gamos* without "benefit of clergy," a desire shared by both Plautine and Aristophanic heroes.

41. The terms of Diabolus' "contract" specify what the twenty *minae* are buying (*Asinaria* 751–754):

> Diabolus Glauci filius Clearetae
> lenae dedit dono argenti viginti minas,
> Philaenium ut secum esset noctes et dies
> hunc annum totum.

> Diabolus transfers to Cleareta, bawd,
> The sum of twenty *minae*, all in cash. This deal

> Makes Philaenium stay with him both day and night
> This next entire year . . .

42. It is true that Pseudolus ends up with an extra twenty *minae* as a result of the spectacular success of his trickery, but all indications are that the money Simo gives him will be passed on to his master Calidorus, or so Pseudolus states (lines 485–488). The wily slave is really unconcerned with cash; he even offers to refund half to the bamboozled old man (line 1329). In the *Bacchides*, Chrysalus successfully obtains the 200 *nummi* needed to save his master and does set about getting more, but for a special reason (lines 971–972):

> Nunc alteris etiam ducentis usus est, qui dispensentur
> Ilio capto, ut sit mulsum qui triumphent milites.

> Now we need two hundred *nummi* more that we can
>         spread around when
> Troy is taken, so there'll be sweet wine to toast the
>         soldiers' triumph.

Chrysalus wants to double the stakes, so that all can have a party. And yet he insists that it is not his party: *non triumpho . . . nil moror / verum tamen accipientur mulso milites* (lines 1073–1074), "For me no triumph's needed . . . I don't care / I only hope the troops will get their sweetened wine." The others can revel; for Chrysalus, playing the game was sufficient. And he turns every bit of the extra money over to his master: *nunc hanc praedam omnem iam ad quaestorem deferam* (line 1075), "I'll now transfer all of this conquered booty to the quartermaster." Surely Chrysalus and Pseudolus are in the best tradition of the unmaterialistic Plautine slaves who, like Toxilus, cry: *iam nolo argentum*, "I don't *want* money!" (*Persa* 127). Indeed, they love the game and not the prize.

43. Leffingwell (above, Chap. I n. 5), p. 79. Moreover, a slave gathering his own *peculium* enhanced his own value on the market; his ambition would show him to be a willing worker. Cf. *Digesta Iustiniani* 21.1.18. There is no reason to believe that this situation did not prevail even in the earliest times.

44. This rejection of money contrasts diametrically with the desires of the "agelast," a character to be discussed in the next chapter. Unlike Toxilus and other merry Plautine slaves, this anticomic figure wants *only* money.

45. Euanthius (*De Fabula* 3.8) calls this practice of addressing the audience out of character *vitium Plauti frequentissimum*. But such instances are found even in Menander, not to mention Aristophanes.

46. Legrand, p. 317.

47. Huizinga (above, n. 2) p. 13.

48. Freud (VIII, pp. 128ff) discusses the psychogenesis of comedy from "play" in "Jokes and Their Relation to the Unconscious." It is remarkable that the author of *Homo Ludens* never read a word of Freud. On this phenomenon, see R. L. Colie, "Johann Huizinga and Cultural History," *American Historical Review* 69, 3 (April 1964) 626.

49. Cf. *Mostellaria* 976–977:

Et, postquam eius hinc pater
sit profectus peregre, perpotasse assiduo . . .

And following his father's faring forth
For foreign parts, the fellow fell to full-time drinking.

50. These two verbs from the *Mostellaria* do not appear in the *Mercator*. They are used here merely to illustrate my argument.

51. The question of whether Plautus himself coined the *redende Namen* of his characters has long been debated. Duckworth, for example (pp. 347–350), believes Plautus took the names right from his Greek originals, as does Legrand, pp. 842ff. The problem is really part of a larger question, i.e., how much Greek did Plautus' audience know? This is impossible to determine with certainty. Leo's argument (*P.F.²*, 107ff) that Plautus' Greek names are coined in exactly the same manner as his Latin ones still seems convincing. Fraenkel (p. 141) considers Plautus to be the inventor of the girls' names. It may also be pointed out that in contrast to the infinite variety of intriguing female appellations in Plautus, Terence seems content to present "Pamphila" in play after play. But even if our poet did not coin the names, I believe that his audience would still have understood enough Greek to appreciate something like "Pasicompsa," if not "Pyrgopolynices."

There is perhaps an analogy with the French which Shakespeare scatters now and then in his plays. His audience certainly appreciated the humor of King Henry V masquerading as "Harry Le Roy" (IV i 48ff).

52. On the deeper connotations of *pecunia*, specifically the "cattle-money" in Homer, see B. Laum, *Heiliges Geld* (Tübingen 1924) 8ff.

53. The *Bacchides* provides another ready example. Here Chrysalus (somewhat like Strabax in the *Truculentus*) has been given money by a debtor in Ephesus to be delivered to Chrysalus' master, old Nicobulus. But the cash will never reach its rightful owner, and tricky Chrysalus, like Sagaristio in the *Persa*, will transfer these funds to a "pleasure account" (*Bacchides* 230–233):

> Mille et ducentos Philippum attulimus aureos
> Epheso, quos hospes debuit nostro seni.
> inde ego hodie aliquam machinabor machinam
> unde aurum efficiam amanti erili filio.

> From Ephesus, we brought twelve hundred golden Philips,
> A sum indebted by our host to our old master,
> A sum for which today I'll schematize a scheme
> To transfer all this gold to master's lover-son.

54. This very common behavior of Plautine slaves, risking everything for a single day of pleasure (such is Epidicus' attitude in the scene discussed on p. 62) will be fully discussed in Chap. V.

55. Cf. my discussion, in the preceding chapter (p. 17), of the "anti-*pietas*" comedy in these lines.

### III.  Puritans, Principles, and Pleasures

1. Bergson, p. 187.

2. Cicero also employs this term, speaking of Marcus Crassus, *quem semel ait in vita risisse Lucilius, non contigit, ut ea re minus* ἀγέλαστος, *ut ait idem, vocaretur* (*De Finibus* 5.92), "although Lucilius says that (Crassus) did laugh once in his life, this did not mean that he deserved any less the title *agelast*." Refusing food and festivity, sitting aloof from all merrymaking, Demeter is aptly called ἀγέλαστος in *Homeric Hymn* 2.200.

3. Meredith, p. 4.

4. Cf. Tenney Frank, *Life and Literature in the Roman Republic* (Berkeley 1930) 9, 82, and *passim*; also, among countless others, Brinton, p. 106 (see above, Introduction n. 38).

5. Cf. Chap. I, pp. 15ff. The superstitious Romans would worship abstractions somewhat similar to those in Pistoclerus' pantheon. For

one example we may cite the case of Marcus Claudius Marcellus, who, after his success at Clastidium, vowed a temple of *Honos* and *Virtus.* So bound up was he by religious feelings (*religiones tenebant*), says Livy (27.25), that he ultimately built two shrines, one for each divinity.

6. Cf. *Truculentus* 922ff, *Pseudolus* 1255ff. Menaechmus' *voluptas* is discussed at length in Chap. II, pp. 46ff.

7. As may also be seen at the party in the finale of the *Persa,* discussed later in this chapter.

8. Cf. *Menaechmi* 596ff, and my discussion above, p. 50.

9. Northrop Frye, "The Argument of Comedy," *English Institute Essays* (New York 1949) 61.

10. Frye's ideas in the essay cited in the previous note are expanded in his *Anatomy of Criticism* (Princeton 1957). For his discussion of the role of blocking character, see "The Mythos of Spring: Comedy," *ibid.,* pp. 163ff.

11. Cornford (see above, Chap. I n. 38) 131 and *passim.* The pioneering study of the *pharmakos* is J. M. Frazer, "The Scapegoat," in *The Golden Bough* (3rd ed., London 1913) 252ff.

12. Cf. my discussion of the prologue to the *Casina,* Chap. II, p. 52.

13. As, for example, in the bellicose shout of young Strabax in the *Truculentus* (lines 658–659): *nunc ego istos mundulos urbanos amasios . . . omnis eiciam foras!* "Bah, all her lovers, worldly-wise or wise-guys . . . I'll just kick 'em out by force."

14. Duckworth (p. 270) considers Euclio, Ballio, and Pyrgopolynices to be Plautus' outstanding characterizations. All three are agelasts discussed in this chapter. Duckworth adds that in extant New Comedy there are no figures who compare to this vivid trio, and he concludes that, unless they stem through Naevius from earlier Italian farce, these three must be considered uniquely Plautine "creations."

15. A. McN. G. Little, "Plautus and Popular Drama," *HSCP* 49 (1938) 218, 225.

16. Quoted by E. K. Chambers, *The Medieval Stage* (Oxford 1925) I, 282. The "luc" in line 1 is no misprint, although it may have been a scribal error. If the spelling is intentional, it may well be, as my colleague Jeremy Adams has suggested to me, a very refined pun on the Gospel according to Luke, which provides the text for the feast of the Circumcision on which this mass was celebrated. Citations of this Gospel would appear as *Luc,* followed by chapter and verse. Professor Adams believes that such a pun would suit the irreverent atmosphere of the festival.

17. Cf. *Menaechmi* 152, and my discussion above, p. 47.

18. Sandor Ferenczi, *Final Contributions to the Problems of Psychoanalysis,* ed. M. Balint (London 1955) 188.

19. Polybius 31.27.11, quoted above, p. 54.

20. Cf. *Menaechmi* 212, discussed above, p. 47.

21. *Menaechmi* 122–123, 789.

22. The conflict in the *Menaechmi* between *damnum* and revelry that is *sine damno in Epidamno* is in fact introduced by Menaechmus I himself when he first appears. Showing the audience the dress he has stolen from his wife to give to his mistress, he quips: *meo malo a mala abstuli hoc, ad damnum deferetur* (line 133), "From louse to loss, I've filched this for a fine financial damage deal."

23. According to the first *argumentum*, the *Aulularia* ended as follows (*Arg.* 1, lines 13–15):

> Per dolum mox Euclio
> cum perdidisset aulam, insperato invenit
> laetusque natam conlocat Lyconidi.

> Soon Euclio,
> Who'd lost his pot through guile, finds it — complete surprise!
> And joyfully he grants Lyconides his daughter.

The miser has many reasons to be *laetus*. Not only does he receive his pot of gold, but he gains a son-in-law and a grandson at the very same time. (His daughter was made pregnant by the bridegroom nine months before the wedding.) We cannot tell, however, whether or not he *joined* the actual celebrating. Perhaps like Knemon, Menander's Dyskolos, to whom he is frequently compared, Euclio is carried forcibly into the party and compelled to enjoy himself.

24. Fraenkel (p. 140 n. 1) observes that when a πορνοβοσκός (brothel-keeper) appears in Menander, he does not always seem so hateful as the *lenones* whom Plautus loves to depict — and deride.

25. Curculio's entire diatribe runs from lines 494 to 516, punctuated with a few ineffectual retorts by the pimp. His vivid language is in the style which Fraenkel (e.g., p. 36) considers typically Plautine elaboration.

26. Mason Hammond has pointed out to me that the "independent *meretrix*" is never harshly judged like the pimp. Even the cynical Phronesium in the *Truculentus*, who is certainly as rapacious as any *leno*, is not abused. Actually the courtesan is more often a helping than a blocking character. Acroteleutium in the *Miles* is the best example, and it is noteworthy that the fee for her services is never mentioned in the play. She seems to be joining the plot for the fun of it. She says as much when Palaestrio explains the intrigue to her (*Miles* 1159–1162):

PALAESTRIO: . . . nunc hanc tibi ego impero provinciam.

ACROTELEUTIUM: Impetrabis, imperator, quod ego potero, quod
voles.

PALAESTRIO: Militem lepide, et facete et laute ludificarier
volo.

"I'm too sick," he said. "I don't want you to see me like this. And I don't want to see anybody, anyway."

"Well, I'll be home for spring break," I said, "Maybe you'll be feeling better by then."

"Maybe. Stranger things have happened," Ken said. I laughed.

My dad later told me how, the next day, Ken wrote a very affectionate note to him, saying that Ken had made him executor of his will. The note also asked my dad to call the funeral home, where he'd already arranged things. He waited for his friend to go out. Then he lay down on his bed, and took the pill.

I tried then, and still do try without much success, to imagine what that must have been like—how he could have had the wherewithal to put things in order, to pay off the bike, to obtain and set aside the pill, to arrange things with the funeral home, to write the note to my dad, to wait until his friend went out, to think of everything. What troubles me most of all, and what I admire, is how he did *it*—how he died, entirely alone.

My dad told me how a couple of guys from the funeral home had come in a big car to take Ken away. They put on their gloves before touching him, but were still visibly uncomfortable because they knew he'd had AIDS.

"It was very awkward," my dad said. "I can still remember the look on the younger guy's face."

When Ken died, I sort of dissolved. I dropped out of school, and went home. Some days were harder than others. At night I would write about him. At times I felt almost out of my mind with grief, but still found myself able to write down every conversation with him that I could remember. I wrote about him for a few months. To my surprise and relief, I could still hear his voice as I wrote. There was a lot to think about and write and remember. It hurt when I realized that I couldn't remember anything more. The memory is finite in the way a person can live on in your mind, but only up until a certain point. In the end, I had a good fifty pages, now lost, of him—everything I could remember. I'd gotten it, too. I'd gotten him down.

ACROTELEUTIUM:     *Voluptatem* mecastor mi imperas.

PALAESTRIO:     . . . now I'll command you in your line of duty.
ACROTELEUTIUM:   You'll command commendably, I'll do my best
                                               to do your will.
PALAESTRIO:   Lightly, brightly, and in spritely fashion — fool the
                                               soldier boy.
   I command it.
ACROTELEUTIUM:           Your command's a *pleasure*.

Perhaps the significant difference is that the courtesans, unlike the
pimps, are never dour people. These women are "in business," to be
sure, but they seldom stress their fees. Whereas the object in Plautus
is to cheat the *leno*, the *meretrix* is always paid — and lavishly. And
even the bitter Phronesium, once finances are no longer the consideration, can turn wholeheartedly to *gaudium* (cf. *Truculentus* 714), a
state of mind impossible for the agelast-*leno*.

27. Cf. Cicero *Phil.* 2.6.15: *Hodie non descendit Antonius. Cur?
Dat nataliciam in hortis. Cui? Neminem nominabo; putate tum Phor-
mioni alicui, tum Gnathoni, tum etiam Ballioni. O foeditatem hominis
flagitiosam, o impudentiam, nequitiam, libidinem non ferendam!*
"Today Antonius will not come down. And why? He's giving a
birthday party in the garden. For whom, you ask? I won't name
names. Perhaps some Phormio, some Gnatho, or even a Ballio! Dis-
gusting and disgraceful man! What insolence, what depravity, what
intolerable hedonism!"
Elsewhere Cicero refers to Ballio, played brilliantly by his good
friend Roscius, as "that foulest, falsehood-fullest pimp," *ille improbis-
simus et periurissimus leno* (*Q. Rosc.* 20).

28. Some critics have been shocked at what they consider a Plautine
breach of decorum, having a pimp invited to the final *cena*; e.g., Lejay
(above, Chap. I n. 71) 146; Norwood (above, Introduction n. 50) 87.

29. In the harsh treatment accorded Plautus' "aliens," it is not
merely a question of foreign citizenship versus national chauvinism,
which might (in an oversimplified way) be offered as an explanation
for the bamboozlement of non-Greeks in Euripidean melodrama (e.g.
victims like Theoklymenos of the *Helen*, Thoas of the *Iphigenia in
Tauris*, and non-Athenian Xuthus in the *Ion*). Actually, in Plautus the
rationale is quite the reverse: the ill-treated "foreigners" suffer for
displaying native Roman character traits — on a Roman holiday.

30. Outsiders are always victimized if they intrude upon a celebration; cf. Fowler (above, Introduction n. 29) 177: "One of the
most frequent customs at harvest-time used to be, and still is in some
places, for the harvesters to mock at, and even to use roughly, any
stranger who appears on the field . . ."

31. Misargyrides is a comic patronymic formed from μισάργυρος, "money-hater." The humor may lie in the fact that the man's attitude is so at odds with his name, or, what seems to me more likely, Plautus may indeed want us to believe that the slave Tranio has himself concocted this appellation as an ironic insult to the greedy *danista*. Cf. line 569: *salvere iubeo te, Misargyrides, bene*, the only time this name is mentioned.

32. *Aulularia* 302–303, discussed in Chap. II, p. 55.

33. *Curculio* 499ff, quoted above, p. 80.

34. We recall the Plautine youth who worships a "pantheon of pleasure" in *Bacchides* 115–116 (discussed above, p. 71). But in considering this comic religion, we must bear in mind that the early Romans worshiped what we might call a "pantheon of profit." They had a god of silver, *Argentinus*, who was the son of a copper-divinity, *Aesculanus*. This adds an important dimension to the fact that Plautine agelasts are mocked for their religious attitude toward money. (Cf. the Plautine divinity *Fortuna lucrifera* [*Persa* 515] discussed immediately below.) And *lucrum*, the very word which evokes such a Pavlovian reaction in Dordalus, is used several times by Plautus himself in the prologue to the *Amphitruo* to entice his Roman audience to silence (lines 2, 6, 12).

35. E.g., *Persa* 668, 713, and elsewhere with slight variations. This technique of comic repetition is also used with the phrase *surge, amator, i domum* in *Asinaria* 921ff. Of course the master of this kind of joke is Molière. One thinks of the repeated "sans dot" in *L'Avare*, "il m'a pris le ———" in *L'Ecole des Femmes*, "les malheureux coups de bâton" in *Scapin*, and naturally, the most famous "et Tartuffe?" Bergson, p. 108, explains the comic effectiveness of this device.

36. Cf. Little (above, n. 15) 208–209: "[Plautus] rejoices in characters which take a beating . . . The laughter which he raises is not thoughtful laughter, but the universal roar which greets a well-known butt."

37. *Casina* 563, quoted above, Chap. II, p. 51.

38. See above, pp. 88ff.

39. *Twelfth Night* V i 367.

40. Chambers (above, n. 16) I, 122 (italics mine).

41. *Ibid.*, pp. 152–153.

42. Cf. the dialogue when Sir Toby inquires about Malvolio's nature (II iii 127ff):

TOBY: Possess us, possess us. Tell us something of him.
MARIA: Marry, sir, sometimes he is a kind of Puritan.
ANDREW: O, if I thought that I'd beat him like a dog.

TOBY: What? For being a Puritan? Thy exquisite reason, dear
knight.
ANDREW: I have no exquisite reason for't, but I have reason good
enough.

43. Plautus may intend some further poetic justice in his use of
the verb *obstringere*, which can also mean "to choke with *debt*."

44. Frye (above, n. 10) 162, 164. Frye's analysis applies only to the
tradition of New Comedy.

45. Duckworth, p. 236.

46. E.g., Periphanes in *Epidicus* 382ff and Philoxenus in *Bacchides*
408ff.

47. See above, p. 74.

48. It may perhaps be suggested that Theopropides in the *Mostellaria* is a *durus pater*, but it should be noted that as soon as he is
reimbursed for the money spent on the girl he states unequivocally
that his son's roistering does not anger him (lines 1163-1164):

. . . neque iam illi sum iratus neque quicquam suscenseo.
immo me praesente amato, bibito, facito quod lubet.

. . . I'm not angry with the boy, nor peeved in any way.
Right before me, let the boy make love, drink up, do what he'd like!

This explicit encouragement to *pergraecari* is exactly the opposite of
the agelast's cry for restraint. To be sure, Theopropides is still angry,
but at Tranio, the clever slave who has made such a fool of him. This
situation will be examined in the next chapter.

49. In this regard Plautus may share Ovid's famous description of
New Comedy (*Tristia* 2.369):

Fabula iucundi nulla est sine amore Menandri.

Never did charming Menander write a play without love.

50. Cf. "The Glorious Military," p. 55: "Far from being an un-
avoidable necessity of the plot . . . the role of the braggart soldier
was a flexible element . . . the very frequency of its appearance must
itself be regarded as the deliberate preference of Plautus, not an
accident of his sources."

51. *Ibid.*, p. 57.

52. On the use in Plautus of the commercial term *arrabo*, see
Williams, "Some Problems . . ." (above, Introduction n. 13) 425ff.

53. Pliny *N.H.* 7.139ff, discussed above in Chap. II, p. 48.

54. Similarly, Lyco the pimp in the *Curculio* is not only tricked
out of the girl but gives away all her jewels and fancy clothes as well
(lines 432ff).

55. Immanuel Kant, *Critique of Judgement*, trans. J. H. Bernard
(2nd ed., London 1914) 223. Paul Goodman, in *The Structure of*

*Literature* (Chicago 1954) 82, speaks of "deflation" as one of the "purest comic actions," citing Jonson's *Alchemist* as the classic example.

56. *Miles* 1420–1421:

CARIO: Ergo des minam auri nobis.
PYRGOPOLYNICES: Quam ob rem?
CAIRO: Salvis testibus
ut te hodie hinc amittamus Venerium nepotulum.

CARIO: All right, give us gold, a hundred *drachmae*.
PYRGOPOLYNICES: Why?
CARIO: To let you go
Without "testifying" — little grandson of the goddess Venus.

57. *Stichus* 669–670. See Chap. I, pp. 34ff.
58. Plutarch's account of Cato expunging a man from the senate roster for kissing his wife in public is mentioned above, p. 11 (*Cato Maior* 17.7).

## IV. From Slavery to Freedom

1. Chambers (above, Chap. III n. 16) I, 125.
2. Bergson, p. 121.
3. Meredith, pp. 14–15.
4. This is discussed in full by Eric Bentley in *Bernard Shaw* (rev. ed., New York 1957) 93–182. *Pygmalion* is, of course, the most famous example, wherein pupil Liza proves herself in the end to be in many ways superior to Professor 'Iggins. Shaw also writes "true comedy" in the Meredithian sense: his females always end up conquering the "stronger sex," and their wit is as swift as their pursuit is relentless; *Man and Superman* is the classic of this genre.
5. Of course Aristophanes "dethrones" Zeus in such comedies as the *Clouds*, the *Birds*, and the *Plutus*, but we do not actually *see* the god humbled. On the nature of such works as Ζεὺς κακούμενος ("Zeus Befouled") by Plato Comicus we can only speculate.
6. Witness the manner in which Mercury-as-servant is treated, by both Jupiter-Amphitryon and the real, terrestrial Amphitryon. When Mercury interrupts the Olympian "husband" as he bids farewell to Alcumena, Jupiter's outburst is in the typical vein of the angry master in Roman comedy (lines 518–520):

IUPPITER: Carnufex, non ego te novi? abin e conspectu meo?
quid tibi hanc curatio est rem, verbero, aut muttitio?
quoii ego iam hoc scipione —
MERCURIUS: Ah noli!

JUPITER: Gallowsbird! Why, don't I know you? Get yourself out
of my sight!
What's all this to you, to care or even mutter, whipping-post?
Why, I'll take this rod of mine — (*threatening him*)
MERCURY (*cringing*): No, please!

And when the real Amphitryon confronts the celestial edition of his
slave, there is the same angry name-calling, the same threats of a
beating (lines 1029–1030):

Verbero, etiam quis ego sim me rogitas, ulmorum Acheruns?
quem pol ego hodie ob istaec dicta faciam ferventem flagris!

Whipping-post! You ask me who I am? Infernal Welt-*anschauung*!
For those words, by Pollux, I'll be warming you with
whopping whips!

7. Jean-Jacques Rousseau, *Oeuvres* (Paris 1821) XI, 44.

8. Cf. *Odyssey* 17.322–323.

9. *Politics* 1.1253b29.

10. Varro *De Re Rustica* 1.17.1.

11. In *The People of Aristophanes* (Cambridge, Mass. 1951), p.
184, Victor Ehrenberg shows that, in general, Greek slaves were well
treated. Cf. also, *inter alios*, Robert Schlaifer, "Greek Theories of
Slavery from Homer to Aristotle," *HSCP* 47 (1936) 181.

12. *Politics* 1253b4.

13. Chambers (above, Chap. III n. 16) I, p. 331. Cf. also the carol
quoted on p. 320: *asinorum dominus / noster est episcopus . . .*

14. The most recent study of slavery in Roman comedy is Peter P.
Spranger's "Historische Untersuchungen zu den Sklavenfiguren des
Plautus and Terenz," *Akademie Mainz. Geistes und Sozialwissenschaftlichen Klasse* 1960 no. 8. Not only does Spranger provide an
excellent review of scholarship on this subject (pp. 7–15), but his
own argument, after judiciously examining both Greek and Roman
elements, concludes that the importance of the slave-role, especially in
Plautus, is not what it may reveal about contemporary social conditions but what it shows of the playwright's fantasy and the *audience's
great fascination* with this character (p. 117).

15. Fowler (above, Introduction n. 29) 272.

16. Martial 11.6.4. Spranger, p. 117, remarks upon the saturnalian
appeal of Plautus' comedy and its "verkehrte Welt," a coincidental
echo of Bergson's *monde renversé*, the quintessential comic situation.

17. It would be of little service to the general thesis of this chapter
to enter into the debate over whether or not Plautus "invented" the
clever slave (as is argued, for example, by A. W. Gomme, "Menander," *Essays in Greek History and Literature* [Oxford 1937] 287).

We must grant the possibility that among the myriad Greek comedies now lost to us there were characters similar to Pseudolus, Tranio, or Epidicus, although there seems to be little, even in the newer fragments, to invalidate Lejay's appraisal (p. 9; see above, Chap. I n. 71): "les esclaves de Plaute sont déjà les Scapins de la comédie moderne. Ceux de Menandre ont leurs défauts, ils ne sont pas fourbes." On the other hand, even though he is arguing "l'originalità di Plauto," Perna (p. 342) discerns traces of the *furbo* among New Comedy slaves, as does Philip Whaley Harsh, "The Intriguing Slave in Greek Comedy," *TAPA* 86 (1955) 142–145.

For the present study we have adopted the moderate — and I believe incontestable — view expressed by Fraenkel in his chap. 8 (pp. 224ff), that Plautus had a predilection for the clever-slave figure and amplified the role wherever he could. More recently, Williams' detailed study of the *Pseudolus* has demonstrated how the Roman playwright has altered the composition of the comedy to effect: "(a) an enlargement of the slave role and its importance and (b) a deep Romanisation of the elements of the plot" ("Some Problems . . . ," p. 423; see above, Introduction n. 13). Spranger's monograph stresses the significant absence of Pseudolus-types in later Greek comedy (see especially p. 116).

18. Fraenkel, p. 136.

19. Leonida, lines 664ff; Libanus, lines 694ff.

20. Fraenkel (p. 37) believes that all the *lazzi* in this scene, especially the piggyback ride, are Plautine additions (*nescio quae mimica?*). As Professor Mary Lefkowitz observes (in a note to her new translation of the *Asinaria*), there may well be bawdy overtones to the *inscende* of line 702. *Inscendere* ("to mount") is used by Apuleius, for example, to mean "begin the sexual act" (*Metamorphoses* 7.21.16, 10.22.3).

21. The master has appealed to his slave's sense of "propriety" once before, when begging Libanus to allow him to carry the money sack: *magis decorumst / libertum potius quam patronum onus in via portare* (lines 689–690, quoted above).

22. Cf. Henri Lévy-Bruhl, "Théorie de l'esclavage," *Revue Générale du Droit et de la Jurisprudence* 55 (1931) 19. And yet in *Mostellaria* 229–230, young Philolaches suggests that he would *sell his father* to keep his sweetheart in luxury.

23. Thus the protestations of young Phaedromus in the *Curculio* (lines 178–180) that he wants neither wealth nor honor nor triumphs in battle resemble Tibullus' lines (1.1.53–55):

> Te bellare decet terra, Messalla, marique
> ut domus hostiles praeferat exuvias:
> me retinent victum formosae vincla puellae.

It is fitting for you, Messalla, to wage war on land and sea, so that your house may display spoils won from the enemy. But I am held captive by the chains of a beautiful girl.

And like the sentiments of Shakespeare's Antony, "let Rome in Tiber melt," as long as he can be in Cleopatra's arms (his Egyptian "bondage" is often emphasized), these may all be noble expressions of love, but they leave a good deal to be desired from a Roman standpoint.

Cf. also the famous monologue of young Philolaches in the *Mostellaria* on what happens to a lad who was a paragon of asceticism: *parsimonia et duritia discipulinae aliis eram* (line 154). When *amor advenit* (line 142) all "Roman" virtues desert: *nunc simul res, fides, fama, virtus, decus / deseruerunt* (lines 144-145), "My wealth, trustworthiness, my manly worth, good reputation have now / Just fled the camp." The damaging effects of romance were perhaps most succinctly summarized by Lucretius (4.1123-1124):

> Labitur interea res et Babylonica fiunt
> languent officia atque aegrotat fama vacillans.

Meanwhile finances start to slide, cash turns into exotic trappings. Obligations languish, and reputations first tremble and then get sick . . .

And Lucretius' subsequent descriptions could well be read as epitomes of New Comedy plots, as young men waste their whole patrimonies (line 1129 *et al.*). Lucretius may not be speaking from a particularly "Roman" point of view, but there is no question that the sober Romans looked askance at overemotional "slaves of love." It is possible, moreover, that Lucretius' description was influenced by Plautus; Lily Ross Taylor in "Lucretius and the Roman Theater" (see above, Chap. I n. 40), p. 23, argues that the poet was a great "theater fan." Cf. *Trinummus* 243: when love comes, *ilico res foras labitur, liquitur*, "all outside affairs decline, dissolve." Also *Trinummus* 259-260:

> Amor amara dat tamen, satis quod aegre sit:
> fugit *forum*, fugitat suos cognatos.

> Love, however, leaves a bitter taste, and lots of pain.
> Lovers flee the forum, even flee their closest relatives!

24. H. J. Rose (above, Introduction n. 28) 170 (italics mine).
25. Cf. also the finale of the *Pseudolus* (lines 1326ff).
26. Dionysus makes a similar offer to Xanthias in Aristophanes' *Frogs* (line 585).
27. See above, p. 108.
28. Gotthold Ephraim Lessing, *Beiträge zur Historie und Auf-*

*nahme des Theaters*, 4, in *Sämtliche Schriften* (3rd ed., Stuttgart 1889) IV, 191.

29. See n. 6 above. Other novel alterations of the familiar *servus-patronus* theme include Mercury's playing the clever slave to further his "master's" love affair: *subparasitabor patri* (*Amphitruo* 515), and the saturnalian scene in which a bondsman (Mercury-as-Sosia) pours water on the head of the *paterfamilias* (see fragmentary dialogue after line 1034). Also, there is Amphitryon bamboozled, *ludificatus* (lines 1041, 1047), which, mutatis mutandis, adds him to the roster of flim-flammed Plautine masters (see my discussion immediately following, pp. 117ff).

30. Chambers (above, Chap. III n. 16) I, 178.

31. *Ibid.*, p. 306. The merry *deposuit* is not to be confused with the *Depositio Crucis*, the enactment of Christ's burial, a feature of the serious liturgical drama of Holy Week. Cf. Chambers, II, 17.

32. Leo brackets line 1100.

33. Fraenkel, p. 226 n. 1.

34. Cf. Jonson's Sir Epicure Mammon dreaming of the prestige that will be his as soon as he receives the philosopher's stone (*The Alchemist* II i 6–8):

> This is the day, wherein, to all my friends,
> I will pronounce the happy word, *be rich*.
> This day, you shall be *spectatissimi*.

35. Fraenkel (p. 69) noted the similarity between the fooling of Hegio in the *Captivi* and the bamboozling of the old man in the *Bacchides*. The prologue to Terence's *Eunuchus* (line 39) indicates that the tricking of an oldster was a very familiar theme on the Roman comic stage.

36. Duckworth, p. 348.

37. Leo (*P.F.²*, p. 199) argues that Plautine elaboration has "elevated" the character of Periphanes. If this be the case, it would indicate a conscious "saturnalian scheme" on the part of the Roman playwright.

38. Leo brackets lines 518–520, in which Periphanes claims, as do other *senes* we have mentioned, that he would rather have lost more money in a less embarrassing manner. Lines 166–168, spoken by Apoecides, may be echoes of Cato on the *lex Oppia* (cf. Livy 34.4), and Periphanes may be, as Duckworth puts it, "a comic Cato" (*T. Macci Plauti Epidicus* [Princeton 1940], p. 212).

39. Cf. *Epidicus* 406ff. Apoecides joyfully tells Periphanes how the two of them have saved the day, by preventing Periphanes' son from buying the music girl. After praising the part which Epidicus has played, Apoecides remarks on how skillfully he himself *played* his role (lines 420–423):

APOECIDES: ego illic me autem sic assimulabam; quasi
stolidum, combardum me faciebam.

PERIPHANES:                         Em istuc decet.

APOECIDES: Res magna amici apud forum agitur, ei volo
ire advocatus.

APOECIDES: And I — I also masqueraded and pretended
As if I was a stupid blockhead —

PERIPHANES:         Hah — well done! (*They both chuckle; then
                       Apoecides changes the subject.*)

APOECIDES: My friend's important lawsuit's on, I'm for the forum
To be the fellow's advocate.

It should be observed that Apoecides exits on a note of self-impor-
tance. After recounting how wise he had been, he makes sure his
friend knows that he has a "big case" to handle in the forum. Periphanes takes up this hint, and boasts, after his "shrewd" comrade
leaves the stage (lines 427–429):

> Ego si allegavissem aliquem ad hoc negotium
> minus hominem doctum minusque ad hanc rem callidum,
> *os sublitum esset . . .*

> If I had deputized another man for this,
> A man less shrewd, less cunning in affairs like this,
> *I would have been bamboozled.*

How painful will be the revelation for these two pillars of the state
after all this (ironic) self-congratulation!

40. See above, pp. 109ff.

41. Following C. H. Buck, *A Chronology of the Plays of Plautus*
(Baltimore 1940) 23. I have not been able to consult the more recent
K. H. E. Schutter, *Quibus annis comoediae Plautinae primum actae
sint quaeritur* (diss., Gröningen 1952), but my argument does not
call for any alteration of the most commonly accepted production
dates.

42. The attitude toward military matters in the prologues is, however, quite a different story. Here there are some "serious" sentiments
expressed about Roman valor and exhortations to fight on valiantly.
E.g., *Rudens* 82:

> Valete, ut hostes vestri diffidant sibi.

> Farewell, may all your foes be stricken full of fear.

and *Casina* 87–88:

> . . . valete, bene rem gerite et vincite
> virtute vera, quod fecistis antidhac.

> . . . Farewell, continue conquering
> With courage quite as true as you have shown so far!

The prologue *Auxilium* in the *Cistellaria* repeats verbatim the words of the *Casina* prologue above (*Cistellaria* 197–198), and then adds a more specific message (lines 201–202):

> Perdite perduelles, parite laudem et lauream
> ut vobis victi Poeni poenas sufferant.

> Oppose our opponents! Prove your mettle, earn your medals!
> And cause the conquered Punics painful punishment.

43. Freud, VIII, p. 108, quoted above, Chap. I n. 13. Commenting on the figure of the soldier in Plautus, Hanson writes ("The Glorious Military," p. 54): "The aspects of real life which he embodies, the military and the glorious, are an important phase of Roman ideology, treated with utmost seriousness by Romans and Roman historians."

44. "The Glorious Military," p. 55, quoted above, Chap. III n. 50.

45. But cf. Reynolds, pp. 37–45, and, more recently, Mattingly, pp. 414–439 (both cited above, Introduction n. 37).

46. Daniel C. Boughner, *The Braggart in Renaissance Comedy* (Minneapolis 1954) 26.

47. Polybius 6.37.

48. Webster (above, Introduction n. 7) 108.

49. "The Glorious Military," p. 61.

50. Perna (p. 199) cites a host of scholars who believe that there were no real braggart soldiers in Rome at this time, only noble ones. Perna concurs that Plautine comedy presents many soldiers because the audience was vitally interested in military matters, adding that Plautus never presents a "philosopher *gloriosus*" (usually a familiar comic type), because there were no real philosophers in contemporary Rome.

51. "Religion in Plautus," p. 52.

52. Traditionally, the *poeta barbarus* mentioned in *Miles* 211 has been taken as an allusion to the imprisonment of Naevius, a view which has recently been questioned by Mattingly (see above, Introduction n. 37).

53. An argument might be adduced that the characterization of the *miles gloriosus* contains subtle allusions to the most famous Roman general of the day, Marcus Claudius Marcellus. The renowned capturer of Syracuse might well have been referred to as *urbicape* (cf. *Miles* 1055), and the very name Pyrgopolynices might be construed as a comic variation of this epithet. Moreover, the *miles* is also called *occisor regum* (line 1055), and this, along with the braggart's supposed conquest of a man in golden armor (line 16) might be interpreted

# I SEARCH FOR THE NAMES
Babo Kamel

of the little boy
who stared at us, rubble dust and blood
painting his face

of the child
washed up on shore like ocean debris
his sneakers still laced

of the Nigerian school girl
who will never return
to herself


Yesterday was National AIDS Day
and I remember the quilt of names

travelling the country, small stitches
around the squares threading the losses.

Stanley and Terrence and probably Clark
one day getting their own.

One night in 1976, after Terrence's dance performance
he, Clark and I tramped through the snow over the mountain

as a reference to Marcellus' momentous achievement, winning the *spolia opima*, when he personally slew the Gallic king Viridomarus in 222 B.C. Actually, Marcellus was killed in 208 B.C., probably a few years before Plautus wrote the *Miles*, and would hardly have been a name suitable for satire under any circumstances. I do not take my own hypothesis very seriously, but the reader may decide whether or not the "topical possibilities" of the *miles* enhance the comedy of the play.

54. Examples of the *miles* asking for advice include lines 973, 978, 1094–1095. Also note the soldier's reaction after Palaestrio has once again outlined "the best plan" (lines 1120–1123):

PYRGOPOLYNICES: Itan tu censes?

PALAESTRIO:                    Quid ego ni ita censeam?

PYRGOPOLYNICES: Ibo igitur intro . . .

PALAESTRIO:  Tu modo istuc cura quod agis.

PYRGOPOLYNICES:                    Curatum id quidemst.

PYRGOPOLYNICES:  You think so?

PALAESTRIO:                    Would I tell you what I didn't think?

PYRGOPOLYNICES:  I'll go inside then . . .

PALAESTRIO:  Just do your own part well.

PYRGOPOLYNICES (*trotting off*):                    Consider it as done!

55. Palaestrio has also succeeded in putting his own words into the soldier's mouth. Three times the slave "instructs" his master on how best to get rid of the girl Philocomasium, lines 980–982, 1099–1100, and 1126–1127. Finally, in lines 1203–1205, the soldier parrots his slave's advice as if it were his own idea.

Much the same "saturnalian" phenomenon occurs in *Othello*, albeit on a far more sinister level. As Iago's control of his military master increases, the Moor begins to talk like his crafty subordinate. E.g., when Iago tortures Othello with animal images of his wife's supposed infidelity, "were they as prime as goats, as hot as monkeys . . ." (III iii 403), his description so overcomes the Moor that later, in greeting Lodovico, he suddenly blurts out, "Goats and monkeys!" (IV i 256).

56. Pyrgopolynices is not clever enough to be capable of a conscious pun. This observation is also made by Ernout, vol. IV, p. 240 n. 5.

57. Leffingwell (above, Chap. I n. 5), p. 83, lists the *pedisequus* as belonging to the lowest rank of household slaves.

58. The old man's *nequiquam* . . . in reference to the soldier recalls the comments made concerning other lofty characters who end up groveling — to no avail. See above, p. 108.

59. Cf. Periplectomenus' entering remark when Palaestrio calls him and Pleusicles onstage: *Ecce nos tibi oboedientes* (line 611). Young Pleusicles is too dumb — or too much in love — to have any opinion

whatsoever: *quodne vobis placeat, displiceat mihi?* (line 614), "What could be fine with you and not with me?"

60. Cf. K. M. Westaway, *The Original Element in Plautus* (Cambridge 1917) 30: "There is no role which the intriguing slaves love more to adopt in the prosecution of their schemes than that of a renowned and particularly successful general . . . This seems to have been a particularly Roman trait . . . Plautus amplified it."

61. Fraenkel, p. 228, using Livy 41.28.8 for comparison. He also finds similar echoes in *Persa* 754, *Stichus* 402, and *Trinummus* 1182. The relation of Plautine slaves' "triumphal" language and contemporary Roman triumphs is also discussed by Perna, p. 187, and Hanson, "The Glorious Military," pp. 57ff.

62. A great number of the tragedies of the early Republic dealt with matters from the Trojan cycle. Cf. W. Beare, *The Roman Stage* (2nd ed., London 1955) 63. Aeschylus was said to have considered his plays "slices from Homer's banquet," and, if Cicero's observation in *De Finibus* 1.7 is reliable, this was also the case with the great Ennius: *ut ab Homero Ennius, Afranius a Menandro solet* [scil. *locos transferre*]. And, of course, Livius Andronicus' *Odyssey* was the first piece of "Roman literature." Fraenkel (pp. 85–86) argues that the Trojan myths were known at Rome well before Livius Andronicus because of their frequent representation in works of art.

63. See Fraenkel, p. 61 and *passim*, on the "Plautinity" of the passages which compare the assault on a *senex* to an attack on a city (especially Troy).

64. Grimal (above, Chap. I n. 54) 82.

65. *Miles* 814–815:

> Eripiam ego hodie concubinam militi
> si centuriati bene sunt maniplares mei.

> Today I'll snatch the concubine back from the soldier,
> That is, if all my troops are well-centurioned.

66. To cite a few examples: Trachalio (*Rudens* 1266 and 1280), Leonida and Libanus (*Asinaria* 652 and 689), Olympio (*Casina* 739), and Toxilus (*Persa* 842) are all addressed as *patronus*, while Trachalio (*Rudens* 1266) and Olympio (*Casina* 739) are called *pater* as well.

67. Discussing various Florentine "saturnalian" festivals of the *trecento*, Toschi notes that the holiday leaders were all given exalted titles like *gran monarca, principe, re, imperatore,* and so forth (p. 94; see above, Introduction n. 25). These are not unlike the titles assumed by the various Plautine Lords of Misrule.

68. Pinacium, the running slave in the *Stichus*, feels strong enough to scorn royal state, and would knock over any king standing in his way: *si rex obstabit obviam, regem ipsum prius pervortito!* (line 287).

But, to achieve kingly status, the true Plautine slave needs swiftness of wit, not of foot.

69. Some scholars of Greek New Comedy consider the mere presence of the word βασιλεύς to be an allusion to Alexander the Great. E.g., J. M. Edmonds, commenting on Philemon frag. 31, *The Fragments of Attic Comedy* (Leiden 1957) III 18. Fraenkel (p. 184), noting that there seems to be no trace in Greek comedy of a large usage of the adjective and adverb derived from this word, suggests that *basilicus* and *basilice* are Plautine coinages (p. 186). Perna (p. 235) makes a similar observation. More recently, Chalmers (p. 41; above, Introduction n. 11) has proposed that the Roman soldiers learned these words in monarchical Sicily.

70. To what extent Greek New Comedy contained references to Homeric and Hellenistic heroes will continue to be a subject of debate. Fraenkel, of course (pp. 55ff), believes that this kind of name-dropping was a central feature of the Plautine elaboration, especially since it is the "Plautine" clever slave who usually makes the boastful comparisons.

71. Lily Ross Taylor, *The Divinity of the Roman Emperor* (Middletown, Conn. 1931) 44 (italics mine).

72. Beaumarchais, *Le Barbier de Seville* I v. We may cite an outburst of this nature by Chaerea, the young master in Terence's *Eunuchus* (lines 1034–1035):

> O Parmeno mi, o mearum voluptatum omnium
> inventor inceptor perfector, scis me in quibus sim gaudiis?

> O Parmeno, of all my joys the
> Finder, Founder, Fosterer — can you imagine how I feel?

But it should also be borne in mind that Parmeno himself does not perform any "heroic" deed to justify this rhapsody.

73. Contrast with Epidicus in despair, lines 610ff, moaning that even Jupiter and the other eleven gods couldn't save him. Evidently, the slave gets "divine reinforcements" which result in his tremendous victory.

74. Compare with *Curculio* 439ff, where a similar claim is made for a "triumphal" braggart soldier. On the Roman significance of this passage, see "The Glorious Military," p. 56.

75. See above, p. 108.

76. *Odyssey* 10; *Aeneid* 1.

77. Beaumarchais, *Le Barbier de Seville* II i.

78. I have deliberately rendered *renverser* as "turn topsy-turvy" to recall not only Bergson's theory of the comic situation being *monde renversé*, but also Rousseau's accusation that Molière "renverse tous les rapports les plus sacrés . . ." (see above, p. 101).

79. Jonson, *Volpone* III i 7–9.
80. Molière, *Les Fourberies de Scapin* I ii.
81. Cf. Livy 5.48.8–9.

## V. From Freedom to Slavery

1. E.g., *Miles* 494, *Pseudolus* 446, *Rudens* 1098. There are innumerable variations on this derogatory epithet, such as old Apoecides' appraisal of Epidicus as *mancipium scelestum* (line 685), "an evil piece of property."

2. Cf. Chap. I n. 70.

3. For an example of the (occasional) threats hurled at slaves in Terence, we may take *Eunuchus* 1021–1022, where Parmeno is menaced with a hanging-up punishment (*tu iam pendebis*) for having led a youth astray.

4. In the opening repartee of the *Epidicus*, the rascally slave Thesprio remarks that he has been flourishing, thanks to his left hand's ability to steal. Epidicus expresses amazement that his friend's hand has not already been cut off for his thieving: *quam quidem te iam diu / perdidisse oportuit* (line 11A).

5. Plutarch *Cato Maior* 25.

6. Petronius *Satyricon* 53. To emphasize the heartless attitude taken toward slaves, the author depicts an *actuarius* in the employ of Trimalchio reading off a long list of what has happened on the great man's estates. The crucifixion of the slave is mentioned en passant, among other "trivialities."

7. Juvenal *Sat.* 6.219–224. When the husband inquires of his wife what offense has caused her to order the slave to the cross, she replies that she has no reason, but, after all, a slave is not really human: *ita servus homo est?* (line 222). In lines 475ff of the same satire, Juvenal describes a wife who goes calmly about her business while the household slaves are being beaten up.

8. *Catenae singulariae* (*Captivi* 112); *pix atra* (*Captivi* 597); *columbar* (*Rudens* 888); *carnarium* (*Pseudolus* 198); *patibulum* (*Miles* 360, *Mostellaria* 56); *pistrinum* (*Bacchides* 781, *Pseudolus* 534, *et al.*).

9. E.g., *furcifer* (*Captivi* 563 and 577); *mastigia* (*Captivi* 600 and 659); *verbero* (*Captivi* 551). However, there is a great irony here, since these epithets are hurled at Tyndarus, a man known by the audience to be no slave at all.

10. In discussing the references to whippings in Aristophanes, Ehrenberg (above, Chap. IV n. 11), p. 187, cites a word coined by an unknown comic poet to describe a slave put into stocks and whipped: κλῳομάστιξ from κλοιός, wooden collar. Ehrenberg suggests that the various threats were exaggerated for comic effect, which is probably

true for Plautus as well. μαστιγία is an epithet hurled frequently at
slaves in Menander, and, understandably, it is favored by Terence.
On threats in the latter author, see Duckworth, p. 334. There are some
rather "Plautine" references to punishment in Naevius, for example
numbers 15 and 16 of the unassigned comic fragments:

Tantum ibi molae crepitum faciebant, tintinnabant compedes.
Utrum scapulae plus an collus calli habeat nescio.

Great the crunch of millstones there, the chains were jangling too.
I don't know if shoulder blades or collarbones have tougher skins.

11. These passages are frequently cited to prove that the Roman
actors were themselves slaves — and, in fact, that Plautus was one
himself. See below, n. 33.
12. Theodore Mommsen, *Römische Geschichte* (12th ed., Berlin
1920) I, 900.
13. Aristotle *Poetics* 1453.
14. *Volpone* V iii 124. Jonson was criticized for the harsh ending
and replied with a long epistle which he added as preface to the
printed version. His argument reflects the "moralistic" attitude toward
the uses of comedy (*Preface* lines 109–122): ". . . though my *catastrophe* may, in the strict rigour of *comick* law, meet with censure . . .
I desire the learned and charitable critick to have so much faith in me,
to thinke it was done off industrie . . . my speciall ayme being to put
the snaffle in their mouths, that crie out we never punish vice in our
*enterludes*, etc. I tooke the more liberty; though not without some
lines of example, drawne even in the ancients themselves, the goings
out of whose *comoedies* are not alwaies ioyfull, but oft-times, the
bawdes, the servants, the rivals, yea, and the masters are mulcted: and
fitly, it being the office of a *comick-Poet* to imitate iustice, and instruct
to life . . ."
15. Duckworth, p. 290. See also pp. 253 and 288. Spranger, p. 58,
suggests that the insouciant attitude of the Plautine slave may reflect
the actual circumstances of Hellenistic Greece, where there was an
"ungezwungen menschlicher Verkehr von Herren und Sklaven."
16. E.g., Phaniscus in *Mostellaria* 859–884; Harpax, *Pseudolus* 1103–
1122. The *canticum* is generally accepted by scholars as indicating
that Plautus has chosen to emphasize the particular matter he has
transformed into song (and probably elaborated) from the Greek
original.
17. Molière, *Les Fourberies de Scapin* I i.
18. *Ibid.*, III ii.
19. Legrand, p. 110.
20. In n. 3 above, we cited as a Terentian "slave-threatening" scene
*Eunuchus* 1021ff. Here the bondsman Parmeno is menaced with dire

punishment that will serve as a deterrent to potential malefactors. *In te exempla edent* (line 1022), says Pythias to Parmeno, referring to the imminent revenge both his masters will take on him. To this Parmeno replies with an anguished groan (line 10), *nullus sum* (cf. Geta's fear of punishment in *Phormio* 248ff, discussed above, p. 151). In contrast to this fearful attitude in Terence, we have such Plautine instances as the finale to the *Mostellaria*, where the master also threatens to "make an example" of the slave Tranio (line 1116). Unlike Terence's Parmeno, the impertinent Tranio retorts to the threat of "exemplary punishment" with cheeky defiance. Cf. *Mostellaria* 1147: "By Hercules, I'm glad I did it!" This scene is discussed below, pp. 157ff. On further differences between Plautine and Terentian slaves, see Spranger, pp. 91ff.

21. Legrand, p. 455.
22. *Ibid.*, p. 240.
23. Frye (above, Chap. III n. 10) 164.
24. John Gay, *The Beggar's Opera* III xvii.
25. Leo is one of the few editors who bracket line 547.
26. Lucretius *De Rerum Natura* 2.4.
27. *Asinaria* 558–559:

Edepol virtutes qui tuas non possïs conclaudare
sic ut ego possim, quae domi duellique male fecisti.

Pollux! *Noble* deeds of yours you couldn't vaunt too well, and yet
I could cite your negative achievements, at home and in the field.

Earl comments on the Roman significance of Plautus' use of the term *virtus*, "Political Terminology . . . ," pp. 239, 242, and *passim* (see above, Introduction n. 13).

28. *Persa* 21–22:

Plusculum annum
fui praeferratus apud molas tribunus vapularis.

29. Also Lurcio in the same play: *fugiam hercle aliquo . . .* (*Miles* 861).

30. See Chap. IV, p. 122.

31. Chrysalus' name is derived from χρυσός, gold, a fact which he enjoys bringing to the attention of the audience; for example, *quid mihi refert Chrysalo esse nomen nisi factis probo?* (*Bacchides* 704), "What good to have a golden name unless my feats are golden too?"

32. To give the art of Terence its proper respect: Geta's speech closely parallels one by his master which comes immediately before, in which old Demipho muses philosophically on the pains which may await a father who returns home after a long journey (cf. especially *Phormio* 242–246, on which much of Geta's phraseology is patterned). This scene has an admirable ironic texture and is, in the Terentian

genre, excellent theater. Actually, Phormio himself expresses a kind of *non curo* attitude toward potential punishment. But here again in Terence we find significant contrasts with Plautus: Phormio, the *homo confidens*, is not a slave at all. Still more important, the penalty he risks is legal, not physical. Cf. line 133:

> Pater aderit, mihi paratae lites: quid mea?

> Your father, when he comes, will sue. What's that to me?

And Phormio is an absolutely unbeatable legal adversary; he is too poor to be fined (cf. lines 326ff).

33. Very possibly the plays of Plautus, like those of Marlowe ("that atheist Tamburlaine") have misled later generations into drawing deductions about the character of the author himself. Plautus does in fact seem to be "speaking" through some of his clever slaves, most notably Pseudolus, who claims to be working out his plot "just like a playwright" (line 401). In this comedy there are innumerable threats of being sent *in pistrinum* (e.g., lines 494, 499, 500, 534, 1060). Pseudolus even offers to go there forever if his scheme fails (lines 533–535):

> SIMO:  Sed si non faxis, numquid causaest ilico
> quin te in pistrinum condam?
> PSEUDOLUS:                Non unum in diem,
> verum hercle in omnis, quantumst.

> SIMO:  If you don't pull it off, can you give one excuse
> Why not to slap you at the mills?
> PSEUDOLUS:                Not for a day,
> Why, slap me there forevermore.

Varro's life of Plautus (preserved by Gellius *N.A.* 3.3.14) indicates that the playwright spent some time *in pistrino* and even wrote three comedies there. Later, when his first theatrical earnings were lost in a business venture, Plautus (says Varro) found himself in the mills once again. But in light of the many references to the mills in his plays, it is not unlikely that this story contains more of the histrionic than the historical.

34. P. S. Dunkin, *Post-Aristophanic Comedy: Studies in the Social Outlook of Middle and New Comedy at Both Athens and Rome* (Urbana 1946) [Illinois Studies in Language and Literature 31, nos. 3–4] 86.

35. *Ibid.*, p. 104. It was not surprising to discover that this view has been expressed in recent years by Russian and Polish scholars. Plautus as social(ist) critic is the argument of Oktawiusz Jurewicz in "Plautus, Cato der Aeltere und die römische Gesellschaft," *Aus der*

*altertumwissenschaftlichen Arbeit Volkspolens,* ed. J. Irmscher and K. Kumaniecki (Berlin 1959), pp. 48ff. Jurewicz' book (in Polish), *Niewolnicy w komediach Plauta* (Warsaw 1959), according to Spranger's description (pp. 13ff), presents Plautus at war with the aristocracy, a champion of the oppressed lower class.

36. Bernard Knox, *"The Tempest* and the Ancient Comic Tradition," *English Institute Essays, 1954* (New York 1955) 59.

37. The youth has already transferred his authority to his slave earlier in the play (*Poenulus* 145–146).

38. On saturnalian language in the *Captivi,* see my discussion in Chap. IV, p. 120.

39. When Tyndarus reenters in chains, he complains that life in the quarries is worse than hell (lines 998ff). But we have no knowledge of precisely what he has suffered.

40. In the fragments of Menander's *Perinthia* (393 Kock), there is a scene which is strikingly similar to the assault and "smoking out" of Tranio. This must have been a stock situation on the Greek (and ·Roman?) comic stage, since old Simo in the *Pseudolus* (line 1240) protests that he will not prepare against his bondsman the kind of ambush seen "in other comedies."·

41. Molière, *Les Fourberies de Scapin* III xii. And, like Theopropides (*Mostellaria* 1116), Géronte is anxious to punish the disobedient servant as an example to others: "je prétends faire de lui une vengeance exemplaire" (III vi).

42. *Les Fourberies de Scapin* III xiii.

43. There is, of course, the suggestion of escape or evasion in Scapin's very name, which is related to the Italian *scappare.* This is not unlike Plautine slave *redende Namen* like Palaestrio ("slippery-wrestler"), Pseudolus ("sneaky-tricky"), which also imply "getting away with it." And Spranger (pp. 54, 112) emphasizes that Plautus' bondsmen never bear the slave-names typical of early republican Rome. See also Chap. I n. 82.

44. The altar to which Tranio flees was probably used for ceremonial purposes just prior to the performance of the play. See Lily Ross Taylor (above, Chap. I n. 40) 151.

45. Perna (p. 428 n. 1) regards the ready forgiveness of mischievous slaves as an aspect of "l'originalità di Plauto."

46. Legrand, p. 455.

47. Chambers (above, Chap. III n. 16) I 122. See above, Chap. III, p. 40.

48. Frye (above, Chap. III n. 9) 61.

49. Cicero *Paradoxa Stoicorum* 5. The notion is not new, and the fact that it is essentially a "comic" paradox may explain why we find a very similar sentiment in Menander (frag. 769 Kock):

ἅπαντα δοῦλα τοῦ φρονεῖν καθίσταται.

All things are slaves to intelligence.

50. In *Sat.* 2.7, Horace is lectured by his bondsman Davus on the subject *quisnam igitur liber?* "who, after all, is free?" (line 83). Davus' tone is at first ironic; he is afraid to speak his mind: *cupiens tibi dicere servus / pauca reformido.* This attitude is reminiscent of Epidicus' mock-humble words to the two *senes: si aequom siet / me plus sapere quam vos* . . . (lines 257–258). But the dialogue is set during the Saturnalia and so Davus can take advantage of the *libertas Decembris* to speak out (line 4).

The longer he talks, the more Davus assumes a pose *velut melior* (line 41) and angers Horace by concluding that he, Davus, is wiser (and freer) than his master (line 42). Although Horace wishes to strike his slave for this impudence (line 44) he is forbidden to do so by the rules of the holiday. The slave is immune for the moment, although he is addressed as *furcifer* (line 22) and refers to previous (i.e., non-holiday) whippings: *tergo plector enim* (line 105).

Finally, Horace's ire is so aroused that he threatens to send Davus to hard labor in the country, much the way Grumio threatens Tranio in *Mostellaria* 17. Horace's satire had a direct influence on Persius *Sat.* 5, which takes up the same (Stoic) question of "who is really free?" concluding, of course, that a man must not be a slave to passions like *Avaritia* and *Luxuria.* Persius' moral is Horatian (lines 151–153):

Indulge genio, carpamus dulcia, nostrum est
quod vivis, cinis et manes et fabula fies.
vive memor leti, fugit hora . . .

Go open up your spirit. Now, let's pluck the sweet things. All you have is life, you'll soon be dust and shades, and simply bygones. Live aware of death, for time flees on . . .

51. Herodotus (1.60) writes that Greeks have always been distinguished from barbarians by their σοφία, the Athenians being the shrewdest of all Greeks.

52. In his recent study, *Aristophanes and the Comic Hero* (Cambridge, Mass. 1964) 30, Cedric H. Whitman has pointed out that the Aristophanic protagonist is distinguished by the quality of *poneria*, "an unscrupulous, but throughly enjoyable exercise of craft." Surely its precise equivalent in Plautine comedy is the *malitia* displayed by Epidicus and other clever slaves. As Mercury says in the *Amphitruo* (lines 268–269), *malitia* is the essential weapon (*telum suum*) of the crafty comic slave.

53. See my discussion of the Epidicus "supplication scene" in Chap. IV, pp. 109ff.

54. Similarly, the slave Strobilus in the *Aulularia* has the good fortune to overhear Euclio the miser reveal where he will hide his treasure (lines 608ff). With the gold in hand, Strobilus confronts his master Lyconides and demands manumission (line 823). It is at this point that the text of the *Aulularia* breaks off, but it is safe to assume, using the analogy of Gripus (and to some extent Messenio) that Strobilus was freed in the end. But even so, he belongs to the "dumb and loyal" category, for when he first enters he delivers a monologue similar to that of Messenio in the *Menaechmi* on being a good slave and *avoiding* ill-treatment (lines 597ff, esp. lines 601–602).

55. Cf. *Love's Labour's Lost* IV i 76. Marriage in a Plautine finale, unlike most comic traditions, does not constitute a happy ending, but quite the contrary, as may be seen in the *Trinummus*, where the prodigal son is forgiven by his father since the boy has agreed to get married and "that is punishment enough for one man" (line 1185). With a bit of wry (Plautine) cynicism, we might include marriage as one of the few "punishments" in Plautus that *are* inflicted. Walter Kerr has recently made some interesting observations about the conventional comic marriage-finale, *Tragedy and Comedy* (New York 1967) 57ff.

56. Livy 8.21.

57. Elisaveta Fen (trans.), *Chekhov's Plays* (London 1959) 365.

58. Huizinga (see above, Chap. II n. 2) 9 and 13.

59. C. L. Barber, "Saturnalia in the *Henriad*," *English Institute Essays, 1954* (New York 1955) 189.

60. *The Tempest* IV i 148–150. Once again at the very end of *The Tempest*, Prospero will step forward *as actor* to insist that he really does not possess the magic powers of the character he portrayed, so he needs the applause of the Elizabethan audience if he is to prosper in real life (*Epilogue* 1–10):

> Now my charms are all o'erthrown,
> And what strength I have's mine own,
> Which is most faint. Now 'tis true
> I must be here confin'd by you . . .
>
> .  .  .  .  .  .  .  .
>
> But release me from my bands
> With the help of your good hands.

61. The epilogue to the *Cistellaria* is most often quoted to prove that the actors in Roman comedy were slaves (e.g., Beare [above, Chap. IV n. 62] 157). If this indeed was the case, there would have been an extra saturnalian satisfaction for them to be playing generals, senators, and, in such plays as *Amphitruo*, even gods. But I have quoted these lines merely to show that the general social situation is

to their little basement apartment on Pine Avenue.
(When you looked through their window in daylight
all you could see were anonymous hurrying legs.)
We listened to Bowie, drank hot chocolate
and I fell asleep between them, wearing Terrence's pajamas.

———•·•·•———

Fingers trace the words on the black granite wall
as if somehow, we could reach the dead
who learned to walk as we have done, who learned

the shape of language one guttural at a time
who first wrote their name on a plain piece of paper
the pencil thick, in a small closed fist

returning to normal. Most literally interpreted, the *negotium* in line 783 refers merely to theatrical matters. I do not argue that Plautus himself was conscious of the special "holiday-everyday" significance which I have attributed to these remarks, but they are nonetheless significant for our own understanding of the relation of Roman comedy to Roman life.

62. Once again we must cite the view of Earl ("Political Terminology . . . ," p. 237; see above, Introduction n. 13), who is certain that when Plautus mentions *mos maiorum* it is a deliberate and conscious allusion to the Roman ideal.

## Why Plautus Chose *Amphitruo*

1. See Elisabeth Frenzel, *Stoffe der Weltliteratur* (5th ed. rev., Stuttgart 1981) 43ff. See also, E. Lefèvre, *Maccus vortit barbare: vom tragischen Amphitryon zum tragikomischen Amphitruo*, Akademie der Wissenschaften und der Literatur, Abhandlungen der Geistes- und Sozialwissenschaftlichen Klasse, Jahrgang 1982, No. 5 (Wiesbaden, 1982); and Udo Reinhardt, "Amphitryon and Amphitruo," in *Musa iocosa: Festschrift Andreas Thierfelder*, (Hildesheim and New York 1984) 95ff.

2. Cf. Pauly-Wissowa 1.2.1967ff. For a more recent catalogue see L. R. Shero, "Alcmena and the *Amphitryon* in Ancient and Modern Drama," *TAPA* 87 (1956) 194ff. The latest view put forth is that of H. Tränkle, which suggests a multitude of sources, including Egyptian legend, Euripides, New Comedy, etc., in *MH* 40 (1983) 217–238.

3. Cf. E. Segal, "The φυσις of Comedy," *HSCP* 77 (1973) 129ff. and the recent discussion of R. L. Hunter, ed., *Eubulus* (Cambridge 1983) 4–6.

4. On the phlyax see Shero (above, n. 1) 202; Louis Séchan, *Études sur la tragédie grecque dans ses rapports avec la céramique* (Paris 1926) 48, 241ff; Margarete Bieber, *The History of the Greek and Roman Theater* (Princeton 1961) 132, 151; A. D. Trendall in *BICS*, Supplement 19 (1967) 9ff.

5. S. Freud, *Der Witz und seine Beziehung zum Unbewussten* (Leipzig and Vienna 1905) III:3. For a useful collection of opinions on matrimony and antiquity, see K. Gaiser, *Für und wider die Ehe* (Munich 1974).

6. Cf. *Clouds* 1079–1082.

7. Cf. H. Janne, "L'Amphitryon de Plaute et M. Fulvius Nobilior," *Revue belge de philologie et d'histoire* 12 (1983) 515ff; C. H. Buck, Jr., *A Chronology of the Plays of Plautus* (Baltimore 1940) 25ff; L. Hermann, "L'Actualité dans l'Amphitryon de Plaute," *L'Antiquité classique* 17 (1948) 322; W. B. Sedgwick and C. H. Buck, "Plautine Chronology," *AJP* 70 (1949) 382; F. Della Corte, *Da Sarsina a Roma*

(Genova 1952) 69. Professor Handley concurs in his essay "Plautus and His Public: Some Thoughts on New Comedy in Latin," in *Dioniso* 46 (1975) 117–132.

8. Della Corte (above, n. 7) 259.

9. Zeph Stewart, "The *Amphitruo* of Plautus and Euripides' *Bacchae*," *TAPA* 89 (1958) 364ff.

10. A corroborating example of the contemporary Roman mania for lucre may be found, *inter alia*, in the *laudatio* of Quintus Metellus on his father, cited by Pliny *NH* 7.139ff, and Polybius 31.26.9. In truth, the single thing that could attract the Romans more than sex was money. (For proof of this we need merely adduce the career of Cato the Elder.)

11. Lefèvre (above, n. 1) 25ff, has an interesting discussion of this term, including some consideration as to whether it was in Plautus' Greek model. With Plautus' portrayal of Mercury in the prologue, contrast the Aristophanic Hermes at *Plutus* 1152ff.

12. In "Signification théâtrale du double dans *l'Amphitryon* de Plaute," *REL* 54 (1976) 129–141, F. Dupont describes this play as "une comédie sur la comédie," anticipating the argument developed at length by N. W. Slater that the essence of all Plautine comedy is itself self-conscious metatheatricality (*Plautus in Performance* [Princeton 1985].)

13. Cf. *usura* employed in the mercantile sense by Cicero in *Verr.* 2.3.72.168; *Att.* 9.12.3 and 12.22.3.

14. "Deux visages semblables, dont aucun ne fait rire en particulier, font rire ensemble par leur ressemblance" (*Pensées* 50). On this type of comedy, see H. Levin "Two Comedies of Errors," in *Refractions: Essays in Comparative Literature*, (London, Oxford and New York 1966) 128ff.

15. A point emphasized also by Stewart (above, n. 9) 356 n. 24. Structurally, as E. W. Handley reminds me, the second prologue can be compared to Eur. *H.F.* 821ff and to the dialogue scene at Ar. *Frogs* 738ff.

16. Elsewhere in Plautus we find *surripio* with an overtone of amorous clandestinity, for example *Asinaria*, lines 929ff, *Menaechmi*, lines 200, 394, 510, 1128.

17. Contrast Lucretius 4.1116 *parva fit ardoris violenti pausa parumper*, "for a little while, there is a brief respite from the searing flame."

18. "Religion in Plautus," pp 48ff. According to C. D. N. Costa, "Alcmena is one of Plautus' greatest, if least characteristic creations." ("The Amphitruo Theme," in *Roman Drama*, ed. T. A. Dorey and Donald R. Dudley (New York 1965) 93). In contrast, L. Perelli considers that the characterization includes farcical elements: see "L'Alcmena plautina, personaggio serio o parodico?" *Civiltà classica e cristiana* 4 (1983) 383–394.

19. In this context there is also a sexual undertone to the *dedisse* as

we can see quite clearly in Ovid *Amores* 1.4 when the poet begs his mistress not to succumb to her husband's advances, or at least

> Sed quaecumque tamen noctem fortuna sequetur
> cras mihi constanti voce *dedisse nega!*
>
> (lines 69–70)

> And yet, whatever chances to happen this night, tomorrow —
> in unshaking tones, deny you gave him anything!

20. In fact, the verb *accumbere* occurs several times in Plautus' "twin comedy" to demonstrate the sensuality that is the trademark of the *meretrix* Erotium.

21.

> Non ego illam mi dotem duco esse quae dos dicitur
> sed pudicitiam et pudorem et sedatum cupidinem,
> deum metum, parentum amorem et cognatum concordiam,
> tibi morigera atque ut munifica sim bonis, prosim probis.
>
> (lines 839–842)

> I regard a "dowry" to be other than what most believe:
> Chastity and honor and a passion that is moderate,
> Fear of gods and love for parents, peace with all one's relatives,
> Being a compliant wife that always helps you faithfully.

In his important article, "Some Aspects of Roman Marriage Ceremonies and Ideals" *JRS* 48 (1958), Gordon Williams comments on these verses (p. 19): "The language is solemn and tragic, and reviews the whole life of a married woman, defining the proper behavior to be expected of such a woman in each sphere of relationship: she finds expression for the ideally dutiful relationship with her husband in the word *morigera*."

All throughout the *Amphitruo*, Plautus plays ironically with this matrimonial ideal. For example, when Mercury describes what is going on in the house: "Pater nunc intus suo animo morem gerit" (line 131), "Father is inside complying — to his own desires." And later Jupiter himself announces:

> volo deludi illunc, dum cum hac usuraria
> uxore nunc *mi morigero.*
>
> (lines 980–981)

> Compliant to my own desire, trick the man —
> While I take more interest in his wife's "account."

In this comedy we see not only the deception of a wife and the derision of a husband but indeed a veritable topsy-turvydom of the values of an entire people. One thinks of the Horatian phrase *dos est magna parentium virtus* (*Odes* III.24.21).

22. And later Alcmena pronounces — but to Jupiter in disguise — the legal formula for a divorce (*repudium*): *"tibi habeas res tuas, reddas meas"* (line 928). Cf. the *XII Tabulae* 4.3 = E. H. Warmington, *Remains of Old Latin* (London 1938) 3:442–443; also Cicero *Phil.* 2.28.

23. It is worth citing the moralizing conclusion of Geoffrey Chaucer:

> Grisilde is deed, and eek hire pacience,
> And both atones buryed in Ytaille;
> For which I crie in open audience,
> No wedded man so hardy be t'assaille
> His wyves pacience in trust to fynde
> Grisildis, for in certein he shal faille.

(*The Clerk's Tale*, lines 1077–1082)

24. Cf. *inter alios* Hesiod *Scutum* 1–56; Apollodorus 2.4.7–8; Hyginus *Fabula* 28; Tzetzes *Lycophron* 33, 932. Not to mention Pindar *Isthmia* 7.5.

25. E. Fantham offers some interesting observations on this fragmented portion in "Towards a Dramatic Reconstruction of the Fourth Act of Plautus' Amphitruo," *Philologus* 117 (1973) 197–214.

26. Lefèvre (above, n. 1, p. 37) argues that the finale of the play is "eine echte 'Tragödie.' "

27. To the Roman ear, *bonum would* inevitably have the double connotation of "earthly goods, blessing" and — "morally correct."

28. Albert Grenier, *Les Religions étrusque et romaine* (Paris 1948) 141ff, H. Janne (above, n. 7) 531; L. Hermann (above, n. 7) 321–322.

29. Kurt Latte, *Römische Religionsgeschichte* (Munich 1960) 264–265.

30. Jean Bayet, *Histoire politique et psychologique de la religion romaine* (Paris 1957) 156–157.

31. Grenier (above, n. 28) 147. See also Cyril Bailey, "Roman Religion and the Advent of Philosophy," *Cambridge Ancient History* 8: 428ff, esp. p. 454.

32. W. Warde Fowler, *The Religious Experience of the Roman People* (London 1911) 351. On the influence of Ennius on Roman culture, see also Grenier (above, n. 28) 160ff and Latte (above, n. 29) 265–266.

33. Mercury says:

> Amat: sapit; recte facit, animo quando opsequitur suo.

(line 995)

> He is wise and well he does to love, *compliant* to his will.

Do we not find in *opsequitur* a possible irony like the one discussed above in n. 16? Let us also note the descriptive words of Mercury when he says that Jupiter is embracing Alcmena: *animo opsequens* (line 290).

Williams emphasizes that "In particular, *obsequi* and its derivatives are so frequent in this use that the word seems almost to be a technical term and arouses the suspicion that it may have been pleonastically linked with *morigera*, but survived its disappearance. At any rate, obedience in wives is praised as a virtue on their epitaphs from early times to late: for instance, *Carm. Epigr.* 429.4; 455; 476.4; 765.1; 1140.2; 1258.6; 1604.10; 1988.15 (*obsequium*); 56.2 (*obsequens*); 1846.10 (*obsequi*); 2173.2 (*obsequentia*); 429.13ff (general praise of obedience). Most worthy of mention is probably the *laudatic Turiae* (*CIL* 6.1527*; see the text of *FIRA* 3.69, p. 212), 30ff: *domestica bona pudicitiae, opsequi, comitatis, facilitatis.* . . . "Some of this praise is merely conventional, some is equally sincere; but, whether conventional or deeply felt, there is presupposed a general agreement that such obedience or dutifulness is a positive virtue" (Williams [above, n. 21] 24–25). We once more see that the dialogue resounds with the traditional language of female fidelity, but with the values turned upside down. See also this volume pp. 21–26.

34. Cf. Richmond Lattimore, *Themes in Greek and Latin Epitaphs* (Urbana, Ill. 1962) 295ff and Williams (above, n. 21) 23.

35. *C.L.E.* (Bücheler) 959.B.

36. See above, p. 24.

37. Dionysius of Halicarnassus 2.25; cf. also Plutarch *Romulus* 22.3.

38. Henri Bergson, *Le Rire: essai sur la signification du comique* [1899] (Paris 1940) 72.

39. J. N. Hough, "Jupiter, Amphitryon, and the Cuckoo," *Classical Philology* 65 (1970) 95–96.

40. *Ibid.*, p. 96.

41. The dramatic heyday for this theme was doubtless seventeenth-century England, when adultery seemed to be the theme of almost every comedy. See J. H. Wilson, *A Preface to Restoration Drama* (Boston 1965) 126ff; N. Holland, *The First Modern Comedies* (Cambridge, Mass. 1959).

## Is the *Captivi* Plautine?

1. In "The Plot of the *Captivi* of Plautus," *Acta Classica* 6 (1963) 45, G. van N. Viljoen notes the "unusually serious and tragic tone marking the play throughout." E. W. Leach offers a perceptive reading centering on the unifying role of the parasite Ergasilus but adds that "we cannot separate the serious from the farcical aspects of the play." ("Ergasilus and the Ironies of the *Captivi*," *Classica & Mediaevalia* 30 [1969] 275). Walter Kraus regards the *Captivi* as a tragicomedy, with Hegio the closest to being an Aristotelian tragic hero

("Die *Captivi* im neuen Lichte Menanders," *Latinität und Alte Kirche* 8 [1977] 165–166).

2. Cf. *Amphitruo*, lines 51–53:

Post argumentum huius eloquar tragoediae.
Quid? Contraxistis frontem quia tragoediam
dixi futuram hanc?

Next you shall hear the story of our tragedy.
What — why the frowns? Because I mentioned "tragedy"?

3. See the interesting discussion in R. L. Hunter, *The New Comedy of Greece and Rome* (Cambridge 1985) 118ff.

4. Aristophanes, *Wasps* (57ff), *Peace* (739ff), *Clouds* (537ff), *Frogs* (1ff). In his first edition of the play (Cambridge 1900, rev. ed. Oxford 1930), W. Lindsay adduces a line from a prologue by Naevius:

"Acontizomenos fabula est prime proba."

5. Most recent critical analyses have tended to date the *Captivi* as a late play; for example, J. C. Dumont, "Guerre, paix et servitude dans *Les Captifs*," *Latomus* 33 (1974) 505ff (198 B.C.); P. Grimal, "Le Modèle et la date des *Captivi* de Plaute" in *Hommages à Marcel Renard*, ed. J. Bibauw (Bruxelles 1969) 1:505ff (190 B.C.); K. Wellesley, "The Production Date of Plautus' *Captivi*," *AJP* 76 (1955) 298ff (189 B.C.).

6. E.g., Aristophanes calling the spectators *euruproktoi* at *Clouds* 1098 and *sykophantai* at *Eccl.* 439–440; cf. *Wasps* 74ff.

7. J. N. Adams (*The Latin Sexual Vocabulary* [London 1982] 151) notes the sexual connotations to the verb *rumpere*, which can also suggest exhausting parts other than the vocal chords.

8. Cf. the canzone at the end of Act III of Machiavelli's *Mandragola*: "Si suave è l'inganno / al fin condotto imaginato e caro. . . ."

9. In fact, *scortum* is a more vulgar term than *meretrix*. A character in Terence refers to it as *verbum turpe*, *HT* 1042, cf. Donatus *ad Eun.* 424 and Adams (above, n. 7) p. 217. On the topos at *Captivi*, line 69, see W. G. Arnott, "Studies in Comedy, I: Alexis and the Parasite's Name," *GRBS* 9 (1968) 161ff.

10. Viljoen (above, n. 1) 267.

11. Leach (above, n. 1) 289, 265.

12. Cf. Fraenkel, pp. 133ff and Netta Zagagi, *Tradition and Originality in Plautus* (Göttingen 1980) p. 107 n. 7.

13. Cf. Fraenkel, p. 35ff.

14. J. N. Hough ("The Structure of the *Captivi*," *AJP* 63 [1942] 36) suggests that at least a portion of the Ergasilus scenes came "from some Greek parasite play."

15. Paul Lejay, *Plaute* (Paris 1925) 134.

16. E.g., Kraus (above, n. 1) 166: "Träger solcher Tragik [sc. *hamartia*] ist in den *Captivi* vor allem Hegio."

17. This play contains several hints at the traditional, comic "rebirth motif." Cf. Tyndarus' pun at lines 1006–1008; Hegio's exclamation *iterum gnatus videor* (line 891); and Aristophanes' description of old Philokleon, *Wasps* 1299ff.

18. There may be a sexual innuendo to the pun — appropriate for a character called Scortum — which could have been accentuated by the actor's gesture. Cf. Adams (above, n. 7) 84, who adduces, *inter alia, Asinaria*, line 874. See also Eric Partridge, *Shakespeare's Bawdy* (London 1968) 192, on the bard's use of "stomach" as a euphemism for sexual organs.

19. Note the ironic anticipation of the epilogue's praise of this play as being one *ubi boni meliores fiant* (line 1034).

20. Cf. above, Chapter 4 (pp. 99ff), especially pp. 111–116.

21. Henri Bergson, *Le Rire* (Paris 1940) 72.

22. The verb *inquinare* (line 267) can have scatological connotations. Cf. *Pseudolus*, line 1279 and Adams (above, n. 7) 239.

23. The appeal of the comic miser may be precisely because the Romans in real life were themselves notoriously stingy. Cf. Polybius 31.26.9.

24. Many scholars have called attention to the thematic parallels between the *Captivi* and the "escape" plays of Euripides like *Helen* and *Iphigenia Taurica*. K.-H. Abel, *Die Plautusprologe* (Mülheim and Ruhr 1955) 47, has noted similarities between the *Ion* and the comedy we are discussing. In "Un monologo dei *Captivi*," *Riv. di Filol.* 55 (1927) 25, G. Pasquali remarks "il Tindaro plautino . . . continua in certo modo eroine euripidee."

25. E.g., *Mostellaria*, lines 406–407, *Poenulus*, lines 145–146, *Casina*, lines 738–739; cf. n. 20, above.

26. Hough (above, n. 14) 34 argues that Ergasilus has no real dramatic function in the play.

27. Cf. *Menaechmi*, lines 810ff, esp. 828–829 and *Captivi*, lines 594–596; also, *Menaechmi*, line 890 and *Captivi*, line 598.

28. Cf., for example, the lament of the senex Nicobulus at *Bacchides*, lines 1087ff at his humiliation at the hand of the slave Chrysalus, esp. 1092–1095:

Perditu' sum atque eradicatus sum, omnibus exemplis excrucior.
Omnia me mala consectantur, omnibus exitiis interii.
Chrysalu' med hodie laceravit, Chrysalu' me miserum spoliavit:
is me scelus auro usque attondit dolis doctis indoctum ut lubitumst.

I'm a void, I'm completely destroyed,
     From all manner of tortures I'm crying.
I'm all bruised and abused

And innumerable deaths I am dying.
Chrysalus whipped me and stripped me today,
   The rogue jeered as he sheared all my gold,
Made an ass of a wise man of class in his own wily way.

Chrysalus had earlier boasted of having bamboozled a *callidum senem callidis dolis* (line 643). Compare Hegio's comment that *he* is known through the city as *senex doctus* (*Captivi*, line 787).

29. Yet, curiously, Hegio is not too upset to make puns, cf. lines 724–726. For a similar name-change quip, cf. Chrysalus in the *Bacchides*, fearing that his name will become "Chrysifixion."

30. Grimal (above, n. 5) 398 argues that the entire play is infused with Stoic philosophy. D. Konstan, "Plautus' *Captivi* and the Ideology of the Ancient City-State," *Ramus* 5.2 (1976) 81, argues that the play presents "the clash between two opposing ethical systems . . . the communal ethos of the city-state and a universal humanism." While denying that the drama per se "eine philosophische Aussage enthält," Kraus discerns in the characters' speeches "ein Element popularphilosophischer Reflexion" akin to Menander (above, n. 1) 169–170.

31. The Menandrian source is *Dis Exapaton*, fr. 4. See A. W. Gomme and F. H. Sandbach in *Menander: A Commentary* (Oxford 1973) 125 and W. G. Arnott's remarks in *Menander I* (Cambridge, Mass. 1979) 169, 171.

32. Viljoen (above, n. 1) 21 acknowledges that some of the play's inconsistencies may already have been in the Greek model.

33. Cf. Mercury in *Amphitruo*, lines 984–989.

34. The banquet also includes certain delicacies specifically forbidden the Romans by the sumptuary laws, e.g., *glandia* (line 915). Cf. Pliny *NH* 8.78.209, which discusses the prohibitions. On their flagrant violations by Plautine characters see above, Chapter 2, pp. 47ff and 189 n. 8.

35. Cf. n. 17 above.

36. Fraenkel (pp. 238ff and 408ff) emphasizes that the references to pork are Roman additions (Greeks ate fish).

37. The *puer*'s speech (lines 909–921) is a set piece, a bit of verbal farce, to suggest passage of time.

38. This is the only example of extant Roman comedy where a male character is found to be freeborn.

39. Cf. Viljoen (above, n. 1) 63: "The self-sacrifice of this loyal servant could not have amounted to a stay of more than a few hours in Hegio's stone quarry, especially if we consider that his true identity was revealed only some time after Philocrates' departure, and that after this he still had to be put in chains by a smith and travel to the quarry which is some distance from the town (733–6)! All this greatly reduces the significance of Tyndarus' description of his own toil and suffering (998–1004)."

40. Leach (above, n. 1) 293 remarks upon the "relative joylessness of the recognition scene."

41. Cf. *inter alia* lines 867, 956, 966, 984 (also see below, n. 45).

42. L. P. Wilkinson, *Classical Attitudes to Modern Issues* (London 1978) 136. Wilkinson mentions a *Lex scantinia* passed some time in the second century B.C.; cf. Caelius in Cicero, *Ad. Fam.* 8.12.3 and 8.14.4.

43. Cf. Hunter (above, n. 3) 13. On Men. *Dysc.* 892–893, see the commentary of Gomme and Sandbach (Oxford 1973) 270.

44. This is not beyond dispute, but most critics beleve *Cistellaria*, line 785 indicates that the actors — in some cases — were slaves, and there is another mention of actors being beaten at *Trinummus*, line 990. Cf. Frances Muecke, "Names and Players: The Sycophant Scene of the 'Trinummus,'" *TAPA* 115 (1985) 184.

45. Kraus (above, n. 1) p. 161 suggests that his kidnapper chose the name Paegnium for the lad "in Himblick auf eine Funktion als *catamitus.*"

46. Cf. Wilkinson (above, n. 42) 136–137 on Roman versus Greek mores.

47. In *Plaute et l'impartialité comique* (Brussels 1964) 215–216, M. Delcourt argues that the text implies a prior homosexual dalliance between old Hegio and Stalagmus.

48. Dumont (above, n. 5) 507, arrives at a similar conclusion. His argument bears quoting at length:

> Dans les *Captifs*, la structure de l'intrigue s'apparente pourtant à celle des autres oeuvres comiques: tant les invariants que les variations permettent de préciser la signification des *Captifs*. Le schéma le plus commun selon lequel sont bâties les comédies suppose un couple à réunir pour le γαμος final; on doit surmonter un certain nombre d'obstacles liés généralement à la servitude, à la guerre, au fait militaire: la jeune fille est prisonnière de sa condition, c'est-à-dire que sa condition est d'être prisonnière; il faut pour la libérer forcer une porte, un mur, vaincre un *leno*, un soldat; l'agent de cette victoire sera l'esclave du jeune homme, il aura comme moyen la ruse qui lui permettra de se procurer ou de remplacer l'argent nécessaire à la conquête. Ces éléments ne manquent pas dans les *Captifs:* une ruse d'esclave conduit à une libération, l'insistance mise à rappeler le prix des captifs souligne qu'une substitution de personne équivaut à un prélèvement d'argent . . . dans les *Captifs*, la triade jeune homme–esclave–jeune femme a également subi une réduction à deux éléments.

49. Cf. M. Pârlog, "La Langue de Plaute: Observations concernant le vocabulaire des comédies *Casina et Captivi*" (in Rumanian), *Annales Univ. de Timisoara*, Ser.sc.phil.9 (1971) 244–255.

Morality and Money: The Purpose of the *Trinummus*

1. Several of the metaphorical parallels will be cited in this essay. For a recent discussion of the imagery in the *Mostellaria*, see Eleanor Winsor Leach, "De exemplo meo ipse aedificato: An Organizing Idea in the *Mostellaria*," *Hermes* 97 (1969) 318-332.

2. It is, of course, Terence who employs this term in reference to his *Heauton Timorumenos* (36). Moreover, there is a conspicuous echo of the *Trinummus* in the prologue to the *Adelphoe* (22-23):

> De⟨h⟩inc ne exspectetis argumentum fabulae,
> senes qui primi venient i partem aperient,
> in agendo partem ostendent.

> Hereafter don't expect to hear this play's whole plot.
> The oldsters coming out will let you know a bit
> The rest will come in action.

Cf. *Trinummus*, lines 16-17:

> Sed de argumento ne exspectetis fabulae:
> senes qui huc venient, i rem vobis aperient.

> But don't expect to hear this play's entire plot:
> The oldsters coming out will let you know the tale.

Indeed, various other similarities between the two plays are often remarked upon. See below, n. 31.

3. Though it has been discounted by many critics, Leo's hypothesis on the Philemonian original still seems worth reviving here. Basing his conjecture on *Trinummus*, line 648, where Lysiteles tells Lesbonicus *praeoptavisti amorem tuom uti virtuti praeponeres*, "you preferred a lovelife to a life of loving virtue," (as well as 651, 666 and elsewhere), Leo argues that in the Greek model, there had been a single *amor*, a girl for whom Lesbonicus had gone into debt (*Geschichte der röm. Lit.* [Berlin 1913] I:117, n. 1). This would seem likely Plautine material, and indeed it is the precise situation in the *Mostellaria*. And yet apparently Plautus *noluit*. The play is no richer for the absence of a lively *meretrix* and by George Meredith's standards there can be no true comedy without the fair sex. If Leo is correct, Plautus has here atypically suppressed an inherently good comic situation. There are, however, arguments against Leo's view, as in Günther Jachmann, *Plautinisches und Attisches* (Berlin 1931) 242ff.

4. And yet T. B. L. Webster, for example, dedicates an entire chapter to "Philemon and His Comedy," in *Studies in Later Greek Comedy*, 2nd ed. (Manchester 1970) 125ff. But his conclusions are based

# THERE'S BANISHMENT FROM NATIVE EYES IN SIGHT OF NATIVE AIR

Jen Karetnick

I looked away from my father's bowed head,
the same pale flesh as the oysters he ate
in La Trappiste that he said tasted metallic,
a little too salty, though he drank their liquor
regardless, swallowing down hard on the tears
they loosed, quivering, in their last live moments.

I looked away from my mother who was looking away
from the bread basket filled with the crusty
hard ends she has always preferred to the fluff
of middles, food she can no longer digest
as she told me a story about Dover Castle
and its tunnels where the medics practiced

their craft despite the bombs vibrating
the battlements like mallets on a tuning fork.
She recalled every detail but the one of me,
strolling beside her in the iodine dark, listening
to the audio re-enactment, panicked parables
of a war fought underground. I looked away

mostly on Plautus' plays and Apuleius' observations in *Florida* 16. Also, the problem of using vastly differing plays as evidence for a New Comedy author's style is not unique with Philemon. What of the disparity between "Diphilus' " *Rudens and Casina?*

5. *Trinummus*, lines 843–997. The comic essence of this scene is *sartor resartus*, or as Charmides himself says (line 958) *enim vero ego nunc sycophantae huic sycophantari volo*. This is the rubric Bergson calls a *monde renversé*.

6. *Menaechmi*, line 779. Even the characters within the *Trinummus* are aware of their own long-windedness, as in Megaronides' remark (line 806) *at . . . nimi' longo sermone utimur*. This is unusual. Under normal circumstances, Plautus (and his characters) are acutely aware of audience reactions and remind us that they are trying not to bore. Cf. *Poenulus*, line 1224, *in pauca confer: sitiunt qui sedent*, and the hasty forgiveness proffered at the close of the *Casina* (line 1006), *hanc ex longa longiorem ne faciamus fabulam.*

7. Naturally the question of who invented the prologue has been the occasion of many a Greco-Roman tug-of-war. Fraenkel, citing Wilamowitz and Jachmann, views the entire prologue as completely the work of Plautus (p. 434). Webster (above, n. 4) 140 understandably argues its presence in the Greek, although he concedes that Plautus may have invented the characters' names.

8. In "Plautus' *Trinummus*: The Absurdity of Officious Morality" *Traditio* 35 (1979) 333–345, W. S. Anderson argues that Plautus intended his audience to laugh at the exaggerated moralizing on the part of most of the play's characters. He does, however, concede that the first 800 lines of the play are "boring" (p. 340.) One might argue that too much of Anderson's argument depends on Plautus' hypothetical "surgery" on the Greek original (his excision of the love plot, etc.) Aside from the fact that we do not have the original, are we to assume that Plautus' audience had a detailed knowledge of it and thus would be able to appreciate Plautus' revisions of Philemon? See also R. Hunter, "Philemon, Plautus, and the *Trinummus*," *MH* 37 (1980) 216–230. While he argues that Plautus' adaptation does not consist of "simply random accretions" (p. 230) Hunter does offer support for our own argument by such remarks as "the very Roman colouring of the second part of [Stasimus'] monologue is striking. I find it hard to believe that all this talk of *mores maiorum*, *leges* and *ambitio* and *honor* correspond closely to anything in Philemon."

Interestingly, a general consensus of scholars dates the *Captivi ubi boni meliores fiant* (line 1034) at about the same time as the *Trinummus*, and Wilamowitz noted the similarity in tone between the two plays.

9. Cf. in Lucretius the birds inspired by Venus, *perculsae corda tua vi* (1.13) and esp. 4.1123–1124:

Labitur interea res et Babylonica fiunt,
languent officia atque aegrotat fama vacillans.

Meanwhile your substance dissolves into Babylonian
tapestries,
Your duties are neglected and your reputation sickens
and stumbles.

10. Cf. *Amphitruo,* line 928 and above, p. 233, n. 22. P. E. Corbett (in *The Roman Law of Marriage* (Oxford 1930) 224) cites, in addition to Plautus, Cicero, Martial and the *Digest.* The cry *apage* is used at two other important junctures in the *Trinummus:* when Philto rejects the "haunted farm" (line 537) and when Charmides forswears maritime commerce (line 837).

11. Fraenkel, pp. 188ff; D. C. Earl, "Political Terminology in Plautus," *Historia* 9 (April 1960) 239.

12. Earl (above, n. 11) 236 compares the language of line 651 to Polybius' description of Scipio Aemilianus (31.23), esp. where Scipio defends himself against criticism of his "un-Romanness" — for not taking on cases in the law courts. That Plautus deliberately contrasts the festive activities in his plays with the forum and Roman responsibilities, is argued above in Chapter 2 (pp. 42ff).

13. *Mostellaria,* lines 431ff. By contrast, consider how the slaves in each play greet their newly arrived masters: loyal Stasimus hails "the best man alive" (line 1069), Tranio wishes he would drop dead (*Mostellaria,* 442–443).

14. Cf. lines 853ff. Also eavesdropping, Stasimus plays the sophisticated drama critic, lines 705ff. That Plautus should lavish so much theatrical termiology on the *sycophanta* once again reaffirms where his heart is in the *Trinummus.* By this line of reasoning, we can adjudge Pseudolus his favorite character of all, since he compares his plots and fictions to a playwright's creative process (*Pseudolus,* lines 401ff). Cf. John Wright, "The Transformation of Pseudolus," *TAPA* 105 (1975) 402–416. See, too, N. W. Slater, *Plautus in Performance* (Princeton 1985), esp. chapter 9, "Playwriting as Heroism" (168ff).

15. It was this remark that prompted Friedrich W. Ritschl to propose 194 B.C. as the *terminus post quem* for the *Trinummus* (*Parerga zu Plautus und Terenz* [Leipzig 1845] 349). Aediles took office on March 15 and it seemed likely to Ritschl that the play would have been performed soon after, e.g., at the Megalesia (April 14). According to Livy 34.54.3, the first Megalesian *ludi scaenici* were in 194. A different explanation for this reference to the *novi aediles* is offered below, p. 224.

16. Webster (above, n. 4) 139 sees no reason to believe that most of the moralizing element was not in the Philemon play as well. See also E. Fantham, "Philemon's Thesaurus or Dramatisation on Peri-

patetic Ethics," *Hermes* 105 (1977) 402–421. Fraenkel, pp. 146ff does not argue for total Plautine originality but instead notes how abruptly and without motivation Stasimus' sermon begins. Though moral decline is a traditional motif in both Latin and Greek, this scene is characterized by "molti imbarbarimenti apportativi da Plauto" (p. 148).

17. And yet the Romans must have taken delight in this joke, for Plautus repeats it on several occasions (e.g., *Miles Gloriosus*, lines 327ff; *Stichus*, lines 280, as well as *Persa*, lines 53ff, although it is a *parasitus* who here makes the boast). For the legal details, see W. W. Buckland, *The Roman Law of Slavery* (Cambridge 1908) 76–77.

18. Regarding the specifically Roman connotations of *fidelitas*, see the comprehensive work by J. Hellegouarc'h, *Le vocabulaire latin des relations et des partis sous la république* (Paris 1963) 37–38.

19. "Zur Geschichte des Wortes *fides*," *Rheinisches Museum* 71 (1916) 187ff, rep. in *Kleine Beiträge* (Rome 1964) 15ff. Gordon Williams senses the Roman concept of *fides* in Pseudolus' pointed remarks to Ballio (lines 279ff), "Some Problems in the Construction of Plautus' *Pseudolus*," *Hermes* 84 (1956) 428.

20. Earl (above, n. 11) 235ff. The quotation is from 239.

21. Tenney Frank, "Some Political Allusions in Plautus' *Trinummus*," *AJP* 53.2 (1932) 152ff; Donato Gagliardi, "Aspetti del teatro comico latino: la politica di Plauto," *Le Parole e le Idee* 5.1–2 (1963) 171.

22. C. H. Buck, Jr., *A Chronology of the Plays of Plautus* (Baltimore 1940) 106.

23. On the funding of comedies, see Evelyn Holst Clift, *Latin Pseudepigrapha* (Baltimore 1945) 41–42. Duckworth also suggests the personal supplement by the aediles, p. 74. This has been discussed more recently by A. S. Gratwick in his account of "The Origins of Roman Drama," in *The Cambridge History of Classical Literature*, ed. E. J. Kenney and W. V. Clausen (1982) 2:82.

In "Names and Players: The Sycophant Scene of the *Trinummus*," *TAPA* 115 (1985) 167–168, Frances Muecke offers a metatheatrical interpretation of the sycophant scene, which discusses the trickster's use of technical theatrical terms. Our attention is called to the use of the verb *conducere* (line 853), which would suggest *conductores*, which would indeed be another reference to the aediles. Referring to lines 843–844, she observes: "In the terms of the double vision of the role with which Plautus is operating, the name of the sycophant's day is the same as that of Plautus' day, because the play and day coincide for the actor/sycophant, both the intrigue and the play answering to the description *artes nugatoriae*."

24. And, of course, they were revered in everyday life. Cf. Cicero, *De Senectute* 61: *Habet senectus, honorata praesertim, tantam auctoritatem, ut ea pluris sit quam omnes adulescentiae voluptates*, "Old age, especially if one is held in esteem, has such influence that it surpasses all the pleasures of youth."

25. One example of Plautus' usual treatment of Roman institutions is *Menaechmi*, lines 571ff: *Vt hoc utimur maxume more moro* in which Menaechmus damns the entire system of *clientela*.

26. On *amicitia* and its component features, see again Hellegouarc'h (above, n. 18) 41ff. On the role of *fides*, see pp. 23ff. On the *Captivi*, see above, n. 8.

27. Buck (above, n. 22) 102 generally supports Ritschl's suggestion of 194 or just thereafter (see above, n. 15). There is concurrence in W. B. Sedgwick, "Plautine Chronology," *AJP* 70 (1949) 379, 382; K. H. E. Schutter, *Quibus annis comoediae Plautinae primum actae sint quaeritur* (Groningen 1952) 147–148. Tenney Frank's suggestion of 187 B.C. (above, n. 21) 152ff did not generate much support, but even if corect it in no way alters our argument. In fact, it would lend it support.

28. H. H. Scullard, *Roman Politics 220–150 B.C.* (Oxford 1951) 154.

29. Pierre Grimal, *Le Siècle des Scipions* (Paris 1953) 113.

30. Cf. Scullard (above, n. 28) 112ff. At one point (18.35.1), Polybius indicates that 200 B.C. saw the beginnings of Roman moral decline, although he dates the full extent of the decline only after 167, the end of the Third Macedonian War (31.25.6). Cf. C. O. Brink and F. W. Walbank, "The Construction of the Sixth Book of Polybius," *CQ* 48 (1954) 106.

31. Following the suggestions of Ernout (7:8): "Lesbonicus, 'le vainqueur à Lesbos,' ou le roi des amoureux." Ernout sees the *Trinummus* as a possible *pièce à thèse*, "où s'affrontent deux façons de concevoir la vie . . . de même que dans les Adelphes de Térence s'affrontent deux systèmes d'éducation" (pp. 8–9).

32. Fraenkel, p. 141. Cf. E. W. Handley, *Menander and Plautus: A Study in Comparison* (London 1968) 9.

33. There is a striking similarity between young Lysiteles' grim picture of women despoiling their husbands (*Trinummus*, lines 237ff) and Cato's speech on the very same topic, quoted (paraphrased?) by Livy 34.4.16ff.

34. *Aen.* 6.868–886. Cf. Servius 6.861.

35. Georges Sorel, *Réflexions sur la violence* (Paris 1946) 180.

36. E. Littré, *Dictionnaire de la langue française* (Paris 1882) 3:681. Illuminating is Harry Levin's essay, "Some Meanings of Myth," *Daedalus* 88.2 (Spring 1959) 223ff, rep. in *Myth and Mythmaking*, ed. H. A. Murray (New York 1960) 103ff.

37. This would certainly not have been the case at the end of the *Aulularia*. And cf. the finale of Molière's adaptation: "je suis Don Thomas d'Alburcy, que le ciel garantit des ondes avec tout l'argent qu'il portait" (*L'Avare* 5.5.); also:

ANSELME: Allons vite faire part de notre joie à votre mère.

HARPAGON: Et moi, voir ma chère cassette. (*Finis*)

ANSELME: Let us hasten to inform your mother of our joy.

HARPAGON: And I shall hasten to my dear money pot.

The joy of the *Trinummus* is all too virtuous.

38. Which may perhaps explain why it was far and away Cicero's favorite Plautine comedy (he cites it four times). Of this predilection Wilhelm Zillinger writes: "In general, the play is free of the usual Plautine crude comic elements. It has something of a moral character, as in all the writings of Cicero. It is an excellent character study." *Cicero und die altrömischen Dichter* (Würzburg 1911) 25.

# INDEX of
# PASSAGES FROM PLAUTUS

## Epidicus

11A: p. 211 n. 4
17–18: p. 148
158–159: p. 129
163: pp. 129, 130
166–168: p. 205 n. 38
189: p. 120
257–258: p. 215 n. 50
345–347: pp. 61–62, 195 n. 54
348: p. 143
349ff: p. 184 n. 49
382ff: p. 199 n. 46
406ff, 420–423, 427–429: pp. 205–206 n. 39
517–524: p. 121
592: p. 131
610ff: pp. 148, 210 n. 73
664–665: p. 149
675–676: pp. 133–134
685: p. 210 n. 1
721, 723: p. 109
724: pp. 109–110, 164
725: p. 110
726: p. 164
728: p. 110
728–731: pp. 161–162
730: p. 110
732–733: p. 164

## Menaechmi

3: p. 175 n. 4
7–9: pp. 36–37
10–12: p. 37
100–101, 104: p. 44
114: pp. 23, 189 n. 12
114–118: pp. 44–45
115, 122: p. 46
122–123: p. 196 n. 21
122–124: p. 45
123: pp. 43, 46
127, 129: p. 24
133: pp. 27, 196 n. 22
152: pp. 27, 44, 47, 196 n. 17
189: p. 46
202: p. 188 n. 5
208–213: p. 47
212: pp. 189 n. 9, 196 n. 20
215: p. 47
226: p. 48

258–264: pp. 48–49, 187 n. 80
318: p. 27
473–477: p. 50
569: pp. 23, 47
571ff, 588–589: p. 50
591–595: p. 189 n. 13
596–599: pp. 50–51, 195 n. 8
597ff: p. 216 n. 54
598a: p. 52
601–602: p. 216 n. 54
788–791: p. 46
789: p. 196 n. 21
846ff: p. 182 n. 28
973–977, 985: p. 142

## Mercator

73–78: p. 65
79: pp. 65, 69
93–97: pp. 65–66
98–99: p. 66
319: p. 120
425–427: p. 28
543: p. 27
838: p. 32

## Miles Gloriosus

11–12, 13–18: p. 125
16: p. 207 n. 53
46–47: p. 94
49: p. 125
62: p. 94
75: p. 125
78: pp. 126, 127
138–143: p. 147
147: p. 116
211: p. 207 n. 52
360: p. 211 n. 8
494: p. 210 n. 1
582–583: p. 148
592–595: p. 128
611, 614: p. 208 n. 59
680–681: p. 23
805–806: p. 126
814–815: p. 209 n. 65
861: p. 213 n. 29
952: p. 95
954: p. 126
957: p. 95

from the mud stains, patches like age spots,
marking our pants from the navigation of time-
bitten steps that lead down to the Great River Stour
in Sandwich, where the water lay too low to search
for seals. Instead, we headed upstream under
the old toll bridge, past centenarian Dutch barges
turned into houseboats with names like Dragonfly
and Orca, and hunchbacked banks of reeds,
bent under the weight of their own success,
where so few remain to weave them into shelter,
and I looked away from my own desire for isolation
and the image of myself crashing into the marshes,

disappearing almost instantaneously, out of range
of knees that do not bend and canes that hit
other tourists accidentally in the shins and a memory
that no longer is a busy trade hub but instead
a Cinque Port, socked in, a repository for visitors
who receive the same answers to questions

they have not asked. "Such a lapse could [not] give
them any balm." I looked away from my second pour
of Sauvignon Blanc, my still-full pot of mussels
steamed with garlic, white wine and cream. A few
of them were closed as tight as disapproving lips,
dead already when the chef set them to flame.

# GENERAL INDEX